Crossing Swords

Crossing Swords

Mary
Baker
Eddy

VS.

Victoria
Claflin
Woodhull

And the Battle for the Soul of Marriage

The untold story of America's
nineteenth-century culture war

Cindy Peyser Safronoff

Cindy Peyser Safronoff

this one thing
SEATTLE
2015

www.Crossing-Swords.com

This book is a publication of
This One Thing, LLC, 503 N 36th St., #A, Seattle, WA 98103 USA

First edition 2015
Copyright © 2015 by Cindy Peyser Safronoff. All rights reserved.
Book cover and illustrations by Mark Peyser

Manufactured in the United States of America

Publisher's Cataloging-in-Publication (***Provided by Quality Books, Inc.***)

Safronoff, Cindy Peyser.
    Crossing swords : Mary Baker Eddy vs. Victoria
Claflin Woodhull and the battle for the soul of marriage
: the untold story of America's nineteenth-century
culture war / Cindy Peyser Safronoff. -- First edition.
    pages cm
    Includes bibliographical references and index.
    LCCN 2015900768
    ISBN 978-0-9864461-0-8 (paperback)
    ISBN 978-0-9864461-1-5 (e-book)

    1. Marriage--United States--History--19th century.
2. Culture conflict--United States--History--19th
century. 3. Culture conflict--Religious aspects.
4. Eddy, Mary Baker, 1821-1910. 5. Woodhull, Victoria C.
(Victoria Claflin), 1838-1927.   I. Title.

HQ535.S24 2015   306.810973
                    QBI15-600035

Dedicated to

My Mom and Dad
whose lasting marriage
has been and continues to be
a blessing to me
and all

Table of Contents

Preface..i

Introduction... 1

Marriage and American Freedom................................. 11
    The Puritan Ideal of Marriage 13
    The American Free-Love Movement............................ 37

Here Come the Brides.. 65
    God's Gracious Preparation... 67
    A Great Wail of Agony 89

Preparing for a Mission (1866 to 1869)...................... 105
    Eddy's Primitive Christianity 107
    Woodhull's New Social Order..................................... 111
    Evangel of Womanhood.. 115

Emerging into Civic Life (1870 to 1872) 119
    The Social Freedom Campaign.................................... 121
    Moral Science 135

Will Marriage Survive? (1872 to 1875) 145
    Woodhull's Bomb.. 147
    Eddy's Text Book... 161

Two Worlds Collide (1876) 175
    Eddy's Centennial Celebration.................................... 177
    Woodhull's Boston Lectures....................................... 183

A New Chapter in Life (1877 and Beyond) 207
    Union of Hearts 209
    Becoming a Lady 221

Postscript... 229

Acknowledgements... 237

Bibliography.. 239

Notes 245

Index.. 271

Yes, I am a free lover! I have an inalienable, constitutional, and natural right to love whom I may, to love as long or as short a period as I can, to change that love every day I please! And with that right neither you nor any law you can frame have any right to interfere. And I have the further right to demand a free and unrestricted exercise of that right, and it is your duty not only to accord it, but, as a community, to see that I am protected in it.

Victoria Claflin Woodhull

The last infirmity of error that would fasten itself on society, to see it hop and hobble under a new burden of guilt, is named "free love"; wherein "they declare their sin as Sodom, and hide it not," but the boldness of depravity will show its deformity.

Mary Baker Eddy

Preface

This story came out of my own spiritual quest. I was searching for a higher view of womanhood and a deeper understanding of marriage. I discovered a battle! Opposing visions of womanhood crossed swords. The very soul of marriage in the modern world was at stake in this epic conflict. I had stumbled upon America's nineteenth-century culture war.

This marriage debate in America in the 1870s was new to me, yet surprisingly familiar. I recognized so many social issues that we are debating today. As I learned about the personal lives, professional careers, and political positions of Mary Baker Eddy and Victoria Claflin Woodhull — two historic women leaders representing different perspectives, philosophies, and ways of life — I found clarity I previously lacked. This study of opposites became a new lens with which to view my life experience.

Eddy and Woodhull were both outspoken advocates of women's rights, ambitious achievers of extraordinary accomplishments, and public figures of international acclaim, yet most Americans today are unfamiliar with either of them. In recent years scholars have been rediscovering both women — revisiting the records of their lives, reconsidering their cultural influence, and reconnecting them to American history. This new work made the research and writing of *Crossing Swords* possible.

In this story, our leading ladies each fight against the values and beliefs of the other in the civic dialogue. Eddy and Woodhull never met, but in October 1876 in the newspaper columns in Lynn, Massachusetts, they came as close as they ever would come to a personal confrontation. This exchange has never before been thoroughly examined. Even the most thorough Eddy biographer to date has relegated Eddy's direct criticism of Woodhull to a mere mention in a footnote. I am unaware of any Woodhull biographer who has ever commented on Eddy's attack. The event is worth exploring because of the influence of their values on the shaping of modern womanhood and our current culture.

This story is less about historical events and more about the development of ideas. It begins with an overview of the evolution of culture and marriage law in America and from there explores nineteenth-century alternative relationship models. This background is useful for understanding the positions of Eddy and Woodhull on these issues. The heart of the story is a marriage debate as women entered the public sphere as outspoken leaders in religion, culture, and politics — and especially as women began to demand suffrage. The legal changes required to allow women the right to vote seemed to shake the foundation of the male-female relationship. What would become of the institution of marriage? What about children and the family? Eddy and Woodhull had opposing viewpoints.

I began my exploration by searching the writings of Mary Baker Eddy on the topics of love, marriage, and womanhood. To better understand seemingly contradictory statements, I put Eddy's statements in chronological order, and then correlated them with events in her life and career. Through this process, I saw how she expressed her vision of enlightened womanhood throughout her career in her writings, in her life, and in the structure and rules of her church. To put her work into historical context, I immersed myself in the issues of nineteenth-century America with a focus on the women's rights movement. I saw how Eddy's statements and articles were often written in response to specific issues in the civic dialogue as well as in her life.

Eventually, I focused on Eddy's article "Wedlock," which begins with a statement that her book *Science and Health with Key to the Scriptures* "crossed swords with free-love" in "about the year 1875." I wondered what the term "free-love" meant to Eddy and what she said about it in the 1875 edition of *Science and Health*. I wondered what happened in the mid-1870s. As soon as I began looking for answers to these questions, I discovered Victoria Claflin Woodhull. Like most people today I had never heard of Woodhull, yet she had a remarkable career and was one of the most famous women in America — the first woman to run for United States president! The more I learned about Woodhull's public statements, the more I realized they were the perfect counterpoint for the statements of Mary Baker Eddy.

I came to see Eddy and Woodhull as representatives of opposing value systems that in some ways are still clashing. In their conflicting approaches to fulfilling the promise of the American Revolution, these two empowered women certainly disagreed on how to apply the concepts of liberty, enlightenment, and rights to sexuality. Perhaps on a deeper level, this book expresses a timeless struggle of the human condition.

I grew up studying the Bible and Eddy's Bible-inspired writings. I benefited in so many ways from the strong marriage between my mother and my father. In the contest between Eddy and Woodhull, I cannot help being biased in favor of Eddy. Yet having grown up after the sexual revolution of the 1960s, I also recognize the strong appeal to some of Woodhull's views.

I know I am not alone in having felt at least partly torn at times between these opposing philosophies. In my life, I have seen the conflict between Eddy and Woodhull expressed in so many ways, to the point that I can say that this story is mine — if only my inner battle.

Could it be yours too?

Cindy Peyser Safronoff

Introduction

I am a prophetess – I am an evangel – I am a Savior, if you would but see it; but I, too, come not to bring peace but a sword.

Let him who is without sin cast his stone. . . . I know that many of my self-appointed judges and critics are deeply tainted with the vices they condemn.

Victoria Claflin Woodhull

It was about the year 1875 that Science and Health first crossed swords with free-love, and the latter fell hors de combat; but the whole warfare of sensuality was not then ended. Science and Health, the book that cast the first stone, is still at work, deep down in human consciousness, laying the axe at the root of error.

Mary Baker Eddy

"Figuratively speaking, Mrs. Eddy is already as tall as the Eiffel tower," wrote American author Mark Twain. "She is adding surprisingly to her stature every day." The newly built Eiffel Tower, the main symbol of the 1889 world's fair in Paris, was by far the tallest building in the world at that time. It was hailed as a model of courageous innovation and achievement—a wondrous monument to man's ability. Twain's comparison was a tribute to Mary Baker Eddy's towering accomplishments and her unique fame in the world.

The fact that Twain focused so much of his colorful remarks, critical analysis, and biting humor on Eddy, was a testament to her prominence. Like any popular comedian in any era, Twain explored topics of universal relevance, including current events and the influence of famous people—the things that were on everyone's mind. By 1910 at the height of her career, every move Eddy made was monitored and publicized by the news media. A mere wave of her hand seen through a window could make the newspaper front page headlines in Boston, where her organizational headquarters dominated the city skyline.

When Twain referred to Eddy as "the Boston Pope" it was not a compliment, but it reflected the wide recognition of Eddy's strong leadership within the movement she launched, which Twain noticed was "spreading with a constantly accelerating swiftness." She founded a world religion—a new expression of Christianity for a scientific age, which she called "Christian Science." By the end of Eddy's career there were more than eleven hundred established Christian Science congregations across the globe, with a new church being dedicated every few days. Twain believed that Eddy could very well "conquer the half of Christendom."[1]

Mark Twain was not the only prominent American to recognize the influence of Mary Baker Eddy. One of America's leading journalists, Arthur Brisbane, wrote of her after an interview, "Mrs. Eddy has accumulated power in this world. She possesses it, she exercises it, and she knows it." To women's rights leader

Susan B. Anthony, Eddy's towering accomplishments were a wondrous monument to woman's ability:

> No man ever obtained so large a following in so short a time. Her churches are among the largest and most elegant in Boston, Chicago, and other cities.[2]

In addition to her churches, Eddy established her own publishing company to extend her reach through books, magazines, and literature. Sales of her book *Science and Health with Key to the Scriptures* were brisk and profitable. Eddy had a staff of professionals dedicated to managing her public relations and lobbying lawmakers, and a team of lecturers who took her message to public halls throughout the world. The international daily newspaper she founded, *The Christian Science Monitor*, quickly established itself as a trustworthy news source and a model for American journalism.

Eddy had achieved this prominence despite all normal expectations of her gender. From Eddy's platform of international fame and financial success, she announced that the time had come for woman to be a force in the public sphere:

> In natural law and in religion the right of woman to fill the highest measure of enlightened understanding and the highest places in government, is inalienable, and these rights are ably vindicated by the noblest of both sexes. This is woman's hour, with all its sweet amenities and its moral and religious reforms.[3]

At the very start of Mary Baker Eddy's career in the early 1870s, when she was struggling to find an audience for her ideas, another woman had the attention of the American people. During those years, Victoria Claflin Woodhull was being hailed as "the most prominent woman of our time."[4]

Woodhull ran for president of the United States of America. It was the first time a woman had announced candidacy for the highest place in American government. To support her campaign for the 1872 election, Woodhull published her own weekly newspaper, authored books, and lectured throughout America, frequently filling the largest halls to overflowing.

But in the year 1875, Woodhull was most identified with the philosophy of social freedom, commonly called "free love." Eddy must have had Woodhull in mind when she wrote:

> It was about the year 1875 that *Science and Health* first crossed swords with free-love, and the latter fell *hors de combat*; but the whole warfare of sensuality was not then ended. *Science and Health*, the book that cast the first stone, is still at work, deep down in human consciousness, laying the axe at the root of error.[5]

Those who first read Eddy's words would certainly have remembered Victoria Claflin Woodhull and her campaign. Between 1870 and 1876 when Eddy was laying the foundations of her Christian Science teachings and organization, Woodhull brought free love to the forefront of American thought by publicly declaring war on the institution of marriage and promoting social freedom as the more enlightened alternative. She announced to her audiences all over America:

> I am conducting a campaign against marriage, with the view of revolutionizing the present theory and practice. I have strong convictions that, as a bond or promise to love another until death, it is a fraud upon human happiness; and that it has outlived its day of usefulness. These convictions make me earnest, and I enter the fight, meaning to do the institution all possible harm in the shortest space of time; meaning to use whatever weapons may fall in my way with which to stab it to the heart, so that its decaying carcass may be buried, and clear the way for a better institution.[6]

Woodhull waged her ideological war against marriage with a take-no-prisoners intensity. In an attempt to weaken the institution of marriage and demoralize its defenders, she triggered the most explosive sex scandal of the nineteenth century involving some of the most prominent public leaders in the country.

Eddy entered the war in defense of marriage. Within a short chapter called "Marriage" and throughout the 1875 first edition of her book *Science and Health*, she weighed in on marriage-related issues being discussed in the civic dialogue. Eddy's disagreement with free-love philosophy turned into a public confrontation in 1876 when Woodhull came to lecture in Eddy's home town of Lynn, Massachusetts.

Victoria Claflin Woodhull and Mary Baker Eddy were not the only public figures to frame their issues as a battle. In the dynamic American society dedicated to "life, liberty, and the pursuit of happiness," the discussion around the institution of marriage was often phrased in terms of warfare. The American Civil War was still a fresh memory at that time. It was a violent conflict over African slavery and also whether the union between the states could be dissolved. The nation faced the question of whether individual rights and liberty belonged equally to all or only to a portion of the population. Through the loss of about one million American lives, it was resolved that the union could not be broken and that slavery would no longer be tolerated in America.

During this same time period, the women's rights movement was gaining momentum, questioning whether women were really free citizens. The nature of the marriage union was directly or indirectly the focus of much of the women's rights debate, which from the very beginning often used emotionally charged terms associated with warfare and slavery. The free-love movement took those analogies to their logical conclusion by declaring marriage to be the worst form of slavery and setting a goal of abolishing the institution.

Meanwhile, Mary Baker Eddy was fighting for a higher platform of human rights through Christian Science, which she saw as a return to the spirit of the very earliest Christians who were healers. To Eddy the worst form of slavery was the belief that a mortal material body is the master of mankind. She described the war she was fighting:

It is a revolutionary struggle. We already have had two in this nation; and they began and ended in a contest for the true idea, for human liberty and rights. Now cometh a third struggle; for the freedom of health, holiness, and the attainment of heaven.[7]

But Eddy's revolution involved improving marriage, not abolishing it.

Looking back on the ideological conflict of this period, Eddy framed the free-love issue in biblical terms—as she did in writing on any topic. Just as a tree is known by its fruit, so would free love be known by its fruit. Eddy's efforts to lay "the axe at the root of error," was the sort of biblical battle weapon expressed in this citation:

the axe is laid unto the root of the trees: therefore every tree which bringeth not forth good fruit is hewn down, and cast into the fire. (Matt. 3:10, Luke 3:9)

Eddy believed her teachings would eliminate free love from society, not through coercion or physical force, but by causing a change in human consciousness—a shift away from materialism, selfishness, and sensuality.

There was a very personal dimension to Mary Baker Eddy's war against free love as well. Biographer Robert Peel briefly mentioned that in the gossip around the town of Lynn, Massachusetts, Eddy was accused of practicing free love. In a footnote, Peel attributed this gossip in part to the public influence of Victoria Woodhull, whom he described as a "flamboyant exponent of free-love." In the early to mid-1870s, Eddy was teaching small classes on her healing method, developing a theology, and writing manuscripts for her small circle of students. By 1876 her theology would be more defined and she would begin establishing it under the name Christian Science. But in this early phase of her career, the townspeople of Lynn, Massachusetts, were not sure how to think about her unconventional activities.[8]

On top of this, circumstantial evidence supported the distrustful suspicions of her neighbors. Eddy was a single woman at that time, known to be charming and attractive, but also carrying the social stigma of separation and divorce. Some of her early students were young single men who frequently visited her at home. This alone was enough to suggest improper behavior. But in fact, there was much more going on within her close community of students to fuel the flames of the local gossip.

To really understand how and why Eddy crossed swords with free love in the mid-1870s, the story needs to start at the very beginning of the American experience. Mary Baker Eddy's revolution had deep roots in Protestant Christianity. Likewise, Victoria Claflin Woodhull's revolution was an outgrowth of the American free-love movement, which had begun several decades after the establishment of the American Republic—this "new nation, conceived in liberty, and dedicated to the proposition that all men are created equal" as United States President Abraham Lincoln famously described it. The undeveloped American continent offered European settlers the opportunity to create new forms of community to express their ideals. It was an unprecedented era of reform, change, and experimentation. Rethinking society also meant rethinking marriage. The Protestant Christian establishment and the counterculture free-love movement were both made possible by American freedom.

And so the battle for the soul of marriage begins.

AMERICA'S NINETEENTH-CENTURY
CULTURE WAR

Horace Greeley

Lucy Stone

Isabella Hooker

Elizabeth Cady Stanton

Mary Livermore

Susan B. Anthony

Martin Luther

Mary Baker Eddy

Victoria Claflin Woodhull

Emanuel Swedenborg

John Calvin

Henry Beecher

Theodore Tilton

Andrew Davis

John Winthrop

Harriet Beecher Stowe

THE BATTLE
FOR THE SOUL OF
MARRIAGE

Steven Andrews

John Humphrey Noyes

Abigail & John Adams

Antoinette Blackwell

Maggie & Katie Fox

Karl Marx

Marriage and American Freedom

As dutiful descendants of Puritans, let us lift their standard higher, rejoicing, as Paul did, that we are free born.

Mary Baker Eddy

Free love means nothing more and nothing less, in kind, than free worship, freedom of the press, freedom of conscience, free trade, free thought.

Victoria Claflin Woodhull

The Puritan Ideal of Marriage

"My ancestors came to America to worship God according to the dictates of conscience," Mary Baker Eddy wrote in her monthly magazine, *The Christian Science Journal*. "The first settlers of the State, they planted the standard of pure and undefiled religion before God and man. So shall the children of Puritans speak at this day in the words of St. Paul, 'I was free born,' and seek a higher inheritance, even the liberty of the sons of God."[9]

To say that Eddy valued her Puritan heritage would be an understatement. She praised her own religious education received from Puritan parents. She described the Puritan character of marriage as "its true basis." She saw "puritanical honesty and virtue" in marriage as the "stability of this covenant." In her scathing rebuke of Victoria Claflin Woodhull, Mary Baker Eddy clearly aligned herself with Puritan values on marriage when she wrote:

> For one, we honor the Puritan faith and fidelity of our mothers and fathers in the relations of husband, wife, or parent, and say let well enough alone.[10]

In the Puritan faith, relations of husband and wife were modeled on their concept of marriage as partnership, companionship, even friendship. Their marriage ideal was central to their culture and it may have been one of their most influential and long-lasting cultural innovations. Eddy considered herself and her followers to be among the "dutiful descendants of Puritans." Within her own religious denomination, Eddy honored and encouraged marriage as well as many other aspects of the Puritan culture upon which New England and the city of Boston were founded.[11]

John Winthrop and the City on a Hill

On June 6, 1630, after two storm-tossed months at sea, the Winthrop Fleet of eleven sailing ships was only a few days away from its destination of Massachusetts Bay. America was in sight—the New World. It may have been at this moment, aboard the ship named *Arbella,* that John Winthrop wrote these now famous lines:

> we must consider that we shall be as a city upon a hill. The eyes of all people are upon us.[12]

Originally designed for carrying freight, the ships on this voyage were carrying a cargo of 700 colonists, including men, women, and children of all ages, 240 cattle, 60 horses, 40 goats as well as other animals, one ton of baggage per family, plus a crew of 400 sailors. They all had left the Boston, England, area in early spring and were on their way to their new colony in New England where they would found the city of Boston, Massachusetts. This was the first large wave of the Great Migration, which brought about twenty thousand English emigrants to America over a period of about two decades from 1620 to 1640.[13]

The potential for economic opportunity was a strong incentive for these early colonists to uproot themselves from their ancestral homes, perhaps never to return. In England, many of them had been essentially serfs, laboring their whole lives on someone else's land with no hope of ever improving their lives. Even John Winthrop, the landowner of Groton Manor and a college-educated lawyer, had felt a discouraging financial strain caused by recent economic hardships and a heavy tax burden imposed through dubious means by an unpopular king. But in New England, anyone could own land and keep the fruits of their own labor.[14]

The incentive may have been largely financial, but what inspired and motivated the Great Migration was religious zeal. Among this group were some of England's most fervent Christians, who had been recruited for the colonization project by the most reform-minded Christian clergy. Winthrop had had a transforming religious experience during a sorrowful time where God filled him with "such power of faith" and "sense of his love" as made his "heart melt with joy." After this deepening of his religious convictions, Winthrop, like many others in this group, was no longer content with the Church of England at that time, which seemed to many of these devout Christians to be hopelessly corrupted. The move to America offered the opportunity to improve their society, government, and church—to create a civilization that was more pure than that of England. In the metaphor of Jesus' Sermon on the Mount (Matt. 5:14), they would be a city on a hill, a radiating light shining brightly in dark times.[15]

As the *Arbella* neared its destination of Massachusetts Bay, John Winthrop outlined the spirit of the new nation he hoped to help establish in America in his now-famous work, "A Model of Christian Charity." Winthrop had been elected governor of the colony even before the group left England because of his reputation for integrity. In his mission statement, he made high demands:

> That which the most in their churches maintain as truth in profession only, we must bring into familiar and constant practice. . . . [W]e must love one another with a pure heart fervently.

He envisioned a society where every member—rich and poor, prominent and lowly, righteous and regenerate—would be knit together into one united body, charitable toward each other even in financial concerns. Winthrop concluded with a charge of responsibility similar to that which Moses had given to the Israelites as they prepared to enter the Promised Land. These New England settlers had been given a "special commission" by God and must be faithful in their Christianity, strictly observe God's commandments, and avoid "the common corruptions of this evil world," otherwise their new civilization would certainly experience a figurative shipwreck. Winthrop warned:

> if our hearts shall turn away, so that we will not obey, but shall be seduced, and worship other Gods, our pleasure and profits, and serve them; it is propounded unto us this day, we shall surely perish out of the good land whither we pass over this vast sea to possess it.

In Winthrop's role as governor, he worked with clergy and other community leaders to create a new form of government for the colony that supported their religious ideals. At times Winthrop was challenged by people who disagreed with his approach. Roger Williams and Anne Hutchinson were two such influential individuals in the earliest years of the new settlement of Boston. They each actively promoted their alternative views to the point that it threatened the unity of the colony. Winthrop handled their challenges by inviting them to go start their own colony in Rhode Island, and he banished them from Massachusetts.[16]

Even at the time, Winthrop was severely criticized for his banishments, especially of Anne Hutchinson, by those who expected the newly settled American colony to practice greater religious tolerance. A theological aspect of the Hutchinson conflict was her objection to New England leaders putting so much importance on law and right living—an approach she condescendingly called "legalism." To Winthrop supporters, she and her followers were "opinionists." Winthrop believed Hutchinson's views to be "dangerous errors" that would encourage sexual licentiousness. The leading Boston clergyman, Reverend John Cotton, who wrote the first legal codes for Massachusetts, agreed with Winthrop that without a focus on encouraging right behavior, "more dangerous evils and filthy uncleanness and other sins will follow than you do now imagine or conceive!"[17]

As governor, Winthrop confronted every type of issue in the colony, including all sorts of sexual activities that he believed "tended to the frustration of the ordinance of marriage." His approach to elevating humanity was to set a high standard for behavior through law that recognized the covenant between God and man. He expected people to "quietly and cheerfully submit unto that authority" in order to preserve their own liberties.[18]

Winthrop recognized two types of liberty: natural and civil. "Natural liberty" meant the choice to do anything, good or evil. Natural liberty was "that great enemy of truth and peace, that wild beast, which all the ordinances of God are bent against, to restrain and subdue it." To Winthrop, "civil liberty" meant the moral law. This was "a liberty to that only which is good, just, and honest. This liberty you are to stand for . . . . It is of the same kind of liberty wherewith Christ hath made us free."[19]

Winthrop was a prominent community leader for nearly twenty years, an important historian of early American settlements, and as early as a generation later, Winthrop was extolled as "the father of New England." Two and a half centuries later, a statue of John Winthrop would be installed in the National Statuary Hall in the United States Capitol Building to represent the state of Massachusetts. He has sometimes been referred to as an American founding father. Today he is remembered as a Puritan.[20]

Among the millions of immigrants who eventually came to the region later known as the United States of America, the Puritans were a tiny minority, yet their influence on America has been disproportionately large because of their foundational role. They laid a legal and organizational framework for a new society, which influenced neighboring settlements as they developed. Alexis de Tocqueville, in his 1835 commentary *Democracy in America*, wrote:

> The civilization of New England has been like a beacon lit upon the mountain tops which, after warming all in its vicinity, casts a glow over the distant horizon. . . . The founding of New England was a novel spectacle and everything attending it was unusual and original.[21]

Even in today's culturally diverse America, representing immigrants of every race, culture, and religion in the world, the United States Presidential Proclamation for the Thanksgiving Day national holiday typically includes mention of the 1620 arrival of the sailing ship *Mayflower* at Plymouth Rock near Boston. As part of their first history lessons, young school children in America draw pictures of early colonists wearing black hats with flat brims, sharing the harvest of their first crops with friendly indigenous people. United States politicians often refer to the Winthrop's vision of America as a city on a hill. These New England settlers who had such an influence on the shaping of America were also the cultural and religious influence for Mary Baker Eddy, including her views on marriage.

Martin Luther and the Protestant Christians

Those whom historians have called Puritans would not have used that label to describe themselves. They called each other "the godly." The term "Puritan" was coined in the mid-1500s as an insult. It was a politically motivated smear against nonconforming Christians — those who called for change in the Church of England, which was a state-run church controlled by a monarchy. In a social context, Puritan was a derogatory term for a person who would stay at home on a Sunday to read the Bible instead of playing games or dancing. Historians use the term for a Christian movement between the early 1500s and 1700 that originated in England.[22]

The Puritans wanted to reform and revitalize Christianity — to purify it! They were part of a larger Protestant Christian movement that protested the long-standing control of religion and government throughout Europe by the Roman Catholic Church.

Martin Luther was one of the first and most famous Christians to reject Catholic teachings on salvation. All Christians agreed that humanity was corrupt. In the Bible, the first man and woman, Adam and Eve, disobeyed a commandment of God; they sinned. This "original sin" caused all humanity to be cursed and banished from paradise, thus explaining the woeful human condition. But Protestants and Catholics disagreed on how sinners could be redeemed, or saved from destruction—the way of salvation.

Catholic practices in the early 1500s included church fund-raisers where people could buy their salvation. In 1517 Martin Luther publicly disputed this theological approach in favor of seeing salvation as a gift of grace from God. To Luther, salvation could not be bought with money or earned through doing good works, and it did not require the intervention of priests. Accepting as authority the Bible—not priests—and having become "convinced by the testimony of Scripture" that his thinking conformed with biblically based divine law, Luther expressed the spirit of the Protestant movement when he told church authorities, "My conscience is captive to the Word of God. I cannot and will not recant anything, for to go against conscience is neither right nor safe. Here I stand; there is nothing else I can do. God help me. Amen."

Likewise, following the dictates of conscience, in 1526 William Tyndale translated the New Testament of the Bible into English and published it in defiance of church rules. Church officials eventually punished him for his defiance by having him burned at the stake—the standard punishment for religious heretics. Tyndale's risk-taking is an example of how fervently the Protestant Christians wanted everyone to read the Bible for themselves in their own language, and to own a copy of the book.

To the Puritans, no possession was more valuable than the Bible, and no activity more important than reading it, studying it, discussing it, and striving to follow the teachings of it. They believed the Bible described timeless principles for living a godly life, which could be thoughtfully applied to their own lives in their own era. The Bible was the final authority in how to live a God-centered life. Biblical "law spiritually interpreted," according to William Tyndale, came through grace and an absolutely sincere Christian love, which "written in thine heart, are the keys which open all the scriptures unto thee." In the same spirit of biblical interpretation, Mary Baker Eddy would write her book *Science and Health* and eventually call it "Key to the Scriptures."[23]

The Puritans valued heartfelt transformation of personal character and moral conscience. They adhered to John Calvin's Reformed branch of the Protestant movement, which took the rejection of Catholic theology a step further than Luther. To Calvin, Christian salvation required overcoming sin through repentance, reformation, and regeneration. But God's gracious salvation was not chosen by the individual through free will. Salvation was initiated by the sovereign God, acting according to a divine plan established before the world began. Because it seemed that not everyone would be transformed before death, and thus saved from eternal punishment, it logically followed that only some were predestined for salvation—God's elect. Presumably, the Puritans were God's chosen people, and the human experience was a time to do preparation work for eternal life. This Calvinist doctrine of predestination was adopted by the Congregational and Presbyterian denominations of Reformed Protestant Christianity.

Puritans observed the Sunday Sabbath by reserving the whole day for church services and meetings, charity work, prayer, reading the Bible, and household discussions on Christian teachings. They were prolific writers on theology for a broad audience (writing in English, rather than Latin), tireless evangelizers, and outgoing teachers, spreading their views throughout Europe, and later in the American colonies.

Puritan views of church and Christianity were not welcome within the state-controlled Church of England, so the nonconforming Puritan religion developed as a subculture outside the church in homes and local communities. But all residents in England were required by law to attend their local Church of England. In their reform efforts, Puritans wanted simpler, more substantive religious worship. They wanted church edifices without elaborate ornamentation, services with less ritual and more inspired sermons, and biblical scholars for clergy. As the religious movement grew, government church officials saw it as a political threat. Puritan efforts to resist papist influences under Catholic-leaning King Charles I were sometimes disruptive and even destructive. Those participating in the rebellion were removed from their church roles and sometimes faced criminal charges. The religious and political conflict in that period was the reason for the Great Migration of the 1630s—both why Puritans wanted to go to America, and why the king was glad to have so many of them leave England.[24]

Some early Boston-area settlers first lived as political refugees in the more culturally diverse and religiously tolerant country of Holland, a center of commerce and international trade. But one leader, William Bradford, cited "the great licentiousness of youth in that country and the manifold temptations of the place" as one of the motives for leaving Holland for Plymouth colony in America. Ultimately, these devout Christians preferred the risks of the long, dangerous journey across the Atlantic Ocean and a difficult life in the undeveloped American colonies of New England over exposing their children to what they saw as corrupting cultural influences.[25]

Puritan religious leaders were college-educated at a time when most people in English society were illiterate. Between all the graduates from Oxford and Cambridge colleges who immigrated to America, plus graduates from Harvard College—founded in Cambridge, Massachusetts, a few years after the first Puritans landed—first-generation New England America may have been the best-educated community in the world. This early focus on education would continue as the Boston area became an American center for higher education—the home of some of the most prestigious colleges and universities in the world.[26]

In New England, the Puritans created an egalitarian middle-class society where everyone could learn to read and write, home ownership was normal, and all laws applied equally to rich and poor, highborn and lowborn, master and servant. They organized themselves into small township communities of subsistence farms and home-based businesses centered around their church and governed democratically at the local level. They intended to create a highly religious society (even a theocracy), but in the spirit of the Protestant reformation, they immediately established more separation between church and the government than there was in England and Europe.

As a side note, as important as their religion was to them, Puritans did enjoy leisure activities too. They played games and sports and had feasts to celebrate special occasions. They wore fashionable, bright-colored clothes — although they chose simple and modest clothing design. It was only on Sunday that they wore the black formal clothes with which they have since been associated. Puritan clergy wore black to distinguish themselves from Catholic priests who wore white.[27]

Boston clergyman John Cotton formally separated from the Church of England and established the Congregational Church to be a more pure church for God's elect. Attendance at Cotton's church was voluntary, and membership was selective. To become a member, an applicant needed to agree with church doctrines, show evidence of right living, and profess faith by publicly testifying about conversion through divine grace. The Congregational Church had similar Calvinist reform theology as the Presbyterian denomination established in England and Scotland, but following the "New England Way," as promoted by Reverend John Cotton, each Congregational Church was governed democratically by the local members. This was Mary Baker Eddy's church until she founded her own.[28]

Protestant Reformation of Marriage

During the Protestant Reformation Era, Catholics and Protestants disagreed on many points of Christian theology. The definition of marriage and views on sexuality were among the most contentious of their disagreements. The doctrine of the Roman Catholic Church, which had dominated Europe for a thousand years, promoted abstinence as necessary for living a truly Christian life. The church clergy — priests, nuns, and monks — took a vow of celibacy and lived apart from ordinary society. To Catholic clergy, marriage was for common people — God's provision for preventing sinful promiscuity among those too spiritually weak for celibacy.[29]

In contrast, Protestant leaders saw marriage as an important part of God's design. They focused on the statement of God in the Adam and Eve story of creation in the Bible, "It is not good that the man should be alone" (Genesis 2:18). Not long after he wrote his widely published criticism of church policies, Catholic priest Martin Luther broke his vow of celibacy to marry a nun, and together they had six children. He set a new standard for marriage among clergy, which has since been followed by Protestant Christians.

Luther believed laws prohibiting priests from marrying were "of the devil." Another Protestant leader, Heinrich Bullinger accused Catholic clergy of being dishonest in their celibacy. Bullinger thought singlehood was more sinful than married life. He wrote:

> For if we judge the tree by the fruits, I pray you, what fruits of the single life may we recite? What filthiness, what bawdry, what adulteries, what fornications, what ravishings, what incests and heinous copulations may we rehearse? Who at this day liveth more unchaste or dishonest, than the rabble of priests and monks do?[30]

Another point of disagreement between Catholics and Protestants was the nature of the marriage commitment. Catholic doctrine defined marriage as an indissoluble bond. Marriage vows were an oath to God, which according to the biblical law of Moses could not be taken back, therefore divorce was not an option. A legal separation was possible after blatant adultery, but remarriage was forbidden. A marriage could be annulled, which left both husband and wife free to remarry because the first marriage was ruled invalid, but this was extremely rare. The effect in common practice when a marriage became intolerable was abandonment, often followed by unmarried cohabitation that produced children outside wedlock. These informal marriages were problematic because neither society nor the law recognized the family relationships as legitimate.[31]

Protestants objected to the extent of church control over marriages in Europe. Catholic officials established a highly restrictive set of rules for marriage eligibility, but church officials could grant exceptions. Because marriage determined property ownership, family alliances, inheritance rights, and succession of government positions, the church held powerful authority and control over individual lives. It seemed sometimes that church officials decided on marriage eligibility for political reasons. The most famous case was England's King Henry VIII who wanted to remarry so he could have a legally recognized son to succeed him as king. When for apparently political reasons, the Catholic Church refused to annul his first marriage to his brother's widow, in 1534 King Henry VIII separated England from the Catholic Church. He established the Church of England and put more sympathetic church officials in charge of the decision on his marriage annulment.[32]

When the Puritans came to America they had the freedom to establish laws that reflected their religious beliefs, including their idea of marriage. In their first legal codes they established marriage as a civil matter, governed by a civil magistrate and civil courts. They wanted marriage to be governed by impartial law, not the whims of politically influenced clergy. Yet they still considered marriage a holy union. The government was separate from the church, but civil authorities, including those who oversaw marriage, were devout Christians. One Puritan wrote that marriage is a

high, holy and blessed order of life, ordained not of man, but of God, . . . wherein one man and one woman are coupled and knit together in one flesh and body in the fear and love of God, by the free, loving, hearty, and good consent of them both, to the intent that they two may dwell together as one flesh and body, of one will and mind, in all honesty, virtue, and godliness, and spend their lives in equal partaking of all such things as God shall send them with thanksgiving.[33]

The Puritans also changed marriage law in America by allowing divorce in the earliest colonies. Divorce was not common or socially acceptable, but it was possible. The intention was to prevent the disintegration of the family from marital problems. This early legalization of divorce (it would be more than two hundred years before England legalized divorce) reflected the desire of the settlers of New England for all marriage-like relationships to be legally recognized unions.[34]

New England law supported marriage to the extent that husband and wife were required to live together, and if an Englishman immigrated to a Puritan colony without his wife, he could be sent back to England on the next ship. Or if a man relocated to another town without his wife or moved in with another woman, he might be fined by authorities and sent back to his wife.[35]

In another divergence from English law, the Puritans forbade wife beating. Puritans objected to the "rule of thumb" standard of law common in Europe, which allowed a husband to physically punish his wife for disobedience so long as the stick used was thinner than a man's thumb and the beating did not draw blood. Puritan law, theology, and customs required husband and wife to live together peaceably. Benjamin Wadsworth put it this way in his book *Well Ordered Family*:

The Great God commands thee to love her. How vile then are those who don't love their Wives. . . . If therefore the Husband is bitter against his wife, beating or striking of her (as some vile wretches do) or in any unkind carriage, ill language, hard words, morose, peevish, surly behavior; nay if he is not kind, loving, tender in his words and carriage to her; he then shames his profession of Christianity, he breaks the Divine Law, he dishonours God and himself too, by this ill behavior. The same is true of the Wife too. . . . The indisputable Authority, the plain Command of the Great God, required Husbands and Wives, to have and manifest very great affection, love and kindness to one another.[36]

To the Puritans, marriage held a high place in the life of a Christian. There was no family member or relationship more important in a person's life than a husband or wife. In a book on godly household government, Thomas Gataker wrote:

There is no society more near, more entire, more needful, more kindly, more delightful, more comfortable, more constant, more continual, than the society of man and wife, the main root, source, and original of all other societies.[37]

A primary motive for marriage was companionship. A wife ideally was "a friend and comfort for society, but also a companion for pleasure." Husband and wife were to be "two sweet friends" who share whatever comes along in life. Richard Baxter described marriage this way:

It is a mercy to have a faithful friend that loveth you entirely, . . . to whom you may open your mind and communicate your affairs. . . . And it is a mercy to have so near a friend to be a helper to your soul and . . . to stir up in you the grace of God.[38]

With companionship being such an important part of marriage, Puritans married for love. But love was expected as a result of marriage, not necessarily as a prerequisite. Puritans tended to be rational, careful, and prayerful in selecting a marriage partner. According to Puritan scholar Edmund Morgan, they thought of love not as romantic madness, but something "warm and tender and gracious." Clergy encouraged the marriage of equals, using criteria that included similarity of age, wealth, social status, and religious faith. The selection of a marriage partner involved both the young adults themselves and their parents. Parents could not force their children into marriage, nor could a son or daughter marry without the permission of both sets of parents, who negotiated inheritance and gifts of property to the couple as part of the engagement contract.[39]

The love and companionship aspect of the Puritan ideal may seem unremarkable to us today because this standard is so widespread now, but before the Puritan era, this was not the expectation of marriage. For thousands of years in Western culture, marriage was primarily about forming family alliances, strategic financial interests, producing heirs, and getting work done, and it was sometimes socially acceptable to seek love outside the marriage relationship. The Puritans established a standard of strictly monogamous marriage as a partnership. But along with the new model came new expectations and challenges.[40]

Puritan preacher Thomas Hooker, suggesting marriage as being for this mortal experience only, was certain there is "no marrying in Heaven." The secret to success in marriage, according to New England minister Thomas Thatcher, is to have low expectations:

> Look not for Perfection in your relation. God reserves that for another state where marriage is not needed.[41]

Another area of disagreement between Catholics and Puritans during the Reformation Era related to sexual intercourse. Catholics defined chastity as virginity. Catholics saw sexuality—even within marriage—as an evil to be abstained from as much as possible. Sexual intercourse was for procreation only. Church officials designated an abundance of holy days throughout the year when married couples were prohibited from having sex. Puritans had no such holidays. They taught that married sex is chaste. They encouraged abstinence from sex before marriage, and "active, honest, and devoted love" during marriage.[42]

The youth in Puritan culture did not always follow the teachings on abstinence. There were brides in colonial New England who were already pregnant on their wedding day. But abstinence was upheld as the cultural norm and as the best practice.

A custom in the northern American colonies, called "bundling," allowed couples to occasionally share a bed for the night in the girl's family home as part of their courtship before marriage, especially during engagement. This was done in the winter months when days were short, nights were cold, and a social visit might require a walk of ten miles or more. Home furnishings did not include any couches then, and bed sharing was common even between strangers.

In bundling, the courting couple was expected to stay clothed and sometimes a board was put between them or other physical restraints. They could enjoy the intimacy of pillow talk into the night, and it was a more practical choice than having the couple sit up all night burning firewood and candles, or sending the young man to walk through the bitterly cold night back to his own home. Visitors from Europe were surprised by the uniquely American custom of bundling. The practice showed a high level of confidence in youth to abide by the cultural expectation of abstinence.[43]

Sexual offenses were taken seriously in early New England. According to American law historian Lawrence Freidman, fornication (nonmarital sex) was the most commonly prosecuted crime in Massachusetts. Punishment typically included some element of public shaming, with a goal of reforming the offender and encouraging marriage. The punishment for "ante-nuptial defilement" (premarital sex), even during engagement, might include a fine and a whipping — a much less severe punishment than for extramarital sex, but still a strong incentive for keeping clothes on.[44]

The Puritan view of sexuality is summarized in this part of John Milton's epic poem, *Paradise Lost*:[45]

Hail wedded love, mysterious law, true source
Of human offspring, sole propriety
In Paradise of all things common else.
By thee adulterous lust was driven from men
Among the bestial herds to range, by thee
Founded in reason, loyal, just and pure,
Relations dear, and all the charities
Of father, son, and brother first were known.
Far be it, that I should write thee sin or blame,
Or think thee unbefitting holiest place,
Perpetual fountain of domestic sweets,
Whose bed is undefiled and chaste pronounced.

However much Puritans sometimes seemed to glorify marriage and the loving companionship it ideally represented, the most important relationship to the Puritan was one's relationship to God. All other loves, including the very best love marriage could offer, needed to be subordinate to a love for God. To support that sentiment, public display of affection was discouraged — it was considered "lewd and unseemly behavior" — and even private communications between husband and wife showed some level of restraint. Marriage, however wonderful it might be, must serve God. The purpose of marriage for a couple was, according to one Puritan minister, "Not for their own ends, but to be better fitted for God's service and bring them nearer to God."[46]

Thomas Hooker and other American Puritan clergy believed God graciously prepared the human heart for salvation and spiritual life through stages of regeneration; the first stage was a broken heart and loss of confidence in worldly ways. This was the activity of the divine, driving the individual away from sin, through reformation, and into union with Christ.[47]

The Godly Household

The household was the most important institution in Puritan society. The success of church and state depended on the orderliness of the households, which were expected to uphold Puritan values of Godliness. The household was in many ways the most important level of government. If an individual got in trouble with the law, the courts would often release the criminal to the head of that person's household for sentencing and punishment.[48]

The household was a school for proper behavior, work ethic, career skills, reading, and writing. The typical Puritan household was an extended family, including elderly members as well as children, plus boarders, live-in servants and apprentices. Parents commonly sent their teenage children to live in other households, contracting them out to work as servants in exchange for vocational training. Girls learned household management, and boys learned a professional trade through an apprenticeship. All children learned discipline and good manners. The household was an important educational institution — a home-based vocational school system used by people of all economic levels.[49]

The husband was responsible for performing the daily duties of leading the household in prayer and study of the Bible in the morning and evening — a practice that created a culture intimately familiar with the Bible. Puritans commonly read the entire Bible at least once a year and memorized many citations and sections. Husbands were required by law once a week (at the least) to teach their children and servants "in the grounds and principles of religion." To convey the Calvinist doctrines that summarized their theology, they used a teaching method called catechism — a question and answer form of teaching where children read, memorized, repeated aloud, and then explained their understanding. The husband led the ministry and his wife assisted.[50]

In Puritan society, the husband was the head of the household. A wife was expected—even implored by ministers—to submit to her husband's authority. Husband and wife were unequal under the law, yet husband and wife, of all unequals in Puritan society, were "nearest to an equality, and in several respects they stand upon even ground," as Puritan author Samuel Willard wrote. In practice, the wife was in charge of managing the household, including the children and the domestic servants. Willard explained, "for tho' the Husband be the Head of the Wife, yet she is an Head of the Family."[51]

Puritan society was hierarchical, with men having all official authority, but this had less to do with superiority and more to do with division of responsibility. The husband was the head, and the wife was the heart—equally appreciated and indispensable parts of the body of the household.

Puritan views included the theological germ for both the equality of the sexes and racial equality. Seen spiritually, everyone had equal value, according to the religious teachings of Willard:

> All the Members in a Family are therein equal, in that they have Souls equally capable of being saved or lost: And the Soul of a Slave is, in its nature, of as much worth, as the Soul of his Master.[52]

Likewise, the prolific writers of the Puritan movement voiced the idea of the inherent equality of the sexes, as in this statement made by Robert Bolton in the mid-1600s:

> Soules have no sexes. . . . And if thy wives soule were freed from the frailty of her sexe, it were as manly, as noble, as understanding, and every way as excellent as thine own.[53]

Because of a wife's value as a marriage partner (the most important relationship in life) and as manager of the household (the most important level of government), a married woman held a high status in Puritan society.

According to historians Catherine Clinton and Barbara Epstein, in the early Puritan colonies women were treated better and had more rights than perhaps anywhere else in the world — certainly in Western civilization. Women could not be forced into marriage, were protected from physical assault, had direct access to the courts for redress of grievances, and could divorce if necessary. Husbands were expected to treat wives as partners, not servants. Also, women were educated to a level that was unprecedented.[54]

The fact that Anne Hutchinson regularly led theological discussions with dozens of women and some prominent men in her large home across the street from Governor John Winthrop shows a remarkable openness to female leadership in the earliest Puritan colonies. In fact, she developed such a large following that she influenced the outcome of elections. However, Hutchinson's eventual banishment from Massachusetts reinforced the traditional notion that beyond the household was the realm of men — even in this revolutionary new civilization of New England. Two centuries would pass before that tradition would be challenged. Yet Puritan theology recognized a great potential for women, exemplified by this statement by Samuel Torshell in his 1645 book *The Woman's Glory*:

> Women are capable of the highest improvement and the greatest glory to which man may be advanced.[55]

Mary Baker Eddy saw no conflict between her heritage of "the Puritan standard of undefiled religion" and her leadership as a woman. Eddy wrote:

> As dutiful descendants of Puritans, let us lift their standard higher, rejoicing, as Paul did, that we are *free born*.[56]

In Mary Baker Eddy's later life, she adapted the Puritan model of the household as a vocational and religious school to her work as a spiritual teacher. At the height of her career, Eddy had a large household full of her religious followers who worked in housekeeping, cooking, grounds keeping, or secretarial duties. Residents read the Bible daily and were given assignments for spiritual practice along with their household duties. Just as the Puritans brought their practice of religion into every activity they did, so Eddy's household workers were expected to bring their spiritual practice into their daily chores. Some of these workers received special teaching such that after three years of faithful service they received a Divinity degree. One significant difference between Eddy's early twentieth-century household and the typical seventeenth-century Puritan household was that the household was headed by a woman.[57]

The Revolutionary Pursuit of Happiness

English Puritans were not the only immigrants who came to America. Even on the earliest ships to New England some did not share the Puritan religious zeal or theology. Catholics, Anglicans, Quakers, and people of other religious affiliations also came to America, and there were early French, Dutch, Finnish, Swedish, and Spanish settlements. But the English Puritans' family oriented colonies had a much higher growth rate than the others, and by 1660 they were the largest European population in America. Then, for a century after the Great Migration, few additional immigrants made the voyage, allowing the Puritans to firmly establish their culture throughout New England before waves of other types of immigrants arrived. Their Calvinist theology became the standard against which all other variations of Christianity in America would be compared for at least the next two centuries.[58]

By one estimate, as many as 90 percent of American citizens at the time of the American Revolutionary War shared a general religious culture of Protestant Christianity. Even as an increasing number of immigrants come to America for different reasons and from different religious backgrounds, the Puritan establishment was effective in maintaining a strong cultural influence through its educational system, including Harvard College, which trained clergy and government leaders.[59]

Even as the population expanded westward and new states were established, Massachusetts was directly or indirectly the model for the laws of other American states as they were created. Monogamous legal marriage was codified in law and any other form of sexuality was a crime. For nearly two centuries after the recognized end of the Puritan Era—certainly through the 1860s—Puritan-influenced Protestant Christianity dominated American culture and marriage law.[60]

Of all the founders of the American Republic, John and Abigail Adams had one of the most interesting and influential marriages. Harvard College graduate John Adams led the cause of independence from the British monarchy in 1776, helped lay the philosophical foundation for the federal government, and became the first vice president and second president of the United States of America. Throughout the revolutionary activities and his presidency, his wife, Abigail, was involved as his primary political advisor, and she maintained a remarkable level of financial independence and self-determination within their marriage. He was always faithful to his wife and called her his "best, dearest, worthiest, wisest friend in this world." In so many ways, their partnership marriage exemplified the Puritan ideal, which essentially became the American ideal of marriage.[61]

The American Revolutionary War had many causes. Disagreement over the concept of marriage was one of them. During the 150 years between the arrival of the *Arbella* and the Declaration of Independence, when the American colonies had been mostly left alone to write their own laws and govern themselves, most states adopted marriage laws similar to Massachusetts, where marriage was administered by the government and divorce was allowed. In the early 1770s when Britain was trying to assert greater control over the colonial governments, they aggravated conflicts with the American colonists by imposing English marriage law.

Thomas Jefferson wrote in the Declaration of Independence about "repeated injuries and usurpations" of England's King George III and his refusing "his Assent to Laws, the most wholesome and necessary for the public good." One of the ways Jefferson was personally affected was the overturning of a Virginia divorce bill he had written. Britain would only allow the colonists to write laws in accord with English law, and because divorce was not allowed in England, British officials voided divorce laws enacted by American legislatures and nullified American divorces that had already been granted.[62]

After independence, the revolutionary generation had the opportunity to begin rethinking their whole legal system as part of the American experiment, summarized by this key sentence from the Declaration of Independence:

> We hold these truths to be self-evident, that all men are created equal, that they are endowed by their Creator with certain unalienable Rights, that among these are Life, Liberty and the pursuit of Happiness.

In Virginia, Thomas Jefferson immediately began changing the area of the law that would eventually become known as "family law." In the spirit of revolution, he wanted laws to be "adapted to our republican form of government, and . . . corrected in all its parts, with a single eye to reason, and the good of those whose government it was framed." The question was what type of laws would best promote the public good in the American Republic?[63]

One shared belief among founders was the importance of integrity, honesty, and virtue in maintaining the republic. In one famous statement, John Adams warned of the dangers of "human passions, unbridled by morality and religion." He expressed the general sentiment of the founders:

> Avarice, ambition, revenge, and licentiousness would break the strongest cords of our Constitution, as a whale goes through a net. Our Constitution was made only for a moral

and religious people. It is wholly inadequate to the government of any other.[64]

Even as America became an increasingly diverse and dynamic society, Puritan-influenced leaders worked to defend their religious ideals and maintain a moral code for America. What Mary Baker Eddy called "the Puritan standard of undefiled religion" was still being preached and practiced in rural New England in her youth in the 1820s and 1830s. At the height of her own prominence as a religious leader, Eddy spoke in glowing terms of the "grand old divines" of the Congregational Church of her childhood. Her admiration of these clergy extended to the figurative battles they fought for their faith:

> Why I loved Christians of the old sort was I could not help loving them. Full of charity and good works, busy about their Master's business, they had no time or desire to defame their fellow-men. God seemed to shield the whole world in their hearts, and they were willing to renounce all for Him. When infidels assailed them, however, the courage of their convictions was seen. They were heroes in the strife; they armed quickly, aimed deadly, and spared no denunciation. Their convictions were honest, and they lived them; and the sermons their lives preached caused me to love their doctrines.

Eddy saw her own theology as an outgrowth of the religious principles taught to her as a "child of the Church, an eager lover and student of vital Christianity" by "those old-fashioned leaders of religion." Like these heroes of her youth, Eddy would in turn spare no denunciation in defense of her doctrines, including her Puritan-influenced views on marriage.[65]

The American Free-Love Movement

"[W]hen [America] realizes that she is the leading nation of the world," Victoria Claflin Woodhull declared to her lecture audiences, "she will rise to the occasion, and shake off the shackles of the Old World's diseased and worn-out social systems which are gradually creeping in and destroying her young life."[66]

To Woodhull, the most diseased and worn-out social system was the institution of marriage.

> I know how long and how powerfully the ideality and sentiment of mankind have clustered, as it were in a halo, around this time-honored institution of marriage. And yet, . . . I believe that in order to prepare minds to contemplate and desire and enact the new and better, it is necessary that the old and still prevalent superstitious veneration for the legal marriage tie be relaxed and weakened; not to pander to immorality, but as introductory to a nobler womanhood and a more glorified womanhood; as indeed, the veritable gateway to a paradise regained.[67]

Woodhull believed that natural love and compelling law were irreconcilably in conflict. She agreed with the free lovers, whose cause of sexual revolution she would champion.

The free-love movement began about seventy-five years after the founding of the American Republic—long before Victoria Claflin Woodhull became its voice and face. In the American cultural melting pot and the free-market of ideas, alternatives to the Puritan model of marriage were beginning to emerge. These competitors included socialistic communities, plural marriage, marriage as a business contract, spiritual marriage, and the doctrine of affinities. Any and all of these exemplified the term "free love" for Americans in the 1870s.

John Humphrey Noyes and the Oneida Community

In 1842 American philosopher and author Henry David Thoreau wrote a poem called "Free Love," which began "My love must be as free as is the eagle's wing" and then suggested any restriction of love to the home as oppressive. John Humphrey Noyes used this poetic term to name his social movement dedicated to abolishing the institution of marriage. Free-love philosophy evolved out of Noyes' rejection of Puritan-influenced Christian theology and the development of his own theology that was sin free.[68]

Noyes went into the Christian ministry after a religious conversion experience at a revival meeting. He studied at the prestigious Andover Theological Seminary and Yale Divinity School, but he began to develop his own unconventional interpretation of the Bible. He concluded that the second coming, or resurrection, of the Christ had already happened in AD 70. Noyes believed that because he had already accepted Jesus as his savior, he had been completely freed from sin. He and the adherents to his theology were released from laws that had previously been needed for sinners, including all restrictive rules for sexuality. This theology was a new covenant for Noyes and his faithful followers:

> Under the old covenant God said: 'Do according to all I command you, and ye shall live.' Under the new covenant . . . he may safely say: 'Do as you please; for I promise that your pleasure shall be mine.'[69]

To Noyes, it logically followed that the institution of marriage was abolished by Jesus himself because of this Bible passage:

> In the resurrection they neither marry nor are given in marriage, but are as the angels of God in heaven. (Matt. 22:30)

Noyes believed Christian perfection was best achieved through nonexclusive sexual relations; furthermore, exclusive sexual relations were selfish and unnatural. He gave the crux of his "idea of Pentecostal love between the sexes" in a letter published in a reform journal called *Battle Axe*:

> When the will of God is done on earth, as it is in heaven, there will be no marriage. . . . In a holy community, there is no more reason why sexual intercourse should be restrained by law, than why eating and drinking should be — and there is as little occasion for shame in the one case as in the other.[70]

Noyes started a Bible school in Putney, Vermont, where he taught his interpretation of scripture, including his unconventional ideas on marriage. A community of thirty-five like-minded people formed around him, which he called a "community of hearts." He and his wife began to have extramarital sexual relations with other married people in the community. Noyes described it this way:

> step by step, the school advanced from community of faith, to community of property, community of households, community of affection.[71]

Not long after these steps were taken, criminal charges of adultery were filed and warrants issued for the arrest of Noyes and his followers. They fled Vermont to start a new community in a region of western New York known for its openness to new ideas.

New York had originally been established as New Amsterdam by a Dutch corporation to be an American commercial center for international trade. The colony leaders took an inclusive and tolerant approach to other cultures and religions, so it became an early safe haven for Quakers, Jews, Muslims, and others. The Dutch approach of tolerance was not motivated by a desire to promote inalienable human rights, but because it was good for business. In fact, for the same business motive the Dutch introduced African slavery in 1626 to New York. Even when the Dutch lost control of the settlement to England, New

York retained the spirit of tolerance for cultural and religious diversity.[72]

The region in New York between the Adirondack Mountains and the Great Lakes in the 1840s was a vibrant economic center for agriculture, food processing, and the shipping trade because of the newly built Erie Canal. It was also the epicenter of revival Christianity. This new type of Protestant Christianity included the belief that anyone can avoid everlasting punishment in the fires of hell and win a ticket to heaven by agreeing to be saved and reforming their lives. In contrast to the college-educated Puritan preachers, in revival Christianity, the only requirement to be a preacher was to be full of the Holy Spirit. Even a child could preach! Roving evangelists set up tents in rural areas and held huge meetings, where they led the crowds into a frenzy of excitement. The region had so often hosted these fiery revival meetings that it was dubbed the "burnt-over district" by Presbyterian preacher Charles Grandison Finney.

Elizabeth Cady Stanton, who attended a women's seminary college in Troy, New York, described her experience at a revival meeting where she heard a sermon by the famous Reverend Finney:

> I can see him now, his great eyes rolling around the congregation and his arms flying about in the air like those of a windmill. . . . He described Hell and the Devil and the long procession of sinners being swept down the rapids about to make the awful plunge into the burning depths of liquid fire below and the rejoicing hosts in the Inferno coming up to meet them with the shouts of the Devil echoing through the vaulted arches. He suddenly halted and pointing his index finger at the supposed procession, he exclaimed:
>
> 'There, do you not see them?'
>
> I was brought up to such a pitch that I actually jumped up and gazed in the direction to which he pointed, while the

picture glowed before my eyes and remained with me for months afterwards.[73]

Christian revivals became a transforming force in the American religious landscape. Inspired and motivated by such exciting sermons, immigrants and the unchurched joined evangelical Christian denominations in droves.[74]

It was in this "burnt-over" region of western New York that the previously obscure Shaker religion flourished—an offshoot of the Quaker religion where believers quivered and shook with religious ecstasy. It was here that the Seventh Day Adventist denomination began, and Joseph Smith founded the Mormon religion after receiving an angel revelation for the *Book of Mormon*. Here antislavery activists like William Lloyd Garrison and runaway slave Frederick Douglas could make highly controversial statements demanding the abolition of the institution of slavery and the immediate integration of the millions of Africans into American society (rather than shipping them back to Africa as most antislavery Americans preferred) without having angry mobs destroy their printing presses, burn down their lecture halls, and cover them with tar and feathers. Here Elizabeth Cady Stanton announced a bold women's rights agenda to the world, and modern Spiritualists launched a new religious movement. And it was here to Oneida County that John Humphrey Noyes came in 1848 to found a community dedicated to the abolition of the institution of marriage through the open practice of nonexclusive sexual relations.

Oneida was not the first intentional community in America to experiment with alternatives to the Puritan model of marriage. The maturing American culture of freedom made it easy for anyone to develop and promote new religions and philosophies and then build new settlements dedicated to solving the problems of humanity—sometimes called utopian communities. New Harmony, Indiana, was one such community, founded in 1824 by a wealthy industrialist from Scotland named Robert Owen. Owen wanted to abolish private property, encourage a nonreligious culture, and redefine marriage as simply a private contract to be made and broken at will by two individuals only. Owen announced his new venture in meetings with United States President James Monroe and other high-ranking government officials, then advertised widely. In response, over one thousand people came to live there.[75]

Other similar communities were inspired by French socialist philosopher Charles Fourier. These early socialistic communities experimented with alternative relations between the sexes. Fourier, who first coined the term "feminist," saw marriage as an oppressive and "indecent custom." He wrote:

> Perpetual fidelity in love is contrary to human nature; . . . the mass of men and women will never be reduced to monogamy.[76]

None of these socialist communities lasted more than a few years before they fell apart. But John Humphrey Noyes knew of them, studied them, and documented them in his book *History of American Socialisms*. These communities were also known and studied by German political activists Karl Marx and Friedrich Engels, who mentioned them in *The Communist Manifesto*, published in London, England, in 1848 — the same year that Noyes started the community in Oneida, New York. Like Owen and Fourier, Marx and Engels called for the abolition of marriage and the family along with the abolition of private property and inheritance rights. As *The Communist Manifesto* explained, marriage would be replaced with "an openly legalized community of women," meaning "community" in the sense of collective ownership, or sharing — essentially what Noyes was trying to accomplish at Oneida.[77]

Noyes developed and promoted a method of birth control to separate procreative and amative sexual intercourse. Initially, the Oneida community focused on amative sex. Under Noyes' strong authoritative leadership, all members were encouraged to let go of their inhibitions and be inclusive of everyone, regardless of age — a concept Noyes called "ascending fellowship." He relaxed prohibitions on incest, restrictions for relatives, which Noyes called "the last citadel of social falsehood." From the elders down to the youth (beginning at puberty), they lived together in one large house and called themselves "the family." All children belonged to the whole community, not to their biological parents. Starting from about a year after birth, children were raised in a separate building by workers who specialized in education. Noyes envisioned the Oneida offspring eventually leaving to form new similar communities elsewhere.[78]

When beginning his social experiment, Noyes widely published his guiding philosophy, sending copies to the state governor and other authorities, so no one could accuse them of being secretly deviant. Oneida would eventually grow to include about three hundred people and become a tourist attraction. The community was a curious showcase of experiments in alternative clothing styles for women, including shorter, looser-fitting dresses and shorter, simpler hairstyles—innovations motivated by a desire to make their female workers more productive in the community's agricultural fields and spoon manufacturing business. Noyes' experiment inspired the formation of dozens of other communities, as well as books and journals dedicated to spreading free-love philosophy all over the United States.[79]

Another small but influential community, called Modern Times, was located on Long Island not far from New York City, the largest city in the United States. Unlike socialist-inspired communes, Modern Times promoted a philosophy of individual sovereignty, with residents declaring their independence from all state and church rules. Its mind-your-own-business culture meant that it was considered rude to ask about anyone's social activities, marital status, or the parentage of their children. Modern Times was not intentionally founded to be a free-love community, but it attracted some of the best-known and most influential free-love advocates. One of the founders was Stephen Pearl Andrews, a journalist, author, and political activist, who later became Victoria Claflin Woodhull's speechwriter and newspaper editor.[80]

Shortly after Noyes established the Oneida community, he left its management to a council of elders, and he founded a branch in Brooklyn, New York, the second largest city in the United States, directly across the East River from New York City. In Brooklyn he published a magazine and continued to develop and clarify his philosophy in a book called *Bible Communism*, which included this summary of his philosophy:

> Variety is, in the nature of things, as beautiful and useful in love as in eating and drinking.[81]

The Oneida community found a champion in Victoria Claflin Woodhull. Although she disagreed with the Oneida approach of forbidding monogamous relationships, she conceded that enforced promiscuity was preferable to enforced monogamy. She preached to audiences across the country:

> Judged by its fruits—by its prosperity, its honesty, its morality, its health—Oneida is the best order of society now on earth.[82]

Brigham Young and Plural Marriage

Meanwhile, in another nationally significant development relevant to the free-love movement, the Mormon religion was evolving an alternative model of marriage that to many Americans was almost synonymous with free love. In the region that would eventually become the state of Utah, followers of religious leader Brigham Young were founding a society around a form of the Mormon religion that included more than one marriage partner. Polygamy (more specifically polygyny, or multiple wives) was such a central element, it was simply called "The Principle." Throughout the American states, the legal term for having more than one marriage partner at a time was "bigamy," and it was a felony crime throughout America. But in Utah Territory, it was called "plural marriage," and it was legal. Not just tolerated, it was encouraged by Mormon church officials who for several decades taught that its practice was required for salvation.[83]

The Mormon religion was started by Joseph Smith, who grew up in western New York when the burnt-over district was establishing its fiery culture of religious conversion. Smith and some of his early followers may have been influenced by the community of Cochranites in nearby Allegany County, New York. Jacob Cochran promoted the idea of a "spiritual wifery" that nullified any preexisting legal marriage ties. Joseph Smith's writings and teachings eventually included a variation of spiritual wifery called "celestial marriage," in which a man and a woman were to be "sealed" to each other for eternity — a higher form of marriage than mere legal marriage which lasted only until death, or "for time."

Although Smith always publicly preached the importance of monogamy, rumors and accusations of extramarital activity came up several times along his path of westward moves from New York to Missouri. In the 1830s, he secretly took his first spiritual wife in addition to his legal wife, then over the next few years, he took many more wives — somewhere between twenty-seven and eighty-four. Historians can only estimate the number because the marriages were intentionally not recorded on paper. Smith's original rationale for plural marriage was apparently the ancient custom practiced by some important figures in early Bible history, but according to historian Richard Van Wagoner, Smith's wives included women who were already legally married and who continued to live with their legal husbands even after being spiritually married to Smith.[84]

Soon other Mormon church officials began practicing polygamy secretly. When the practice became known publicly, it caused rifts within the Mormon community of about sixteen thousand people and hostility with the neighboring communities. In 1838 the Governor of Missouri declared that Mormons should be "exterminated, or driven from the State if necessary for the public peace." Violent skirmishes escalated and Joseph Smith was killed. Most Mormons fled to the undeveloped western deserts of Utah, led by Brigham Young.[85]

From the safety of Mormon-controlled Utah, Brigham Young announced to the world in 1852 that plural marriage was a fundamental principle of the rapidly growing Mormon religion. Although many Mormons quietly refused the practice and the majority of polygamous men had only two or three wives, high-ranking church officials under Brigham Young's leadership were expected to take many wives. Brigham Young eventually had fifty-five wives and fathered fifty-six children.[86]

Free-love communities were small and dispersed, but in Utah the government for the entire territory was controlled by polygamous Mormons. The desire of Utah to join the United States of America as a new state caused polygamy to become a national political issue. If Utah were to become a state, polygamy would have the same legal protection of state sovereignty that had allowed African slavery to continue in southern States.

The political platform of the newly formed Republican Party, whose candidate, Abraham Lincoln, won the United States presidency in 1860, included a pledge to abolish the "twin relics of barbarism": slavery and polygamy. In the years leading up to the Civil War, Republican politicians focused their harshest criticism on polygamy, in part because the slavery issue was too politically sensitive to directly criticize, but the other barbarous twin outside the states was safe to attack. It was understood that criticism of polygamy included that other unmentionable twin.[87]

To counter such politically charged criticism, Utah leaders defended their marriage practices by claiming that monogamous marriage was unnatural and the cause of many societal problems from prostitution to infanticide. They argued that God created men naturally needing a variety of sexual partners, and that men should be able to have as many wives as needed to satisfy their sexual impulses so long as they took care of their wives and children. Plural marriage was Utah's solution to ensure that all women had a respectable and secure place in society, and that men did not have extramarital affairs. In Utah, women had the right to marry, and men had the right to marry more than one woman.[88]

The name Mormon became associated with free love not only because of men having many sexual partners, but also because Utah then had the quickest and easiest divorce process, allowing Mormon converts to remarry within their new faith and neglected wives to be remarried to a more supportive husband. In 1869 when a railroad was completed between the Utah territory and the populous eastern states, the connection meant any American would have convenient access to easy no-fault divorce with only one spouse needing to appear in court. This easy access became an urgent concern for those who saw easy divorce as a form of free love.

Nearly all women's rights activists saw Mormon plural marriage as oppressive to women, even equating it to sexual slavery. They saw no benefit to women in the patriarchal society created by polygamy, and they were certain (although incorrect) that as soon as women won the right to vote in Utah, polygamy would be immediately abolished. Women's rights activists overwhelmingly supported the Republican Party with its promise to abolish both African slavery and Mormon polygamy.

Victoria Claflin Woodhull was one of the few people outside of Utah willing to openly support Mormon plural marriage. In her public lectures she said there were 250,000 professional prostitutes in America, and 2.5 million men visiting them — or 10 male customers for every female prostitute — with New York City and Washington as notable centers of prostitution. She accused Congress of hypocrisy for putting so much effort into trying to abolish polygamy in Utah while allowing prostitution to continue in the capital city.

Consistency is a jewel which Congressmen don't seem to carry about with them. They must be jealous of the Mormons. If the proportions were reversed so that there would be ten women to one man on their side of the question, they would probably let Brigham alone, and think it rather a nice thing to be a Mormon.

Woodhull defended polygamous Mormons for trying to "imitate both the meekest and the wisest of the Biblical fathers." She suggested that women were just as responsible for polygamy as men. She told audiences, "I need not tell you that Mormonism is practiced in *other* places besides Utah." One of these places outside Utah was her own home. Around the time she made these defenses of polygamy, she was publicly known to be living with two husbands and have other lovers on the side. Having Woodhull defend Mormon polygamy only furthered the association in the minds of many Americans between "Mormonism" and free love.[89]

Elizabeth Cady Stanton and the Marriage Contract

The women's rights movement had its own image problems when it came to the topic of marriage and free love. The question driving the women's rights movement was how best to improve the lives of women, but the specifics of legal changes and the potential effect on the marriage relationship was hotly debated. Critics claimed that women activists were undermining the institution of marriage and the family — and could even be interpreted as promoting free love. This was mostly because of Elizabeth Cady Stanton, an influential leader from the beginning of the women's rights movement, who wanted to fundamentally change the institution of marriage to be more like a business contract.

American women had long held an expectation that women should share in the benefits of the American Revolution. Abigail Adams had warned her husband in their private discussions about the Declaration of Independence that if lawmakers did not "remember the ladies" and address this expectation, women would "foment a rebellion." During the Revolutionary War while their husbands and fathers were away fighting the British, American women were forced by circumstance to expand their typical roles to manage farms, run businesses, and conduct trade, and they sometimes surprised even themselves how well they managed things. But when the war ended and the men returned home, women were expected to go back to their previous domestic roles. A later generation of women would foment Abigail's predicted rebellion.[90]

During the first century of the American Republic, the economy shifted from predominantly subsistence farms with home-based businesses in rural areas to urban centers where men competed for jobs outside the home in an industrial market. Men socialized more frequently outside the home as well, often in taverns where it was socially acceptable to drink alcohol, gamble, and use prostitutes. Women were left alone at home in charge of the children and expected to maintain a domestic atmosphere of purity. More than ever, men and women seemed to live in two different worlds. This cultural phenomenon of "separate spheres"was sometimes celebrated in the early nineteenth century. But women in the early 1840s began speaking out against this model for society. Women began entering the public sphere in what became known as the women's rights movement.[91]

Until the mid-1860s, there was little formal organization or structure within the women's rights movement. This was intentional because there were so many styles, approaches, opinions, and agendas. Early leaders were concerned that too much organization would cause divisions among participants. National and local women's rights conventions were simply a forum for a diversity of ideas to be expressed through speeches and papers. The women and men participating were also involved in efforts to abolish slavery, in the temperance movement to reduce the abuse of alcohol, and other reforms.[92]

The very name of the movement—women's rights—reflected a shared desire for women to always be recognized by the law as individual citizens with full civil rights, regardless of marital status. Most activists found repugnant the prevailing legal interpretation that a woman's body and all her possessions became the property of her husband when she married. Women seemed to have no rights because in fact the law in the early American Republic did not recognize a woman as an individual. A shift toward adoption of English law had occurred during British control in the mid-1700s before the American Revolutionary War, giving, as Abigail Adams described it, "unlimited power to the husband to use his wife ill." Based on the biblical reference of husband and wife becoming "one flesh" (Gen. 2:24), William Blackstone's highly influential 1765 book of English law interpretation, stated that for all purposes of civil law:

> By marriage, the husband and wife are one person in law: that is, the very being or legal existence of the woman is suspended during the marriage, or at least is incorporated and consolidated into that of the husband, under whose wing, protection, or cover, she performs every thing.

Blackstone's law book became a standard legal reference due to lack of any American-originated equivalent. Because the married woman was represented by the husband, she had no separate existence in many areas of law. This legal concept of the male cover, called "coverture," was the reason that a married woman could not collect her own wages, enter into business contracts, have custody of her child, or own property separate from her husband. Women's rights activists sought a higher level of individual self-determination than coverture allowed. They wanted civil rights for women regardless of marital status, including suffrage — the right to vote. One of the first legislative victories for the women's rights movement was a law enacted in 1848 in New York granting separate property rights to married women.[93]

Elizabeth Cady Stanton lobbied for this change in law. She was one of a variety of leaders through the long history of the women's rights movement. Although today Susan B. Anthony is perhaps the best known of these leaders, and in 1979 she became the first woman to be memorialized on an American coin, Stanton, Anthony's close associate for fifty years, was also an influential leader. In 1848 she organized the first women's rights convention in Seneca Falls, New York, where she presented the *Declaration of Rights and Sentiments*, a women's rights agenda patterned after the American Declaration of Independence. Stanton was a highly engaging public speaker, but she was also one of the most controversial figures in the movement, partly because of her bold and abrasive style, but also because of her consistent focus on changing marriage and divorce law. Stanton's desire to redefine marriage to make divorce easier was not shared by most women's rights activists.

After Stanton had her disturbing encounter with the fire-and-brimstone sermons of revivalist Charles Grandison Finney during her seminary experience, she completely rejected organized religion. She came to see Christian clergy as woman's greatest enemy, and she wanted to completely remove their role in the institution of marriage. She felt it was especially unjust that a marriage could not be dissolved by mutual consent.

Ultimately Stanton believed marriage should be a simple business contract between two people alone who could make or break the contract without involvement by the clergy or government officials or anyone else—an extreme view like that of Robert Owen, the founder of the New Harmony community. At the 1860 national women's rights convention—the last convention before the Civil War—Stanton presented the business contract model for marriage, called for liberalized divorce laws, and referred to marriage as legalized prostitution and slavery. Her speech raised the disagreement, contention, and division within the women's movement to a whole new level. Many participants felt Stanton had gone too far.[94]

Stanton's views on marriage and divorce turned some powerful people against the cause of women's rights. For example, Horace Greeley moved from being an early supporter to openly opposing woman suffrage. Greeley was the founder of the innovative *New York Tribune* – perhaps the most influential American newspaper of the nineteenth century. Greeley had hired Margaret Fuller in 1844 as America's first woman journalist, and his *Tribune* reported on the early women's rights movement in the 1850s when it was too new and controversial to be considered newsworthy by other newspapers. But Greeley supported the view of marriage as an indissoluble bond, both personally (he was always faithful to his own unhappy marriage) and politically. As a US Congressman he represented a district dominated by Irish Catholic immigrants, who believed in marriage as an indissoluble bond — although Greeley did support New York law which allowed divorce for adultery. Greeley promoted the indissoluble bond viewpoint in a *New York Tribune* debate on marriage and divorce law in the months leading up to Stanton's contentious convention speech.[95]

This was not the *Tribune's* first marriage debate. In recent years Greeley had debated Henry James, Sr., a prominent proponent of allowing divorce by mutual consent, and Stephen Pearl Andrews, the famous individual sovereignty free-love advocate. Now over several months in early 1860, Greeley debated the son of New Harmony community founder Robert Owen, Robert Dale Owen, who as a legislative representative had sponsored liberalized divorce laws for the state of Indiana. Greeley called Indiana "a Paradise of free-lovers" because of its "state of laws which enable men and women to get unmarried nearly at pleasure" — laws based on Owen's "lax principles."[96]

"God forgive you, Horace Greeley, the inhuman sentiment!" Owen was indignant that Greeley wanted to leave the "pure, gentle, blameless, Christian wife" in the "foul pit of degradation" because she innocently married a "miserable loafer and sot," a scoundrel, or a drunken brute. Such a woman would be subjected daily to "heartless deeds of anger, strifes, selfishness, cruelty, ruffianism." Owen claimed that Indiana's laws that allowed divorce for any cause had compassionately improved "the holiest of earthly institutions" by "dissolving misery-bringing unions." In contrast, New York's stricter law, which allowed divorce only for adultery, had produced elopements, adultery, free-love, and "that most terrible of all social sins, prostitution."[97]

In his rebuttal to Owen, Greeley countered:

[W]hat *is* Marriage? . . . Dr. Webster's great Dictionary says:

"MARRIAGE: The act of uniting a man and woman *for life*; wedlock; the legal union of a man and woman *for life*. Marriage is a contract both civil and religious, by which the parties engage to live together in mutual affection and fidelity *till death shall separate them.*"

I am perfectly willing to see all Social experiments tried that any earnest, rational being deems calculated to promote the well-being of the human family; but I insist that this matter of Marriage and Divorce has passed beyond the reasonable scope of experiment. The ground has all been traveled over and over—from Indissoluble Monogamic Marriage down through Polygamy, Concubinage, easy Divorce, to absolute Free Love, mankind have tried every possible modification and shade of relation between Man and Woman. If these multiform, protracted, diversified, infinitely repeated experiments have not established the superiority of the union of one man to one woman for life—in short, Marriage—to all other forms of sexual relation, then History is a deluding mist, and Man has hitherto lived in vain.[98]

At this point, Elizabeth Cady Stanton joined the public debate on marriage and divorce. At the contentious 1860 women's rights convention, other leaders had blocked her motion supporting marriage as a business contract by arguing that marriage and divorce law were irrelevant to the cause of woman suffrage. Stanton took her failed resolution directly to the people by submitting it to the *New York Tribune* for publishing. She argued:

Now, it must strike every careful thinker that an immense difference rests in the fact that man has made the laws, cunningly and selfishly, for his own purpose. From Coke down to Kent, who can cite one clause of the marriage contract where woman has the advantage? ... Is not the very letter and spirit of the marriage contract based in the idea of the supremacy of man as the keeper of woman's virtue, her sole protection and support? Out of marriage, woman asks nothing at this hour but the elective franchise. It is only in marriage that she must demand her rights to person, children, property, wages, life, liberty, and the pursuit of happiness.[99]

In Stanton's controversial resolution, she stated that the contract between "matrimonial partners" should be "no more perpetual" than between business partners, government office holders, or any other relationship in life. Greeley responded:

E. C. S. writes us an elaborate essay on Marriage and Divorce, intended to show that the Law of Marriage, as it now exists, is unequal, and does injustice to Woman. . . . This is the broadest and fullest assertion of the right of Divorce at the pleasure of husband and wife — nay, of either of them — that we ever confronted. The doctrine is in our eyes simply infernal, and calculated to plunge the world into a bottomless abyss of sensuality and lewdness. There are fifty thousand men in this city who would each take a new wife at least as often as he ordered a new coat if the laws were modified into accordance with the above propositions; and they would have little difficulty in finding wives to take. God pity the generation of children doomed to grow up under such a dispensation![100]

Greeley further declared that "the good citizen will cheerfully bear the ills of an unfit marriage rather than seek its dissolution at the cost of the general good."

Greeley did not sway Stanton. She held to her views on marriage and divorce. When the women's rights conventions resumed after the Civil War, she continued the debate using increasingly provocative language. In 1870 Stanton expressed herself this way:

From a woman's standpoint I see that marriage, as an individual tie, is slavery for woman, because law, religion, and public sentiment all combine . . . to hold her true to this relation, whatever it may be, and there is no other human slavery that knows such depths of degradation as a wife chained to a man whom she neither loves nor respects.[101]

From the opposing side of the marriage question, women's rights leader Lucy Stone denounced "all this loose, pestiferous talk in favor of *easy divorce*." Stone believed that Stanton's position, "legitimately carried out...[would] abrogate marriage . . . and we have then the hideous thing known as 'free love.' Be not deceived," Stone warned, "*free love means free lust*."[102]

World-famous American novelist Harriet Beecher Stowe started to get involved in the women's rights movement after the Civil War. Anthony and Stanton hoped Stowe would rally support for the cause of woman's rights as she had done for the cause of abolishing African slavery with her international bestselling book *Uncle Tom's Cabin*. But after brief involvement with Stanton, Stowe abandoned the movement and even became somewhat hostile to it. She privately referred to Anthony and Stanton's organization as "Mrs. Stanton and the free love roost of harpies generally." In fact, Stanton would become the biggest supporter of Victoria Claflin Woodhull's participation in the women's rights movement. As if to respond to Stowe's public withdrawal of support, Stanton made this equally public statement:

The men and women who are dabbling with the suffrage movement for women should be at once therefore and emphatically warned what they mean logically if not consciously in all they say is next social equality, and next Freedom, or in a word Free Love, and if they wish to get out of the boat, they should for safety get out now, for delays are dangerous.[103]

Spiritual Marriage and the Doctrine of Affinities

Around the same time as the first women's rights convention, and not far from Seneca Falls, New York, another movement was just beginning, which would have huge significance for women's rights, free love, and the American religious landscape. In 1848 in Rochester, New York, the first rappings of modern American Spiritualism were heard.

The local news was abuzz about reports of communications from the spirit world and people from all over were coming to witness the phenomenon. It all began in a farmhouse in rural Hydesville, New York. Two teenage sisters, Maggie and Katie Fox, claimed to be able to communicate with a local ghost. They proved to their superstitious mother that they could ask the ghost questions and he would reply with strange knocking sounds, called "rappings." Their mother told all the neighbors about it and soon the neighbors wanted demonstrations too.

At first the ghost could only answer yes or no questions by replying with one or two raps. But soon a helpful neighbor printed the letters of the alphabet with corresponding numbers on a board. By counting the number of raps, the girls could take dictation of letters then combine them into words, phrases, and even whole sentences. Because no one could find a physical source for the sounds, witnesses concluded that the rapping sounds must be coming from the spirit world. People were fascinated and the newspapers reported on the mystery. The news spread throughout the country.

No one seemed to notice that the ghost communication was first reported by two bored teenagers on the eve of April Fools Day. Forty years later Maggie Fox publicly declared it was all merely a childish prank that got out of control. She confessed that she and her sister made the ghostly rapping sounds by cracking the joints in their toes. But hoax or not, large crowds of paranormal curiosity seekers arrived and began camping out around the farmhouse. To escape the crowds, the teenaged sisters were moved to the home of their older sister Leah in the nearby city of Rochester, New York.[104]

Leah was a single mother who worked as a piano teacher to support herself and her daughter since being abandoned by her husband. Leah promoted demonstrations of the Fox sisters' communications with the spirit world for her own profit. The demonstrations evolved into a religious service, called a séance—similar in form to sessions held by Anton Mesmer throughout the United States for group mesmerism, later called hypnotism. In the séances, participants sat in a circle around a table, held hands, said prayers, and sang a hymn. Then the Fox girls would fall into a trance and Leah would begin asking the spirits questions. The mysterious rapping sounds would be heard in response. Leah charged $1 per person to attend the séances. She collected huge sums between $100 and $150 a day.[105]

One early regular to the séances called the raps a "spiritual telegraph." Just a few years earlier, Samuel Morse had invented the telegraph and a system of taps called Morse Code that allowed people to send messages across geographic distances through wires. It was a small leap of logic for many people of that era to believe a similar communication system could exist between the mortal world and a spiritual afterlife.[106]

People eagerly came to the Fox sisters hoping to hear from deceased loved ones. With help from oddity showman and circus founder P. T. Barnum, the Fox sisters held séances in New York City where their fee was raised to five dollars per person, and many prominent and influential people were convinced by their demonstrations. Soon people all over the country were serving as mediums—falling into trances and channeling messages from the dead for a fee. Spiritualism became a significant movement with believers in the millions, supported by over one hundred periodicals.[107]

The success of the Spiritualist movement showed how much a culture of religious freedom and tolerance had developed throughout America by the mid-nineteenth century. In the 1600s "consult[ing] with a familiar spirit" was a crime of heresy for which there were hundreds of executions in England. Even in the more religiously tolerant American colonies, in a famous incident known as the Salem witch trials, nineteen people were executed in one day in Massachusetts in the 1690s. But in 1848, many Americans approached the modern necromancy promoted by the Fox sisters with open-minded fascination.[108]

Spiritualism was appealing to many women, as mediumship provided a new career path when most careers were closed to women. It did not require any formal education or any approval by male-controlled organizations to become a medium. Séances were typically practiced in private homes, safely within woman's domestic sphere. And best of all, as the Fox sisters proved, it could be very lucrative!

Mediumship also offered a socially acceptable way for women to enter the public sphere. In the 1850s it was so unconventional for a woman to speak in public to mixed-gender audiences that when Harriet Beecher Stowe went on lecture tour for *Uncle Tom's Cabin* during this period, she wrote out her speech and had her brother read it to the audience. However, women spiritualists were allowed to speak in public to mixed audiences because it was understood that they were merely channeling messages from the spirits of deceased men. The first women public speakers many Americans ever saw were in trance. To some, the remarkable eloquence of these young women proved the transforming power of mediumship. To others, it demonstrated women's capabilities as public speakers. The effect was that Americans became more accustomed to women speaking to mixed audiences. Many women's rights activists adopted or at least dabbled in Spiritualism, and most Spiritualists supported the women's rights movement.[109]

Spiritualism quickly evolved into a decentralized system of nonbiblical religion with its own theology, which generally included some form of spiritual marriage. Emmanuel Swedenborg, an eighteenth-century Swedish theologian, is often credited with directly or indirectly influencing every variation of American spiritual marriage. It is no wonder that Spiritualists were interested in Swedenborg, because he claimed to have had visits by spirit angels and deceased friends who revealed knowledge of life after death and heaven and hell, which he described in great detail in his books. In his 1768 best-selling book *Conjugal Love,* he described the delights of true marriage. It is an eternal ever-increasing mutual love between a man and a woman predestined for an "inner union of souls" so perfect that together they meld into a perfect whole — "for in heaven a couple are not two, but *one* angel."[110]

According to Swedenborg, true spiritual marriage rarely occurs on the earthly plane because of interference from selfish, lustful, economic, and other superficial influences. But if both the man and woman of the predestined pair believe in perfect unions and keep themselves free from distracting influences, when the two meet they will both immediately recognize that they were made for each other as though an inner voice announced it. Swedenborg claimed to have recognized his true partner, but unfortunately she was already married to his close friend. He remained a celibate bachelor and looked forward to uniting with his soul mate in heaven.

But nineteenth-century American Spiritualists were not always so patient. They wanted to experience perfect spiritual union in earthly life, but unfortunately, the identity of their other half was not always clear. Andrew Jackson Davis, a spiritualist theological leader and lecturer who believed in "one true marriage, namely: the marriage of the right man with the right woman, forever," faced public criticism for an affair with a married woman, for later divorcing a wife he had claimed was his soul mate, and for the fact that two of his three wives had divorced their husbands to marry him. This unconventional relationship pattern seemed scandalously sinful to devout Christians, but Spiritualists were developing a different view.

Within the Spiritualist movement, the concept of Swedenborg's spiritual union merged with ideas from the 1809 novel *Elective Affinities* by German author Johann Wolfgang von Goethe, which compared the attraction and bonding between lovers with the newly developing science of chemistry. The novel suggested that just as some physical substances have a reactive chemical affinity for each other and can combine to form a stable compound, so it is with people and marriage. Just as the introduction of a new physical element or compound may cause the chemical breakdown of the original compound and a recombining to form new stable compounds, so it is with affairs, divorce, and remarriage. Goethe suggested that in love it is not so much a question of morality — of right and wrong, good and evil — but simply irresistible natural forces at work. In Spiritualism, this became known as the "doctrine of affinities," and for those who accepted it, it replaced the biblical concept of adultery and sin.[111]

In the quest to find the right marriage partner with whom they might experience the heavenly delights of true spiritual union here on earth, some gave "spiritual affinities" as the reason for having extramarital affairs, ending marriages, and remarrying, or even rejecting marriage completely. James Towner, a Universalist minister who became interested in Spiritualism then later joined the Oneida free-love community, described his change of thought this way:

> Spiritualism undermined and destroyed my respect for marriage. It led me to look on that institution in the light of a doctrine of affinity, and to regard it as a union or arrangement which the parties to it were at liberty to make or remake to suit their own notions of interest and convenience. . . . In process of time, I became what is called a Free Lover.[112]

Many Spiritualists condemned Christian churches for perpetuating teachings oppressive to women and repressive of the progress of freedom. Andrew Jackson Davis' theology rejected all Christian concepts of sin, judgment, hell, and even the need for a Christ savior or atonement — in favor of his harmonial philosophy of beautiful and benign nature. Spiritualists tended to support some type of free-love philosophy, and free lovers generally adopted Spiritualism as their religion. Author Alfred Cridge went so far as to claim that "free love is the doctrine of Spiritualism."[113]

Much of Victoria Claflin Woodhull's writing and speeches used the language of the doctrine of affinity. At the height of her career, a book publisher in Boston released a new English translation of Goethe's novel *Elective Affinities* and asked Woodhull to write the introduction. Woodhull explained that "the subtle insinuation of a great revolutionary doctrine pervades the whole" book. She wrote:

> Undoubtedly, he shocked the age he lived in, both by his writings and by his life, even in Germany, where the puritanical element has always had less sway than it has had among us; but now, if the book runs any risk of a failure to command the public interest, it will be as I have said, for the opposite reason, that it may be thought not radical and outspoken enough.[114]

To Woodhull, the "great revolutionary doctrine" in Goethe's novel was an early germ of the free-love philosophy she promoted in her career as a public figure—and which she made no secret of following in her own life. Woodhull famously stated, "To preach the doctrine, you must live the life!"[115]

Woodhull supported any and every alternative to legally enforced lifelong monogamy. But by the time of her famous career starting in the early 1870s, free love had taken on a negative association to most Americans, so Woodhull worked to rebrand the philosophy under the name "social freedom." But her critics would not let her escape the term *free love*, with its more negative connotation, so she tried to persuade her audiences to think of the term in a positive light—as something people naturally believe in already without realizing it.

> Do you not now begin to understand, that whosoever believes in the better policy, for society, of leaving the love affairs of the community to regulate themselves, instead of trusting to legislation to regulate them, is a free lover; and

that being a free lover no more determines that one is low or promiscuous in one's habits, than believing that people shall have the right to choose their own food . . . and it would be sheer impertinence for me to interfere, even if you should insist on eating very bad food.[116]

Under whatever name, Woodhull's philosophy demanded a complete transformation of society. It was the final and ultimate fulfillment of the promise of the American Revolution to abolish all restrictions on sexual relations. She wanted to leave individuals free "to choose each for himself to which class to belong," whether that be "promiscuousness, variety, or monogamy." But even for those who chose monogamy, five to ten years was the longest one should expect for one relationship.[117]

Woodhull was open and clear that abolishing marriage was only the first step of her revolution. Establishing free love would open thought to a new scientific approach to propagating the human species, a new type of economy, and a new form of government:

> Society, like everything else in the universe, evolves by natural laws. Marriage is not the perfect condition. It will be replaced by another and more perfect, which will be a legitimate outcome of the old. As republicanism in politics is a legitimate child of constitutional monarchy, so in socialism shall personal freedom be the offspring of legal limitation; and when it shall come, not anybody will doubt its parentage or question its legitimacy.

Along with a new political economy, Woodhull preached a new way to think about morality and religion—a replacement for the biblical model then prevalent in America.

> [I]t is the question of a new gospel, of the new 'word of God,' adapted to this age and generation, as the truth of that olden day was to that.[118]

The first obstacle to fulfillment of her vision of the modern world was the American Christian establishment and its model of marriage.

Here Come the Brides

What do you think of marriage?

That it is often convenient, sometimes pleasant, and occasionally a love affair. Marriage is susceptible of many definitions. It sometimes presents the most wretched condition of human existence. To be normal, it must be a union of the affections that tends to lift mortals higher.

Mary Baker Eddy

I supposed that to marry was to be transported to a heaven not only of happiness but of purity and perfection. . . . But alas, how were my beliefs dispelled! Rude contact with the facts chased my visions and dreams quickly away, and in their stead I beheld the horrors, the corruption, the evils and the hypocrisy of society, and as I stood among them, a young wife as I was, a great wail of agony went out from my soul. . . . I soon learned that what I had believed of marriage and society was the nearest sham, a cloak made by their devotees to hide the realities and to entice the innocent into their snares.

Victoria Claflin Woodhull

God's Gracious Preparation

The moral values Mary Baker Eddy espoused in her public career reflected the New England culture of her youth, including its ideal of marriage. Unfortunately, the Puritan influence in her upbringing did not seem to result in a happy or fulfilling life in her early adulthood. Both of her first two marriages were tragic disasters, which seemed to leave her much worse off than before marriage. Eddy fell into pitfalls that exemplified the types of hazards to women that gave rise to the women's rights movement. To some degree Eddy knew from her own experience how marriage "sometimes presents the most wretched condition of human existence," as she would later describe it.

Nevertheless, Eddy's heartbreaking personal history did not cause her to challenge the institution of marriage. When she looked back on her early life, rather than being bitter about her difficulties, she expressed the spirit of the stages of regeneration described by Reverend Thomas Hooker. Eddy framed her experiences as God "graciously preparing" her for her life mission. Without that preparation, she could not have established the "scientific mental healing" that she called Christian Science and explained in her book *Science and Health*. Her healing system addressed all human suffering, including the sometimes "wretched condition" of marriage. To Mary Baker Eddy, Christian Science

> points to the revelation of Immanuel, "God with us," — the sovereign ever-presence, delivering the children of men from every ill "that flesh is heir to."

A few years after writing her book, she described it to a student as "the outgrowth of my whole life." That included her marriages.[119]

Model of Christian Faith

Mary Baker Eddy's family was typical of New Englanders: deeply rooted in Puritan heritage and American patriotism. One distant English ancestor may have been among the earliest Protestant rebels who agitated for the translation of the Bible into English. Her first ancestor to come to America arrived in Massachusetts in 1640 during the Great Migration. This Baker ancestor had a homestead close to the future site of Mary Baker Eddy's Boston church center. Bakers were among the first settlers of the small farming town of Bow, New Hampshire, where Mary was born on July 16, 1821, and spent her early childhood. Here the Baker family tree spread its roots and branches, securely planted for four generations by the Merrimack River, which flowed through the town.[120]

Mary's grandfather had been a leader in the local militia, which actively fought against the British throughout the Revolutionary War, beginning with the April 19, 1775, Battle of Lexington and Concord. Biographer Jewel Spangler Smaus concluded that members of the Baker family were possibly among those roused to take up arms by the network of revolutionary riders that included Paul Revere.[121]

Mary grew up hearing stories about her brave pioneering ancestors and American patriots. Her grandmother read to her from old clippings of newspaper articles describing George Washington's career, from his military leadership at Valley Forge during the Revolutionary War to his distinguished career as the first president of the new American Republic. Eddy considered these news relics to be worthy of honorable mention in her short autobiography as being among "grandmother's treasures."[122]

The Baker family was well connected to the political establishment of that era. They had personal ties to such political leaders as the governor of New Hampshire and the future president of the United States, Franklin Pierce. Mary had both a brother and a cousin who served in the state legislature then ran for United States Congress. The Baker family estate of five hundred acres of farmland was the most valuable landholding in the area, which meant the Bakers were among Bow's most prominent citizens.[123]

Mary's father, Mark Baker, was a farmer, but he was also a community leader. He helped build a school and served on the school board. He had been involved in the local militia, had worked as a chaplain, and he served in the Congregational Church. Mark also served the community as a justice of the peace—an important local judicial role for enforcing law and resolving conflicts. He had no formal legal education, but through his own independent study and his active role in a variety of legal issues, he earned the prestigious title of esquire. He was a gentleman who "treated all men with kindness and respect."[124]

Mary's mother, Abigail Baker, was the daughter of a clergyman and was "a living illustration of Christian faith," having "a strong intellect, a sympathizing heart, and a placid spirit." Abigail was a well-read confident conversationalist, but being true to the Puritan model of female modesty and submission, she kept quiet at church and let her husband lead the daily prayers for the family. Content with a life focused on the domestic sphere, Abigail was dedicated to her children's education and managing the household. Mary saw her mother as a saint who had "qualities to which the pen can never do justice" and "the very dearest of my kindred."[125]

Mark and Abigail Baker's marriage was a perfect example of the Puritan ideal, and their household of six children, an elderly parent, household servants, and frequent guests followed the form of New England traditions. During morning devotions Mark read a chapter or more of the Bible, and the family attended church every Sunday. Mark and Abigail worked hard, lived modestly, were financially secure, and made charitable contributions to less fortunate members of the community. The Baker siblings had close, friendly relationships.

Like all the Baker children, Mary was well-educated by small town New England standards. She attended local schools through the age of twenty-one, including an academy comparable to a private high school. She attended school irregularly because of fragile health as a child, but she also had an older college-educated brother who tutored her and gave her books. She loved reading and was an exceptionally bright student. In line with her Puritan values, her favorite book was the Bible:

> After school I would seat myself in the rocker, and while I rocked read the Psalms of David or the life of the Master. At twelve years of age my dear Book of books was well thumbed and worn, and many of my favorite Psalms and whole chapters of the New Testament I could repeat by heart.[126]

Thus began Mary Baker Eddy's lifelong relationship with the Bible. It would be a close friend, a source of inspiration, a guidebook, and a comfort during difficult times. She later told one of her students, "The Bible and I are inseparable. It has always been so."[127]

Mary was unique among her siblings in the level of her interest in religion. She loved hearing sermons and theological discussions. All six children had grown up with similar exposure to church and the Bible, but Mary was the only one who chose to join the church as a child. Still, even Mary rebelled against Puritan Christianity in her own way.

She had begun to doubt her father's "relentless theology" of a final judgment day followed by merciless everlasting punishment of all except those predestined to be saved. She was especially bothered by the thought that her older siblings could be "doomed to perpetual banishment from God" because they had not yet joined the church or made any profession of belief. Her doubt of key church doctrines caused friction with her father who considered it heresy.[128]

When traveling evangelists came to the area for a weeklong series of revival meetings hosted by the Concord Congregational Church, Mary attended with her parents. It may have been at such a meeting where Mary Baker Eddy described in her autobiography being examined by an "old-school expounder of the strictest Presbyterian doctrines." She told the minister that she refused to join the church if it meant believing in predestination. But she spoke with such sincerity of her desire to trust and follow God that "to the astonishment of many" the minister received her into the church despite her theological protest. She retained her membership with the Congregational Church until 1876 when she founded her first Christian Science organization.[129]

Young Mary Baker was not the only one rebelling against specific Puritan theological points. Around the same time that she had her confrontation with the "old-school expounder," the famous Reverend Lyman Beecher was making his own theological protest. In 1835 he was put on trial for heresy. Beecher's ministry career included defending Boston against the spread of Unitarianism and Catholicism and training clergy to evangelize western settlers, with the goal of maintaining the dominance of Puritan Christianity in America. But he rejected predestination, preaching instead the revivalist gospel of salvation through reformation. Beecher's heresy trial exposed the fault lines within Presbyterian and Congregational churches at that time. Mary's rejection of key old-school doctrines put her in the "new school" of theology with Lyman Beecher.

Despite Mary's strong personal interest in religion, in her youth she had no great ambitions of founding a religious organization with global reach. A conventional young New England woman, she seemed content to stay in the domestic sphere of society. The only indication of her future career was a strong interest from her earliest years in writing. As a child, she had even expressed an interest in writing a book someday. At twenty-one, when she completed her formal education at the local schools, she began submitting poems and articles to local newspapers and literary magazines—a habit she would continue throughout her life. But she did not pursue higher education or an independent career in writing or public speaking as some women had recently begun to do. Like her two older sisters, Mary was happily focused on finding a good husband and the hopeful anticipation of becoming a wife and mother.[130]

In 1835, when Mary was fourteen, the Baker family moved to the larger town of Tilton, New Hampshire. The move meant better schools for the Baker girls and more social opportunities. Mary was an attractive, fashionably dressed, refined young woman who was intelligent, self-confident, and had a witty sense of humor. Besides this, she was a member of the well-connected, financially secure, and reputable Baker family. Consequently, she certainly would have had many good marriage prospects.

A Love Affair

Later in life when Mary Baker Eddy wrote that marriage is "often convenient, sometimes pleasant, and occasionally a love affair," if she was speaking at all from her own experience, her first marriage to George Washington Glover must have been the love affair. Friends remarked on her husband's "tender devotion to his young bride." She married him because she loved him.[131]

George Glover was an attractive man. He was tall and handsome with an athletic build and well-dressed. He looked enough like Mary's older brother George "Sullivan" that she once confused them. Glover impressed ten-year-old Mary when they first met at her brother Samuel's wedding reception. Years later, Eddy wrote about her interaction with twenty-one-year-old Glover:

> The Colonel placed me on his knees, and said: "I shall wait for you to be my wife!" As I scrambled to get away from him he detained me, by showing me his gold watch, —a memorial now owned by our son.[132]

They met a second time five years later when he came to the wedding of Mary's older sister Abigail. The third time Mary saw Glover, she was about twenty and he was thirty-one. He came for a visit to the Baker's hometown of Tilton in 1841, and they reconnected as two young adults. He had moved from Boston to the South to seek his fortune in the construction industry, and he promised to write to her regularly. Glover's knowledge of life beyond small-town New Hampshire must have seemed impressive to Mary. Charming and confident, Glover would take Mary away with him on an adventure to see the world — first to Charleston, South Carolina, in the balmy South, then to the exotic tropical nation of Haiti in the Caribbean Sea.[133]

Unfortunately, Mary's father did not approve of the match. When the weekly love letters arrived at the Baker house, the houseboy brought them to Mark Baker, who kept them from Mary and destroyed them. As a staunch Puritan traditionalist, it is reasonable to assume that Mr. Baker fully expected to have a say over who married his daughter. He did not want George Washington Glover to marry his daughter.[134]

Mary Baker Eddy later said that her father did not want her to marry Glover because he did not want her to go "so far away from home" to live in what seemed, from news reports of disease outbreaks, an unhealthy climate. But there were many other reasons Mark Baker might have discouraged this relationship for his youngest daughter. At twenty-two, Mary was still a bit young for marriage — although her own parents had married relatively young at twenty-two and twenty-three — and the eleven-year age difference between them might have seemed less than desirable. Beyond the question of age, if Mark Baker read any of the love letters, he would have known (if he did not already know) that the level of education of this potential son-in-law was far below the standards of the Baker family — hardly a good match for his bookworm daughter.[135]

There were also significant cultural and political differences between New England and the South. Biographer Irving Tomlinson described Glover as "thoroughly impregnated with the

Southern viewpoint." In one letter to Mary's brother Sullivan, Glover was apparently trying to encourage his friend to move to the South by enticing him with an opportunity to marry an older widow for her wealth and then take his pleasures with the slave girls on the plantation. Perhaps in the letter he was merely jesting with a friend. But even so, it gives a glimpse of the culture where Glover chose to make his home — a culture including sexual practices and marriage law that would have been abhorrent to New England sensibilities.[136]

In South Carolina, it was socially acceptable for white men to have extramarital sex with the black slave women they owned. Furthermore, unlike New England, South Carolina did not allow divorce for any reason, but it did allow men to have a legal concubine in addition to their wife. Slaves did not have the right to legally marry at all. Their sex lives and family relationships were at the mercy of the whims of their masters, who generally treated them and bred them like domestic animals.[137]

Overall, Glover seems to have been more comfortable with life in the slave-based culture of the South than most New Englanders could fathom — even a Jacksonian Democrat like Mark Baker, whose politics put state sovereignty and maintaining the Union as priority over ending slavery. Glover was certainly more eager for personal financial gain than he was indignant over the injustices and inhumanity of the institution of slavery. He planned a honeymoon for his bride in a center of the Southern slave trade. Mark Baker certainly would have considered all this in his unfavorable evaluation of George Glover as a marriage partner for his daughter.[138]

Moreover, Glover's friendship with Mary's brother Sullivan probably weakened his case with Mark Baker. This brother was the "rash, passionate" son who, according to biographer Gillian Gill, was on a wayward path at the time, like the biblical prodigal son. He had left home partly to avoid having to help on the farm with the harvest and partly to escape embarrassing gossip caused by a romantic intrigue of his in Tilton. Out on his own, on a trip to New York City he was involved with a prostitute; he got into drinking and smoking, and he ridiculed the Christian values of his hometown. It is difficult to imagine Mark Baker being swayed by Sullivan's opinion that his friend Glover was "a fine man" who would make "a good husband" for Mary.[139]

This same irreverent brother made Mary's courtship with Glover possible. Sullivan circumvented his father's wishes by taking Mary on a trip with him to the White Mountains for three weeks so she could receive Glover's letters. According to Gill, Sullivan was acting out the sort of defiant courtship scenarios popular in the romantic fiction he enjoyed reading. Before the trip was over, Mary and George became engaged to be married.[140]

Mary later published a fictional short story called "Emma Clinton," which might have expressed her relationship with Glover and the hard feelings it caused with her father. In the story the father of Emma Clinton is dead set against her marriage to Colonel Beaumont. The wedding happens despite his objections, but at the wedding the father tells his daughter he never wants to see her again. After her husband dies of yellow fever, Emma Clinton returns to her father's house, gives birth to a son, and repairs her relationship with her father.[141]

Like Emma Clinton, Mary Baker would go ahead with the wedding despite her father's objections.

Mary Morse Baker and George Washington Glover were married on December 10, 1843, "under the paternal roof, in Tilton" in the presence of family and friends. After a tour of the area, they began the long journey to the South. They took a train to Boston where they stayed with Mary's oldest brother Samuel. Then on Christmas Day they took a ship down the Atlantic coast through stormy winter seas. Mary, who had just become pregnant, struggled with seasickness during the rough ocean voyage. It was a challenging start for their marriage, but they arrived safely in Charleston, South Carolina, where life was very different than in New England.[142]

Like Boston, the city of Charleston was founded in the 1600s by English settlers who established a new culture for their region according to their own vision for American society. The merchants and aristocrats who founded the city had little interest in church purification, Bible scholarship, or higher education. They named their Southern cultural capitol after the king who put an end to Puritan political influence in England. They created a society where extremely wealthy whites lived a life of luxury and pleasure, ruling with absolute authority over a larger population of illiterate involuntary servants. The economy was based on agricultural exports from large plantations that relied exclusively on the labor of black slaves from Africa. Even in the city, slaves did most of the work. The majority of urban households owned at least one slave to take care of the housework. Slaves also worked in the trades. Charleston was a recreational center for the leisure activities of the ruling class.[143]

In the Carolinas the Glovers enjoyed an active social life, horseback riding in the countryside, and a riverboat trip. Mary raved about all the sights and the beautiful subtropical landscape. The newlyweds took advantage of big-city activities like the theater—perhaps for Mary's first time. They attended worship services at an Episcopal Church, a denomination theologically aligned with the Church of England. Also, Mary engaged in civic life by contributing poems and a theatrical review to the local newspapers. Mr. and Mrs. Glover seemed to have had a happy honeymoon while George prepared for their move to Haiti.

However, Mark Baker's brief first letter to Mary since the wedding interjected with a hint of the hard feelings still remaining between Mary and her father. He wrote with sober foreboding:

> I can say with Job—the thing I greatly feared has come unto you. But commit your ways to the Lord and he will sustain you.[144]

By this time, Mary might have better understood some of her father's hesitations about her moving so far away. Although George may have tried to shelter Mary from some aspects of the slavery system, it was all around them. Their home in Charleston, which apparently had slave quarters, was just a few blocks from a slave market where auctions were regularly held. In George's business as a building contractor, he used slave labor. There were already potentially volatile issues emerging between the couple over slavery. Since early childhood, Mary had always been a champion for the weak and oppressed. The Southern viewpoint was difficult for her to accept. "I never could believe that a human being was my property," she later wrote. She began to teach the house slaves how to read, and she initiated discussions with her husband on freeing the slaves—an extremely dangerous topic. It was illegal to set slaves free under South Carolina law and unacceptable in that culture to even suggest it. Meanwhile, the newspapers reported on political turmoil and revolts in Haiti as the Glovers prepared for their move there.[145]

We can only speculate on how Mary would have coped with life in Haiti or how the slavery issue might have affected her relationship with her husband over time because the marriage abruptly ended. During an outbreak of yellow fever, George became sick and died. This happened just after a devastating loss of the uninsured building materials for the Haiti construction project. Despite all Glover's apparent success as a businessman, he left his pregnant widow with almost nothing. Mary returned "to the paternal roof" as a charity case after only a few months away. The love affair was brief and ended tragically.[146]

Back to Her Father's House

A very pregnant Mary made the fourteen-hundred-mile trip back to the Baker home in New Hampshire in only four days. It was a grueling journey involving trains, steamboats, and horse-drawn carriage rides over bumpy roads during hot summer weather. She arrived feeling weak and ill.

While still in mourning for her husband, she was about to become a mother. Unfortunately, circumstances would interfere with her fulfilling a role as a "regular mother" throughout her son's childhood—and even throughout his adulthood. In her autobiography, Eddy wrote about this phase of her life with few words, describing only the very essence of the human events that separated her from her son. She saw no value in relaying the painful details of these severe life lessons except as it showed that her "mortal life-battle" turned her to God and illumined her spiritual understanding.[147]

The delivery did not go well, and the Bakers were not sure Mary would survive. Immediately after baby George Washington Glover, Jr. was born on September 12, 1844, he was sent away to a wet nurse. The Baker's domestic servant Mahala Sanborn was a nurse for Mary.

Mary did survive childbirth and recovered, but she had lingering back pain and digestion problems—health problems she struggled with for years afterward, which sometimes limited her mobility and drained her energy. Even after Georgy was weaned, Mary had difficulty caring for her child. She often relied on help from other family members, including Mary's elderly mother, Abigail, and her then-bachelor brother George Sullivan, who also lived in the Baker household during Georgy's early years. But the question remained how Mary would become independent from her parents again once she regained her full strength.

Mary learned through experience how difficult it was for a single woman to earn a living wage. She tried to earn money by submitting stories, poems, and articles for the local newspapers and magazines. But these publications paid little, if anything, for her work. Women who had never been married could get work teaching school, as she had done briefly as a substitute teacher prior to her marriage, but as a widow with a child, she was ineligible for employment at the local schools. Her family members pitched in to help Mary start her own school—a one-room kindergarten, with forty children—but it was not a profitable business, and it only lasted a few months before she had to close it. Decades later, she would successfully found her own school in Boston: The Massachusetts Metaphysical College. However, at this moment in her life, it seemed that finding a new marriage partner was the best route to independence from her parents.[148]

Mary was unenthusiastic about the available men in her personal network. She adamantly told a friend that she would not marry any of the men she already knew. But as time passed, she became more willing to consider local suitors.

Her first choice was an old friend from her high school days named John Bartlett. After he graduated with a law degree from Harvard College in 1848, John and Mary secretly became engaged. He had to establish himself financially before they could announce their betrothal. Bartlett sought his opportunity in Sacramento, a faraway western city, which was in rapid growth because of the recent discovery of gold nearby. He planned to find employment then bring Mary and Georgy to join him out West. But shortly after arriving in California, he died of illness. Tragedy struck again.[149]

When Mary received the news about the death of her fiancé, she was already heartbroken because her beloved mother Abigail Baker had recently died. Her emotional turmoil continued because after so many years of hard work managing the family farm, Mark Baker was ready to retire to a smaller house in town, and before Mary was ready for a new stepmother, her father was ready to remarry. These big changes meant Mary needed to find a new home for herself and her rambunctious five-year-old son. Her sister Abigail invited Mary to live with her family, but no one in the Baker or Glover families was willing to have Georgy. Mary had little choice but to accept her father's solution.

Mark Baker sent George Glover, Jr. to live with Mary's former nurse, Mahala, who had since married Russell Cheney. The Cheneys took him to their new home forty miles away in the mountain village of North Groton. Mahala would bring Georgy for visits so mother and son could continue their relationship. It was Mark Baker's best attempt to handle a difficult family situation according to the sensibilities and customs of his own era.

One consideration that may have influenced Mark Baker's solution was inheritance. George Glover, Jr. was sent away at a time when issues of inheritance would have been very much on Mark Baker's mind. He had just lost his wife of forty years and was getting ready to remarry a wealthy politically connected widow, Elizabeth Patterson Duncan. In his role as a local judge and a lay lawyer, Mark Baker would have known the legal precedents that applied to this situation. While putting his legal affairs in order in preparation for his remarriage, he may have concluded that his close relationship with Georgy could jeopardize the future of the Baker estate. Mark Baker valued the traditional practice in which one child inherited a man's entire landholdings. Under this system, all the other children were expected to leave home to make their living some other way. It was common for an estate to be given to the youngest son in exchange for caring for the parents in their senior years. When the youngest son was unavailable or unwilling, an established order of succession determined the heir. This eldercare practice also ensured that farmland would not be divided into parcels too small for economic viability.[150]

Another result of this traditional inheritance practice was concentration of wealth, creating a gap between landowners and the landless, both within families and throughout society. In the spirit of the new Republic, founders like Thomas Jefferson worked to establish a new standard of inheritance where all children would receive an equal share of their parents' wealth. But to Mark Baker, it was more important to keep his estate intact and within the Baker family than to spread the wealth.[151]

If Georgy had continued to live in the Baker household and especially if he grew into a role of caretaking for his elderly grandparents, there could have been a presumption that he would inherit the Baker family estate. As the son of Mark Baker's youngest child, Georgy was in the line of succession for inheritance. But Mark Baker wanted to leave his entire estate to his own youngest son, George Sullivan, with the expectation he would then pass it on to his own son, continuing the Baker legacy. There could have been a conflict over inheritance rights in the future.

Mark Baker knew from personal experience the potential problems of having two heirs to an estate. He was the youngest of ten children, and he had received his farm in Bow as an inheritance after caring for his elderly parents, but for years there were contentious problems within the family because he shared the inheritance with another Baker. By removing Georgy from the Baker household, Mark eliminated any potential inheritance contest between family members or any expectation of estate sharing. Mary would have to find a husband who could be a father to Georgy and could provide him with an inheritance. Meanwhile, Georgy would live with the Cheneys in North Groton.[152]

This inheritance model is the reason that when Mark Baker died, though he knew his daughters Mary and Martha were in desperate financial situations, he left his daughters only one dollar in his will—a mere gesture of inheritance. The entire Baker estate went to George Sullivan, to be passed on to his son George. Ironically, of all of Mark Baker's grandchildren, only George Glover, Jr. ever had children and grandchildren. The Glover family line continues to this day.[153]

Regardless of the reasons for sending Georgy away, this was not what Mary wanted. She wanted to be a mother to him. But without any way to earn a living, she could not support her child. Furthermore, as a widow, a daughter, or even as a wife, she did not have the social or legal standing to control what kind of relationship she had with her own son. She later described the separation from George Glover, Jr. as a heartbreaking experience for her as a young mother:

The night before my child was taken from me, I knelt by his side throughout the dark hours, hoping for a vision of relief from this trial.

She called her son the "Star of my earthly hope" in a poem called "Mother's Darling" written shortly after the boy was sent away. Continuing disappointments and frustrations ultimately weaned her from all earthly hope and unfolded a far more expansive sense of motherhood. Eventually, thousands of people would call her "Mother." But this was decades away. In the meantime, her role as the mother of George Glover, Jr. continued to be the focus of her life.[154]

A Convenient Marriage

"My dominant thought in marrying again was to get back my child." In her autobiography, Mary Baker Eddy described her nearly twenty-year second marriage as "very unfortunate." She met Dr. Daniel Patterson unexpectedly. Her second husband admitted that their "acquaintance commenced strangely." She took the wrong train one day on the way to the Concord dentist and found herself stranded in Franklin, where Daniel had his dental practice. Because her toothache was severe, she had Dr. Patterson work on her tooth instead of her usual dentist. Years later, she told a student that her first impression of him was "one of strong dislike." She "was not pleased" when he visited her home to check on her after the dental work. But her father and stepmother encouraged him to visit again. In getting to know him, she discovered that he was a distant relative of her stepmother, Elizabeth Patterson Duncan.[155]

Mary is reported to have said that "his attentions were so disagreeable as to make me sick." Shortly after he began visiting her, she became severely ill. Dr. Patterson played the hero by researching her illness in his medical books and prescribing medicine. The Bakers believed he saved her life and encouraged her to see him socially. She spent time with him "under great obligations," and she said, "in time I learned to love him."[156]

During their courtship, problems arose and at one point she threatened to end the relationship. First there was the issue of religion. He was a Baptist, which to Congregational church members was heretical. They compromised by agreeing to attend neither Baptist nor Congregational, but another Christian church. Then as friends and family shared stories about Dr. Patterson, questions arose about his morality and personal character. He indignantly denied any wrongdoing. One thing that helped their relationship along was Mary's need for dentistry work, and Daniel's willingness to do her work for free.[157]

In a final attempt to persuade her to marry him, Daniel described his feelings for her as "love standing at the very threshold of Idolatry," and he challenged her to love him just as passionately. In one of his letters to Mary, Daniel declared,

> that is the only love that will satisfy me—no ordinary commonplace love will answer my purpose—it must be stronger than the love of life itself . . . . [158]

He promised her that if she were to be his wife, she would not have her "hopes raised only to be dashed to the ground in a few months after marriage." He promised that his attentive care and treatment with medicine or homeopathy would restore her health. But to Mary, his most compelling promise was that he would bring her son to come live with them and would be a father to him. Unfortunately, he could not keep any of these promises.[159]

On their wedding day in June 1853, Daniel Patterson signed legal documents to become the legal guardian of nine-year-old Georgy. But to make those documents legally binding, Patterson had to appear in court. He never did. It may have been jealousy over the affections of his wife, or the unruly behavior of the boisterous young boy. But perhaps the biggest obstacle to completing the transaction was the $400 bond that came with the guardianship agreement.[160]

Daniel Patterson came from a humble family background. He had done reasonably well for himself overall, and he dressed in fine clothes, often wearing a silk top hat and gloves. He was able to afford a small house, which Mary filled with furniture she inherited from her mother. But the newlyweds were on a tight budget. They owned a dairy cow for fresh milk, but not a horse for transportation. The lack of transportation coincided with a decline in his dental practice. Patterson may have been expecting a financial boost from his marriage into the financially secure Baker family, not a new financial burden. If $400 was the price for guardianship of Mary's son, Patterson never made the necessary sacrifices.[161]

After a couple of years, it became obvious that the boy would not be coming to live with them, so the Pattersons moved to North Groton to be closer to Georgy. The mountain village of North Groton was too small for a full-time dentistry practice, so moving there meant a change of income source and decrease of income. Fortunately, Mary's sister Martha owned a small house about a mile from the Cheney household. The Pattersons were able to buy the house on easy terms, and also one hundred acres of forest land. Daniel would supplement his dentistry practice with lumber work to make the mortgage payments to Martha.

With the Pattersons in town, Georgy naturally wanted to see his mother and spend time with her, which meant time away from work chores. Mary also wanted to spend as much time as possible with her son. She especially wanted to tutor the now eleven-year-old boy who was still illiterate. A conflict arose and George's visits to his mother were forbidden by Russell Cheney and Daniel Patterson. But sometimes Daniel would catch Mahala and Georgy visiting Mary when they thought he would be away from the house.[162]

Daniel complained about the visitation issues in a letter to Mary's wealthy sister Abigail back in Tilton, which resulted in Abigail making a visit to North Groton. In her autobiography, Mary Baker Eddy described what happened next this way: "A plot was consummated for keeping us apart." Shortly after Abigail's visit, about a year after the Pattersons moved to North Groton, the Cheneys moved away to a remote frontier homestead in Minnesota and took Georgy with them. The whole Baker family was fully aware of the situation and most likely funded the move. They withheld information on Georgy's whereabouts from Mary. Mary was told by the Bakers that Georgy was lost. The Cheneys told Georgy his mother had died. The temporary arrangement had become permanent.[163]

With all hope of reuniting with her son having been thwarted by her whole family, Mary sunk into the lowest period of her life. She had always been known as a sensitive and delicate woman with chronic health problems, but during the next several years in North Groton she lived as "a helpless cripple." The stomach troubles she had struggled with since a child and the back pains she had since the birth of her child became severe problems. She spent most of her time in bed. Perhaps because of some combination of domestic duties, incompetence, or a poor work ethic, her husband was not consistently earning a livable income. Mary and Daniel went into debt and relied on the charity of the Bakers, causing more family friction. Eventually, her sister Martha foreclosed on their house and the Pattersons were forced to move.[164]

During this period of isolation, depression, and chronic health problems, when her future legacy was unthinkable, these must have been difficult for Mary to endure. In her gloomy state, she wrote this expression of deep frustration:

> Oh! How long must I bear this burden life? This long and lingering passage through darkness and dull decay, uncheered by many of life's last solaces even till now.[165]

Much later in her life, looking back at this midlife period, she saw a hopeful divine purpose in the disappointments:

> The heavenly intent of earth's shadows is to chasten the affections, to rebuke human consciousness and turn it gladly from a material, false sense of life and happiness, to spiritu-

al joy and true estimate of being. The awakening from a false sense of life, substance, and mind in matter, is as yet imperfect; but for those lucid and enduring lessons of Love which tend to this result, I bless God.[166]

At the lowest moment of her life, Mary made a promise to God that if her health were recovered she would devote the rest of her life to helping other people. This was the first glimmer of a higher life purpose.[167]

Mary spent much of her time reading the Bible. She also began studying homeopathic medicine, experimenting with this new alternative treatment on herself and her neighbors. She would later explain in *Science and Health* how she cured patients with placebos or by prescribing such diluted doses that there was essentially no medicine remaining. After these experiments, she lost all faith in material medicine. Although it would be several more years of exploring alternative healing methods before she would develop the healing system she eventually called Christian Science, she was taking her first steps in her practice of healing.[168]

Around this same time, Mary and Daniel began to grow apart. They became frustrated and impatient with each other. Daniel began a pattern of spending increasing amounts of time away from home, leaving Mary with inconsistent emotional and financial support. Presumably he was away pursuing his dentistry work, but apparently he also began to pursue extramarital affairs. Later as his boldness increased, he even tried to seduce one of Mary's closest friends.[169]

Despite their marital problems, there is no indication that either Daniel or Mary ever considered divorce during the 1850s or 1860s while they were living in New Hampshire. Even if they wanted to divorce, it was impractical for them. Although divorce was legal on grounds that included adultery and abandonment of at least three years, it required a public trial in the state supreme court, which involved the "ruinous expense of masses of depositions," as one New Hampshire attorney described it, with no guarantee the divorce would be granted. The Pattersons could barely afford the basics of housing and food, so they could not afford to get divorced.[170]

Daniel became a less and less reliable marriage partner, leaving Mary alone for increasing lengths of time in an unstable and inconsistent home life. Daniel's first extended absence from her was after the start of the Civil War when on a special assignment for the Union army he was captured and held for nine months in a Confederate prisoner of war camp. But even after he escaped and returned to the North, he found other reasons for being away from Mary. Several times he left her without sufficient funds to live on.

Each time when Daniel returned to Mary she accepted him back, until in 1866, after another blatant act of adultery, she finally refused to take him back again. From that time on they lived separate lives. He promised to continue supporting her financially with a meager alimony payment of $200 a year, but even that was a promise he could not keep. He continued to wander until, according to biographer Lyman Powell, he ended up in Saco, Maine, "in the poorhouse." Journalist Sibyl Wilbur reported that he died in a house fire in the cabin where he had been living the life of a hermit.[171]

As her second marriage slowly fell apart, Mary learned how to survive on her own and to think as an independent woman. She managed to maintain her dignity with some help from friends and family. Gradually she worked toward her new occupation as a healer and spiritual teacher.

Finally, after an eight-year separation, Mary legally divorced Daniel. Throughout America, divorce generally became more accessible and less expensive after the Civil War, although it was still not socially acceptable. Mary could have proved adultery in court, because an arrest warrant had been issued for Daniel after he eloped with the wife of a prominent businessman. But in cases of adultery, it was common to divorce on the grounds of abandonment because it was less scandalous and it generally allowed even the guilty party to remarry. Mary asked the court for a divorce on the grounds that Daniel had abandoned her because he feared arrest for adultery. Her hybrid approach resulted in a quick, simple trial and a divorce decree.[172]

After Mary Baker Eddy had gained a national reputation as a religious leader, one student, Janette Weller, was shocked to learn that her beloved teacher had once been married to the notorious Dr. Daniel Patterson. Much of the story of Mary and Daniel's relationship was recorded by Weller — how they first met, how she had felt disgust on first meeting him, and many other details. Eddy concluded her conversation with Weller by saying, "if it had not been for that man, I should never have given the world Christian Science."[173]

Some insight into that statement can be seen in her poem written shortly after losing the house in North Groton to foreclosure:

Ode to Adversity

Am I to conflicts new to be innured?
No! I have long the utmost wrongs indured
And drawn fresh energies from sharpest blows
Thus from rude hammer strokes or burning heat
With each successive change refined complete
The gold is purged of dross and brightly glows [174]

Drawing on biblical imagery of a purifying metal refiner's fire, she would express a similar sentiment in her later writings on marriage:

Sorrow has its reward, and never leaves man where it found him; it is the furnace that separates the gold from the dross, and gives back the image of God.[175]

The hardships of her first two disastrous marriages were not something to regret, but a hot forge for refining her character, reinforcing her inner strength, and inspiring her heavenward — God's gracious preparation for her life mission.

The moment had arrived for her "heart's bridal to more spiritual existence."[176]

A Great Wail of Agony

Victoria Claflin Woodhull did not consider the adversity sometimes associated with marriage to be a refining fire. She condemned marriage as a "hot little hell." She came to believe that
most married people are "unconsciously dragging out a miserable social existence of domestic wretchedness." Those words
could easily describe her parents' marriage as well as her own
first marriage.[177]

The profound disillusionment she experienced colored her
view of marriage. She told her audiences:

> I supposed that to marry was to be transported to a heaven
> not only of happiness but of purity and perfection. . . . But
> alas, how were my beliefs dispelled! Rude contact with the
> facts chased my visions and dreams quickly away, and in
> their stead I beheld the horrors, the corruption, the evils
> and the hypocrisy of society, and as I stood among them, a
> young wife as I was, a great wail of agony went out from
> my soul. . . . I soon learned that what I had believed of mar-
> riage and society was the nearest sham, a cloak made by
> their devotees to hide the realities and to entice the innocent
> into their snares.[178]

Knowing even a little about her first husband and her introduction to marriage at an unusually young age, it is easy to understand why she thought of marriage as a trap. In addition to
her own difficult life experience, Woodhull spoke of "the tales
of horror, of wrongs inflicted and endured," which she heard
from people all over the country through her clairvoyance practice as a Spiritualist. These stories from her unhappy customers
awakened her to a "realization of the hollowness and the rot-
tenness of society." She eventually concluded that the marriage
institution was the cause not only of her own misery but of all

human wretchedness. She saw marriage as "the most terrible curse from which humanity now suffers."[179]

A Child Without A Childhood

Victoria Claflin Woodhull grew up about as far away from Puritan New England as an American could in the 1840s — both geographically and culturally. The Claflin family was less like a rooted tree and more like a tumbleweed blown around by the winds on the western American frontier. By the time Victoria's father Reuben Buckman Claflin became an adult in the mid-1810s, he was wandering from town to town. This nomadic pattern would characterize the Claflin family for decades.

Early in his life, Buck Claflin worked as a logger and a riverman. Later his career shifted to self-employment in profit schemes involving theft, counterfeiting, blackmail, and fraud. He wore a black patch over his right eye to cover an injury, and one local who knew him during his one decade of stability said Buck "could see more deviltry to do with that one eye than any 2 men with their 4 eyes."[180]

Victoria's mother, Roxanna "Annie" Hummel, grew up in the German-influenced culture of central Pennsylvania and always spoke with a thick German accent. There are several different stories of her family background told by Victoria or her biographers, but Annie herself told a news reporter that she came from "Nowhere." She was most likely an illegitimate child.[181]

Children born to unmarried women were considered "illegitimate," because the law did not recognize parental custody rights, inheritance rights, or a host of other rights relating to children. The child was considered to be an orphan with no relatives. Communities prior to the American Civil War took care of such children by placing them in a household that needed domestic help. A binding legal agreement called an "indenture" formalized the exchange of work for room and board, which lasted until the child reached legal adulthood. Indentured servitude had been a normal part of the American experience from the earliest colonial era. It was used as a system of credit to pay for travel expenses, health care, and education. It was also used as a welfare system for the poor and a foster care system for children born to unmarried women, rebellious children, orphans, and the children of impoverished or "unfit" parents. An indentured servant was one step up from a slave, and one step down from an employee. After the Civil War, when the Thirteenth Amendment to the US Constitution abolished all involuntary servitude, the child adoption model we know today phased into existence.

Annie grew up working as a domestic servant and never learned to read or write. She lived in the household of John Snyder, a wealthy bachelor playboy who loved racehorses, in the town of Selinsgrove, which had ten taverns for every church. Buck Claflin came to the Snyder estate one day to try to sell some stolen horses. John Snyder apparently admired Buck and hired him to be a manager for his racehorse stable. Snyder also invited Buck out for nights of gambling, drinking, and visiting brothels. In the Snyder household, Buck had a room next door to Annie. This is how they came to know each other.[182]

Buck and Annie were married in December 1825, and Annie's first child was born four months later. For the next eleven years, the Claflins moved from town to town, with Buck working as a card-counting gambler, and Annie working as a palm-reading fortune teller. In 1837, after their sixth child was born, they invested their earnings in property in the small town of Homer in central Ohio. Their property included an orchard, a flour mill, and a small run-down, one-bedroom house. For the next nine years, this was home for the Claflins. It was the longest stretch of stability the Claflin family would ever have.

Victoria remembered attending Methodist church meetings as a young child in Homer with her mother, who would "pour forth passionate hallelujahs that sometimes electrified the worshippers." When the roving revivalists came to town that first winter in Homer, the Claflins attended and Annie whipped herself into an emotional frenzy, spinning round and round. According to Victoria, it was after such an excitement on Christmas in 1837 that she was conceived by her parents in the back of the revival tent behind the benches. In that one-bedroom house in Homer, Victoria California Claflin was born on September 23, 1838, and lived her early childhood with her parents and nine siblings.[183]

The most famous Claflin child besides Victoria was Tennessee Celeste, the second youngest daughter. Nicknamed "Tennie," she would eventually become Victoria's business partner. One more baby girl, Zilpha, was added to the Claflin family by Victoria's older unmarried sister.[184]

Victoria claimed that her mother Annie was a Spiritualist even before the rappings of Rochester. At a local fair, Annie had seen a student of Anton Mesmer cure a patient with therapeutic magnets. After losing two of her children to illness, Annie began treating her children with the electrical energy, or animal magnetism, believed to be produced by the laying on of hands, and she went into trances. The Claflin girls followed their mother's example in their own approach to spirituality and healing.[185]

Victoria's first biographer, Theodore Tilton, who knew Buck and Annie Claflin personally and worked closely with Victoria on the biography, described Buck as "impartial in his cruelty to all his children." Buck was an alcoholic who often severely beat his children for no apparent reason. He kept braided willow branches ready at all times and would whip the children until they bled. Victoria's mother was an "erratic" woman with a "fickleness of spirit" who was "never wholly sane." Annie would sometimes watch the beatings and laugh hysterically. The Tilton biography described Buck and Annie this way:

> This eccentric old lady, compounded in equal parts of heaven and hell, will pray till her eyes are full of tears, and in the same hour curse till her lips are white with foam. The

father exhibits a more tranquil bitterness, with fewer spasms. . . . It is said that a fountain cannot send forth at the same time sweet waters and bitter, and yet affection and enmity will proceed from this couple almost at the same moment. At times, they are full of craftiness, low cunning, and malevolence; at other times, they beam with sunshine, sweetness, and sincerity. I have seen many strange people, but the strangest of all are the two parents whose commingled essence constitutes the spiritual principle of the heroine of this tale. . . . The whole brood are of the same feather — except Victoria and Tennie. What language shall describe them? Such another family-circle of cats and kits, with soft fur and sharp claws, purring at one moment and fighting the next, never before filled one house with their clamors since Babel began. They love and hate — they do good and evil — they bless and smite each other.[186]

Victoria was "a child without a childhood," and her home not a sweet home, but one where she was treated with cruelty. The Claflin children lived in poverty in a disorderly house and sometimes begged for food from neighbors. Victoria attended school for only three years. During the rest of her childhood she worked, first as a household servant. A highlight of her childhood was a yearlong relationship she had with a neighbor woman who took a special interest in her. This young woman invited Victoria to visit her beautiful well-kept home every day and gave her food, attention, care, and taught her how to read.[187]

In January 1848 after Buck was suspected of burning down his own mill building for the insurance money, the townspeople of Homer were ready to be rid of the Claflins. The members of the Presbyterian church held a fundraiser to buy a horse and wagon for the family, then asked them to leave town. After they left, townspeople discovered a stash of undelivered mail from when Buck had served as the local postmaster. Buck had opened the letters and stolen the enclosed money.[188]

The Claflins lived next in Mount Gilead, Ohio, another small town about thirty miles away. They moved in with their eldest daughter Margaret Ann, her middle-class working-man husband, and their three children. It was here in the early 1850s that Victoria had her first experience working as a clairvoyant.

News of the rappings of Rochester and the Fox sisters' séances had spread throughout the country, and people all over the United States launched their own careers as Spiritualist mediums. Buck Claflin recognized this new movement as a lucrative business opportunity. He rented a room in a boardinghouse and advertised two of his daughters as a spiritualist duo similar to the Fox sisters. He chose fourteen-year-old Victoria and her seven-year-old sister Tennessee. When young Victoria objected, saying she did not know how to read minds, her father simply told her to "be a good listener." Victoria and Tennie conducted séances and channeled messages from the dead for one dollar per visit, just like the Fox sisters. Buck provided the girls with supportive research from local graveyards and town directories.[189]

Marriage as an Escape

Victoria Claflin Woodhull later referred to her first marriage as "an escape." Interpreting the historical record of Victoria's childhood, biographer Barbara Goldsmith saw suggestions of incestuous sexual abuse by her father. Other biographers have suggested it was the pressure of being a child performer she was escaping. Victoria described herself at this stage as "a daughter whose sorrow was ripening her into a woman before her time."[190]

Dr. Canning Woodhull was called to help when Victoria was suffering with an illness. After she recovered, he asked her to go with him on a picnic in a park on the fourth of July. He was twenty-eight, just recently relocated to Homer from Rochester,

New York. After the Independence Day festival, he let her know that he wanted her for a wife.

In November 1853 when Victoria had just turned fifteen years old, she married Canning Woodhull and left the Claflin troupe. Unfortunately for Victoria, her great escape left her in a worse state. It turned out that her new husband, besides not being a very good or successful doctor, was addicted to alcohol and his mistresses. He regularly spent nights at brothels, beginning the third day after their wedding. He fathered at least one illegitimate child and spent nights away, leaving young Victoria alone for as long as a month at a time. When Victoria left to visit her parents, her husband brought a prostitute into their home and left the mess for Victoria to clean up when she returned. As described in her first biography:

> She was stung to the quick. The shock awoke all her womanhood. She grew ten years older in a single day. A tumult of thoughts swept like a whirlwind through her mind, ending at last in one predominant purpose, namely, to reclaim her husband.[191]

Victoria summoned the courage to find her husband and confront him. She interrupted some uncomfortable scenes in brothels, but she succeeded in bringing him back to their home.

After fifteen months of marriage, while living in Chicago, Victoria gave birth "in almost mortal agony" attended only by her drunken husband. It was the middle of winter and there were "icicles clinging to her bed-post." After the delivery, she became deliriously ill. The neighbors gave her meals until her mother arrived and nursed her back to health. The Woodhulls found that their son Byron was not a normal child. He never developed teeth, never really learned to speak, and was never able to take care of himself.

> When I found that I had given birth to a human wreckage, to a child that was an imbecile, my heart was broken.[192]

Victoria came to believe that it was her husband's drunkenness and the lack of love in their marriage that caused her son's severe disabilities. She would eventually tell audiences all over the country about the tragedy of her son's defects as a teaching point on the dangers of relying on marriage for human reproduction. To sell free love philosophy to the American people, she would preach about how children conceived in short-term passionate relationships were healthier, happier, and better adjusted than those conceived in loveless legal marriages.

At this point in her life as a teenage mother in a difficult marriage, her main focus was survival. In addition to having a drunk and "habitually unchaste" husband who could barely make a living, now she had a mentally retarded child to care for. Out of sheer necessity Victoria began to take more responsibility for the family. She planned a move to give Canning an opportunity to reestablish his neglected medical practice in the West where doctors were needed. She hoped that getting away from her husband's mistresses would provide a fresh start for their marriage. So the Woodhulls took a steamer ship to San Francisco.[193]

San Francisco was a boomtown. After gold was discovered in California in 1849 the population grew from fifteen thousand to three hundred thousand in seven years. The vast majority who came were men hoping to get rich quick. In fact, twenty times as many men as women came there. The city quickly developed such a culture of drinking, gambling, prostitution, and general lawlessness that one world traveler who visited San Francisco during the gold rush era dubbed the city "Sodom-by-the-Sea" — a biblical reference to the ancient city of Sodom that was destroyed by God with brimstone and fire as punishment for its sins.[194]

Because of the extreme shortage of wives throughout the American West in this period, prostitution flourished. Women who had been shunned by their families and friends for non-marital sexual activity or who had been divorced, widowed or abandoned by their husbands could find a career in the sex industry. The most beautiful and charming women in their prime boarded at luxuriously decorated parlor houses where they wore the finest clothing and dined on the best foods while they entertained and pampered the wealthiest and most powerful men. Customers paid as much as one hundred dollars per visit. Older or less beautiful women worked in brothels ranging from high-class to low, serving multiple men each day. From there, these women either moved up into brothel management, out into independent practice, or down to become street walkers, living and working in back alleys.[195]

These women in "the sisterhood," as they called it, were shunned by society both during and after their prostitution careers, even by their male customers. But besides the social stigma, they also faced occupational hazards of arrest or fines for lewd behavior, infections from "removal of obstructions" (abortions of unwanted pregnancies), exposure to venereal disease, addiction to alcohol and opiate drugs, physical abuse, murder, and suicide.[196]

Of the few women in San Francisco during the early California gold rush period, most of them were dance hall girls or prostitutes. These workers, sometimes referred to as "public women," were primarily Irish, Mexican, American Indian, or African. Toward the end of the gold rush, San Francisco took the sex industry to a whole new level with the introduction of Chinese prostitutes.

To meet the growing demand for prostitutes, they were imported from China. Preteen girls were sold by their impoverished parents, kidnapped, or tricked into indentured servitude, shipped across the Pacific Ocean in cargo crates, and then forced to serve their term in the sex industry. The most beautiful Chinese girls worked in the elite parlor houses or were mistresses to wealthy businessmen, but the rest were kept confined in tiny four-by-six-foot rooms called cribs where they served twenty to thirty men a day. Their customers, primarily railroad workers, sailors, and other laborers, paid as little as twenty-five cents per visit. Chinese prostitutes began their careers as early as nine years old, and by the time they were twenty most had contracted a venereal disease. When the girls were no longer fit for prostitution work, they might become cooks, laundresses, or farm laborers. Technically, these girls were not slaves, but they were traded and treated as slaves. They were kept in the district of San Francisco that became known as Chinatown. Although this sex trade was illegal, it was protected by pimps, gangs, bribes, and financially invested powerful men.[197]

Early San Francisco did not have the kind of atmosphere most women would want for raising their family, but by 1858 the gold rush was winding down. The boomtown was beginning to develop into a permanent city. Property owners were replacing hastily constructed canvas and wood buildings with brick and stone ones. The city government was paving dirt roads with cobblestones and erecting gas street lamps. The rapid development offered enticing new opportunities for those willing to make the long, difficult, and dangerous trek across the undeveloped continent by horse, wagon, or on foot. When Mr. and Mrs. Woodhull were looking for a place to start fresh, fierce competition in the advancing transportation industry led to bargain prices for travel from New York to San Francisco by steamboat, making the move out West not only more affordable, but an easier journey for women and children. This is how eighteen-year-old Victoria came to San Francisco in 1858 with her husband Canning and four-year-old son Byron.[198]

Unfortunately, the change of location did not cause a change in Canning Woodhull. Even with San Francisco's great need for doctors, Canning failed to establish a medical practice and fell back into his old habit of drunkenness. Victoria ended up having to support her husband and son financially. Although there were many job opportunities for men, there were very few for women. First, she got a job selling cigars at a tavern, but she was fired after one day of work for not being able to handle the crude treatment by the customers. Next, she tried making a living as a seamstress, going door to door to find work, but she could not support her family on the going rate of three dollars a week. She finally found a well-paying job when one of her seamstress customers, a stage actress named Anna Cogswell, invited Victoria to try acting. For the next two years, Victoria worked as an actress earning fifty-two dollars a week.[199]

The life of an actress in this period was a step up from being a prostitute, but only a step. Like dance hall girls, actresses often wore provocatively revealing outfits, entertained fans more privately after the show, and often received gifts from wealthy men who expected sexual favors in exchange. Victoria's acting debut was in "New York by Gaslight," a play about prostitution, theft, murder, and drunkenness in New York City's nightlife. Her last role was in "The Corsican Brothers," a play about twin brothers who supernaturally feel the pain of the other. One night on stage during a performance she saw a vision of her younger sister Tennessee calling out to her, "Victoria, come home!" She left the stage, packed their bags, and the Woodhull family took a steamboat back to New York City and then a train to Columbus, Ohio, where they reconnected with the Claflins.[200]

Spiritualist Clairvoyant

Back in the Midwest and far from the theater, Victoria launched her next career as a Spiritualist. Throughout the 1860s she advertised her services as a "Clairvoyant Medium and Magnetic Healer." Her introduction to that career as a fourteen-year-old girl had been under pressure from her father, but now as a twenty-year-old woman supporting her own family, she chose this career for herself. No doubt her two years of experience in theater helped improve her performance conducting séances.[201]

Her sister Tennie was now fourteen and had seven years of experience working as a medium. More recently, Buck had been focusing Tennie's career on alternative healing, to promote a bottled medicinal drink that the Claflins produced and sold. Buck advertised Tennie's special abilities: "She can see and point out the medicine to cure the most obstinate diseases."

Consultation with Tennie was one dollar, and it was two dollars for a bottle of "Miss Tennessee's Magnetic Life Elixir" — a cure-all brew that Annie made from alcohol, opium, herbs, and molasses.[202]

During this period before the Civil War, the field of medicine was completely unregulated. Regular physicians still used bloodletting, prescribed toxins such as mercury for medicine, and performed surgery with butcher knives. Those inclined toward Spiritualism tended to distrust regular male physicians and to believe that female mediums could heal the body as easily as they could convey messages from the dead. The Claflins catered to this demographic group.[203]

Tennie worked thirteen-hour days and could earn one hundred dollars a day. Reflecting back on this period, Tennie later said, "It was a hard life. I was forced to humbug people for the money." Victoria later claimed that when she and Tennie worked together as a Spiritualist duo, they were able to earn as much as $100,000 in one year.[204]

Tennie had been supporting the Claflin family. Victoria supported the Woodhull family. When Victoria and Tennie partnered, the two sisters supported the entire family clan of as many as twenty people. This included their older sisters Margaret Ann and Polly, who had both been divorced by their husbands for adultery, and various other family members. Biographer Theodore Tilton described the Claflin family economy this way:

> But for years there has been one common sentiment sweetly pervading the breasts of a majority towards a minority of the offspring, namely, a determination that Victoria and Tennie should earn all the money for the support of the numerous remainder of the Claflin tribe — wives, husbands, children, servants, and all. . . . It is the common law of the Claflin clan that the idle many shall eat up the substance of the thrifty few. Victoria is a green leaf, and her legion of relatives are caterpillars who devour her.[205]

Throughout the 1860s the Woodhull and Claflin families moved from town to town and state to state offering their services. Sometimes Victoria teamed up with Tennie and the Claflins, and sometimes she traveled and worked on her own. Sometimes Victoria's husband was with her, and sometimes he was not. What was consistent during this period were the threats of mob attacks, lawsuits, and criminal prosecution that came up along the way. Charges included fraud, unpaid debt, prostitution, adultery, blackmail, and disorderly conduct. But they always managed to stay one step ahead of the police. When they heard that charges were being pressed and arrest warrants issued, they quickly moved on.[206]

Just before the start of the Civil War, during a period when the Woodhulls were in New York City living in a rented room, Victoria gave birth to a second child, a daughter named Zula Maude. A half-drunk Canning assisted with the birth and botched dealing with the umbilical cord. He then abandoned his exhausted wife and bleeding newborn baby for several days. Victoria banged on the walls of their rented room until someone in the building finally came to help her. Victoria later described this as the moment when she gave up on her marriage to Canning Woodhull. She asked, "Why should I any longer live with this man?"[207]

Married by the Spirits

Shortly after the Civil War, Victoria was married by the spirits to her second husband. In most short descriptions of Victoria's life, especially the ones written for children, the story goes that her first husband abandoned her, and so she divorced him and then later married her second husband, who was also divorced. But the full truth is probably more complex. Exactly what happened is unclear to historical researchers today — whether they were both divorced and whether they were ever legally married — and it was just as unclear in the early 1870s when the topic came up in a court case involving Victoria and her second husband. By this point in her life, Victoria was unconcerned about what she later called "the old and still prevalent superstitious veneration for the legal marriage tie."[208]

When they met in St. Louis, Missouri, after the Civil War, Victoria Claflin Woodhull and James Harvey Blood were united by their mutual interest in Spiritualism. Blood had lived in St. Louis since 1857. After an economic downturn he and his wife and parents moved west from rural Massachusetts to make a fresh start as so many Americans did. He got a job working for the city government. Just a few years later when the Civil War started, he left his wife and young children in the care of his parents while he went off to fight on the side of the Union. During his three years of active duty in the Union army, Colonel Blood fought in almost all of the western battles and was said to have taken as many as seven bullets in the war. He returned to St. Louis in the spring of 1864 to a hero's welcome. He ran for public office and won a three-year term as auditor, one of the highest paid positions in the city government with an annual salary of $2,500. But immediately after the election, he left it all behind for Victoria.[209]

Blood was a founding member of the St. Louis Society of Spiritualists, and upon his return from the war, he was elected president of the organization. So when Victoria came to St. Louis to work as a medium under the name Madam Holland, of course Blood was interested in a consultation. According to biographer Barbara Goldsmith, when Woodhull first met Blood he was with his wife, who was interested in the advertised "wonderful cures of female complaints by means of clairvoyance." According to Victoria, during her first private consultation with Blood, "to their mutual amazement," their future destiny together in marriage was revealed to them by the spirits while Victoria was in a trance. They became married immediately "by the powers of the air." They both abandoned their families and left St. Louis together to travel around the Midwest as a Spiritualist team, calling themselves Dr. and Mrs. James Harvey.[210]

Whether Victoria's union with James Harvey Blood was legal or not (and it seems it was not), their 10-year marriage was highly unconventional. Victoria continued to use the last name of Woodhull—a practice that was extremely unusual at the time. But what was most unusual was their open marriage. Victoria was known to have several intimate and probably sexual relationships with other men during their marriage. Blood must have known about these affairs, but they did not seem to bother him. In fact, he may have even encouraged these relationships as strategic alliances that served to advance their mutual career ambitions.[211]

Blood's tolerance for having other men around included Victoria's first husband. Only a few months after Blood and Victoria connected, Canning Woodhull came to live with them in Cincinnati, Ohio. He continued to be a regular part of Victoria's household for the next seven years until his death in 1873. When he was around, he was the primary caretaker for their two children while Victoria and Blood were busy with the money-making activities that supported the family. In her publicity efforts, Victoria described her continuing cohabitation with Canning as a noble and selfless act of charity toward a "wretched wreck" of a man.[212]

Ironically, around the same time that Victoria united with James Harvey Blood, she had a Woodhull family portrait created. She commissioned an oil painting of herself, Canning, Byron, and Zula Maude—the four Woodhulls standing together looking like the perfect family. The portrait package included a miniature, which she kept inside her pocket watch for the rest of her life.[213]

While Victoria was traveling with Blood, Buck was using Tennie for increasingly risky business ventures. Buck had rented out an entire hotel and advertised it as a cancer treatment center, with himself as "Doctor Reuben B Claflin, American King of Cancers," promising a cancer cure in forty-eight hours.

Annie and Utica Claflin brewed a salve of sheepfat, lye, and scent, which was strong enough to act as paint remover. Tennie applied the salve to the skin of patients under the philosophy of burning the cancer out of them. After the excruciatingly painful death of a patient, charges of manslaughter were made against Tennie. When the police raided the hotel, they compared the living conditions there to a notoriously gruesome Southern prisoner of war camp. Meanwhile, the Claflins had already left town and were headed for the state border.[214]

In the next Claflin venture in Chicago, Buck had his daughters Margaret Ann, Polly, Utica, and Tennie entertaining men. All the Claflin daughters were beautiful women. Tennie had an especially attractive figure and a provocatively unconventional approach to dressing. Historians disagree on whether the Claflin daughters actually worked as prostitutes or if society simply misunderstood their Spiritualist services. Either way, accusations of prostitution along with fraudulent fortune-telling were a recurring issue.[215]

"My God, have I got to live this life always?" was a statement attributed to Tennessee Claflin. When she reflected back on this period in her life, she said, "I was almost lost." At this point Victoria and Tennie joined forces. Whatever Buck had Tennie doing for money, Victoria rescued her from it. The "two united defiers" of their parents' ambitions formed their own partnership for a career that they controlled. Although Victoria and Tennie were never able to free themselves from financially supporting their extended family, the overall male leadership shifted from Buck to Blood. Victoria Woodhull and Tennessee Claflin became an almost inseparable duo for the next twenty years. They would become famous for many extraordinary activities in the public sphere. But what attracted the most attention was their challenge to the Puritan ideal of marriage.[216]

Preparing for a Mission (1866 to 1869)

I shall fulfill my mission, fight the good fight, and keep the faith.

Mary Baker Eddy

The Spirits . . . have entrusted me with a mission and I have done and shall do everything and anything that is necessary to accomplish it.

Victoria Claflin Woodhull

Eddy's Primitive Christianity

Mary Baker Eddy's life mission—her "calling" as the Puritans would say—came into focus during the year 1866. She believed she had made a great scientific discovery, comparable to the recognition of the law of gravitational force by English physicist Isaac Newton when he saw an apple fall from a tree. Newton's insight inspired him to write his revolutionary mathematical work *The Principia*. Eddy's insight two centuries later inspired her to write her book *Science and Health*. Eddy's falling-apple realization included an understanding of how sickness is healed through prayer. She later wrote:

> The miracles recorded in the Bible, which had before seemed to me supernatural, grew divinely natural and apprehensible; though uninspired interpreters ignorantly pronounce Christ's healing miraculous, instead of seeing therein the operation of the divine law. Jesus of Nazareth was a natural and divine Scientist.

She concluded that by using the scientific method to reduce spiritual healing to principles, she and others could learn to follow Jesus' command to his disciples to "heal the sick, cleanse the lepers, raise the dead, cast out demons" (Matt. 10:8). She would eventually establish an organization with a mission to "reinstate primitive Christianity and its lost element of healing."[217]

Eddy had been trying for twenty years to understand how disease is cured. Besides conventional and homeopathic medicine, she had experimented with special diets, and even tried hydrotherapy, also called "the water cure." More recently she had taken regular treatment with a magnetic doctor, Phineas P. Quimby. He massaged his patients, believing he was generating a curative fluid or bodily electricity, which magnetic doctors sometimes called "animal magnetism." While working with

Eddy, Dr. Quimby came to realize that a crucial element of magnetic treatment was the power of suggestion. This was an early form of hypnotherapy. Eddy had experienced startling temporary relief from chronic back pain under Quimby's treatment. But she was not satisfied with temporary relief. She wanted complete and permanent healing. She eventually sought answers in the Bible.

She had always read the Bible daily as she had been trained from her early youth, and she prayed to God for comfort in times of trouble. But in 1866 when she turned to the Bible for answers to questions of life and health, she was more receptive to its message of healing.

Eddy was in bed suffering from spinal and internal injuries from a bad fall onto a street curb after slipping on an icy sidewalk in February 1866. As she read in Matthew chapter 9 the story of Jesus telling a bedridden man "Arise and walk," it was as though the Christ was speaking directly to her. She herself arose and walked. She spent the rest of the year pondering what had happened, trying to formulate a scientific theory that could be tested, proved, practiced, and taught to others. She believed if she could achieve this, it would transform science, theology, and medicine.[218]

The period between 1866 and 1875—from her falling-apple realization to the publishing of her book *Science and Health*—she later called her "pregnant years." Her insight into healing was a "wonderful germ" steadily growing in her thought. For the first three years she worked to gain clarity in her own thought and test her theories.

> It was practical evolution. I was reaching by experience and demonstration the scientific proof, and scientific statement, of what I had already discovered.[219]

At the same time, Eddy became a more purposeful writer. She focused her talent on explaining spiritual healing and interpreting the Bible.

During this period of her life, she could have felt forsaken and desolate. Daniel Patterson had recently eloped with another woman. Her son Georgy, with whom she had reconnected during the Civil War through letters, was out of contact again. Her father had recently died (leaving her only a token inheritance of one dollar), and her remaining brother, Sullivan, was blind and dying. Her relationship with her two sisters was strained and distant because they disapproved of her unconventional interest in alternative healing methods. Quimby, who had become a friend and mentor to her, had died earlier that year. Despite all this, her overall mood was "buoyant with hope" because of her new concept of Christian healing. In her autobiography, she compared this period of her life to childbirth:

> When a new spiritual idea is borne to earth, the prophetic Scripture of Isaiah is renewedly fulfilled: "Unto us a child is born, . . . and his name shall be called Wonderful."[220]

Eddy was becoming known within her circle of acquaintances as an effective healer. She did not advertise or try to establish a professional practice or even ask for payment for her healing work. She simply healed people who came into contact with her. The first ailments she healed included a painfully infected finger, a delirious fever, and a walking disability. As her reputation spread, she began receiving requests for healing from friends of acquaintances.

Eddy also began teaching. Between 1866 and 1869 she gave private instruction in her healing system to three students in exchange for room and board in their homes. Her method would be fully proven only through the successful application by her students, so she encouraged them to go into the professional healing practice. She guided their efforts and helped with their difficult cases. Although the first student, Hiram Crafts, gave up after only a few months under pressure from his wife, her second and third students, Sarah Bagley and Sally Wentworth, were successful in making a comfortable living as healers for many years.

This practical application was crucial for clarifying what she eventually named Christian Science. The first name Eddy gave her system related to something she discovered early in her healing practice: a connection between the moral, the spiritual, and the physical. As an example, the wife of one of her early patients, whom she healed of abdominal illness and a bowel stoppage, said in response to the cure:

> Oh, how I thank you for restoring my husband to health, but more than all, I am grateful for what you have done for him morally and spiritually.[221]

The man became more affectionate to his children after he was healed and promised his wife, "I am going to be a better man." Years later Eddy wrote: "Healing morally and physically are one." In the spirit of that statement, the first name for her healing method was "Moral Science."[222]

However beneficial her healing work was for her patients, she had already encountered resistance and reaction to it. The successful practice of her system meant crossing swords with the materialism that would discount the message of the Bible. But this realization only inspired her perseverance, as she later wrote:

> Error will hate more as it realizes more the presence of its tormentor. I shall fulfill my mission, fight the good fight, and keep the faith.[223]

Woodhull's New Social Order

Having advertised as a magnetic healer since the early 1860s, Victoria Claflin Woodhull could attest to healing and other phenomena of alternative methods. Biographer Theodore Tilton told of special abilities she possessed since the age of ten. Woodhull claimed to have cured her younger sister Tennessee of a fever, healed a sick woman whom physicians expected to die, and to have brought her own son back from death after an illness. Tilton's biography further explained her abilities:

> She straightened the feet of the lame; she opened the ears of the deaf; she detected the robbers of a bank; she brought to light hidden crimes; she solved physiological problems; she unveiled business secrets; she prophesied future events.

But Woodhull's life mission was not about developing her special healing abilities or teaching others how to go and do likewise. Victoria was a prodigy selected by the spirits for a special mission. Her spirit guides followed her around everywhere she went, carried heavy burdens for her, healed the sick and raised the dead for her, and spoke to her. Occasionally, they took her spirit "gliding through the air" on visits to the spirit world while her body was left behind, appearing to be dead. These spirits guided her every action and gave her their authority. Her primary spirit guide was the ancient Greek statesman Demosthenes, who had been in the world of the living in the fourth century BC. She also claimed to be able to summon other spirits for face-to-face conversation "at her pleasure."[224]

The only church Woodhull attended was the "solemn temple" of her rooftop where she communed with the spirits beneath the starry sky. In the Tilton biography, which was given out to delegates at a national Spiritualist convention, her second husband James Harvey Blood described how the spirits communicated with Woodhull:

At about eleven or twelve o'clock at night . . . Victoria and I hold parliament with the spirits. . . . Victoria goes into a trance, during which her guardian spirit takes control of her mind, speaking audibly through her lips, propounding various matters for our subsequent investigation and verification, and announcing principles, detached thoughts, hints of systems, and suggestions for affairs. In this way, and in this spiritual night-school, began that process of instruction by which Victoria has risen to her present position as a political economist and politician. During her entranced state, which generally lasts about an hour, but sometimes twice as long, I make copious notes of all she says, and when her speech is unbroken, I write down every word, and publish it without correction or amendment.[225]

By claiming dictation from the spirits, Woodhull was following the precedent set by the famous Spiritualist Andrew Jackson Davis who claimed to have written his theology books while in trance. By advertising her claims of healing and spirit dictation, she increased her political support among Spiritualists.

According to Woodhull, her spirit guide appeared to her in a vision in 1868, and instructed her to move to New York City where her life mission to establish a new social order was revealed to her. According to biographer Lois Underhill, Victoria and Tennie moved to New York City to establish a connection with the famous New York business tycoon Cornelius Vanderbilt. State legislators were starting to put spiritualists out of business by developing medical standards and banning séances, so Victoria and Tennie, needing to make a strategic career change because of the shifting American legal landscape, wanted to become Vanderbilt's personal mediums.[226]

Cornelius Vanderbilt, nicknamed "The Commodore," may have been the richest man in American history. By the end of his long career, he had amassed wealth totaling over 1.5 percent of the entire United States economy. He is famous for his ruthless business practices in the transportation industry, including steamboats and railroads. There were things about Vanderbilt that Victoria Woodhull might have learned through magazines or during her several previous visits to New York City. He loved horses, Spiritualism, and extramarital affairs. He also had an open-door policy at his office, which made it easy for Victoria and Tennie to meet him.[227]

Whether led by a spirit guide or by a business strategy, in 1868 the Woodhull-Claflin family clan rented a house just a few doors down from Vanderbilt's office on Great Jones Street. At age seventy-four, Vanderbilt was in the last decade of his life. Not long after their first visit to the Commodore's office, the sisters became members of Vanderbilt's personal inner circle. Victoria became Vanderbilt's favorite medium and Tennie became his favorite mistress. They frequently shared meals with Vanderbilt and accompanied him on his carriage rides. Through their intimate association with him, the sisters learned how to interest, tease, manage, and manipulate the great tycoon. They also learned how he conducted his business.[228]

Vanderbilt came to enjoy Tennie's companionship so much that when his wife died that year after fifty-five years of marriage, he asked Tennie to marry him. But even if Tennie had wanted to become the next Mrs. Vanderbilt, that opportunity was inconveniently complicated by her legal marriage to a man in the Midwest several years earlier. Tennie's marriage only lasted a few weeks before it soured, but rather than get a divorce she had paid her husband to leave her alone and simply reverted to using her maiden name. Having a prominent marriage partner like Vanderbilt might attract the attention of her first husband and invite criminal charges of bigamy or threats of blackmail. Rather than give Vanderbilt an answer of yes or no, Tennie put off the question. Meanwhile, the Commodore's oldest son, William, began to play matchmaker for his father, and within a year the elder tycoon married a woman of William's choice.[229]

The new Mrs. Vanderbilt made it difficult for her husband to continue his relationship with Victoria and Tennie, forcing the sisters to consider yet another career change. During their close association with Vanderbilt, they were educated in strategic thinking in business and politics. Victoria learned how to play a much bigger game with the most powerful players in the country. She saw that she could take her talents to a higher level where anything would be possible if she played her game with the same sort of cleverness, confidence, and ruthless ambition as Vanderbilt did.[230]

Evangel of Womanhood

By 1869 many Americans were looking for an evangel of womanhood to transform society. One generation earlier, journalist Margaret Fuller set the expectation in her influential 1843 work *Woman in the Nineteenth Century* in which she called for "inward and outward freedom for Woman as much as for Man" to be "acknowledged as a *right*, not yielded as a concession."

> We would have every arbitrary barrier thrown down. We would have every path laid open to Woman as freely as to Man. Were this done, and a slight temporary fermentation allowed to subside, we should see crystallizations more pure and of more various beauty. We believe the divine energy would pervade nature to a degree unknown in the history of former ages, and that no discordant collision, but a ravishing harmony of the spheres, would ensue.

Fuller predicted the full appearance of the ideal of woman, which previously in Western history had only been partially glimpsed. She wondered whether this ideal woman would be named Victoria, the "name of the queen of our motherland," or Virginia, "the virgin mind with maternal wisdom." Would this ideal woman express the spirit of the absolute monarch dominating the world with economic and military power, or the Christian humility exemplified by the virgin Mary, the mother of Jesus? Fuller suggested perhaps she could exemplify both.

> And will not she soon appear? The woman who shall vindicate their birthright for all women; who shall teach them what to claim, and how to use what they obtain? Shall not her name be for her era Victoria, for her country and her life, Virginia? Yet predictions are rash; she herself must teach us to give her the fitting name.[231]

According to Robert Peel, author Nathaniel Hawthorne read Fuller's article and several years later he concluded his 1850 best-selling novel *The Scarlet Letter* with the main female character, Hester Prynne, assuring other women that someday the male-female relationship would change for the better:

> at some brighter period, when the world should have grown ripe for it, in Heaven's own time, a new truth would be revealed, in order to establish the whole relation between man and woman on a surer ground of mutual happiness.

In Hawthone's story, set in early colonial New England, the fictional character Hester had been convicted of adultery and was coping with the public shame of the punishment of having to wear a red letter "A" on her clothes for the rest of her life. Hester predicted that "the angel and apostle of the coming revelation must be a woman" and she must be "lofty, pure, and beautiful, and wise."[232]

In the spirit of Margaret Fuller's ideal of woman, at the conclusion of the 1869 woman suffrage convention in Washington, DC, Elizabeth Cady Stanton called for a higher level of female leadership. Referring to the political discussions of the day, from westward expansion to monetary policy issues, Stanton declared:

> The need of this hour is not territory, gold mines, railroads or specie payments, but a new evangel of womanhood, to exalt power, virtue, morality, true religion, to lift man up into the higher realms of love, purity, and thought.[233]

Woodhull was there at that convention listening to Stanton's words. She was learning about the women's rights movement as she was considering her next career change. Wanting to do much more than merely win the right to vote, Woodhull was excited about her potential in politics. Elizabeth Cady Stanton had recently run for United States Congress. Woodhull later wrote that "visions of the offices I might one day hold danced before my imagination."[234]

With the stage of expectation set, it is no wonder that Woodhull pointed out the prophetic significance of being named after

Queen Victoria and born the same year England's monarch began her long reign over the British Empire. As if to erase any lingering doubt, Woodhull eventually published this significant statement: "I am the evangel—I am a savior if you would but see it."[235]

Victoria adopted the ambitious goal of achieving the highest level of influence and power attainable. She was sure that she was destined to eventually rule the world. She would use her Vanderbilt connection to launch a new career then unite a broad political coalition under the banner of social freedom. But her identity as a visionary and leader would always be rooted in Spiritualism.

> The Spirits . . . have entrusted me with a mission and I have done and shall do everything and anything that is necessary to accomplish it.[236]

Emerging into Civic Life (1870 to 1872)

It must be concluded then, if individuals have the Constitutional right to pursue happiness in their own way, that all compelling laws of marriage and divorce are despotic, being remnants of the barbaric ages in which they were originated, and utterly unfitted for an age so advanced upon that, and so enlightened in the general principles of freedom and equality, as is this.

Victoria Claflin Woodhull

Infidelity to the marriage covenant is the social scourge of all races, "the pestilence that walketh in darkness, . . . the destruction that wasteth at noonday." The commandment, "Thou shalt not commit adultery," is no less imperative than the one, "Thou shalt not kill." Chastity is the cement of civilization and progress. Without it there is no stability in society, and without it one cannot attain the Science of Life.

Mary Baker Eddy

The Social Freedom Campaign

Victoria Claflin Woodhull achieved several noteworthy accomplishments that have earned her at least a mention in American history. But perhaps the biggest impact Woodhull made was a result of her social freedom campaign. Her opportunity for influence came after her first success at playing Vanderbilt's game.

It all began on Wall Street. Woodhull had a friend from her two years in San Francisco who now worked as a high-class prostitute in New York City and whose client Jim Frisk was a business rival to Vanderbilt. Woodhull was able to get inside trading information through this connection, and she passed it on to Vanderbilt during a séance as coming to her from the spirits. In exchange for the tip on Frisk's plans to manipulate the gold market, Vanderbilt offered his favorite medium a percentage of his profits. The result was the infamous "Black Friday" stock market crash on September 24, 1869. On that one day, Vanderbilt netted extraordinary profits while investors across the country lost their wealth. Victoria later reported her share of the profit to be $700,000.

Using this enormous fortune, some clever strategic leverage from her Vanderbilt connection, and business support from her husband James Harvey Blood, Victoria launched her new career. In February 1870 she and Tennie opened a stock brokerage company called Woodhull, Claflin & Company. The brokerage was instantly popular with investors who assumed the company was supported and advised by Vanderbilt. The sisters drummed up business by extending office hours into the evening, holding open houses, and sending out personal invitations to influential people. Curious government leaders, businessmen, and reporters came to meet the two female stockbrokers. Victoria and Tennie shocked visitors by modeling boyish haircuts and innovative clothing inspired by men's business suits.

Newspaper articles and political cartoons presented Woodhull and Claflin as the "bewitching brokers." Susan B. Anthony and Elizabeth Cady Stanton featured Victoria and Tennie in their women's rights newspaper *Revolution* as an example of extraordinary female success.[237]

Leveraging her fame from the stock brokerage publicity, Victoria launched the next phase of her career. In April 1870 she announced that she would run for president of the United States as the woman suffrage candidate against incumbent Ulysses Grant and challenger Horace Greeley for the 1872 election. Arguably, she was the first woman to run for president in America. The argument enters in because technically she did not meet the age requirement for the office. But Woodhull made a sincere campaign effort, creating her own independent political party and organizing a convention of delegates and supporters for her nomination.

To top off her bold ambitions, she published a proposal for a global government based in America—a Constitution for the United States of the World. Then she launched her own newspaper and set up a staff of journalists to run *Woodhull & Claflin Weekly*. Woodhull relocated her family to a luxurious rental home in the wealthy neighborhood of Murray Hill where she hosted gatherings of her new circle of friends and professional associates.

In the fall of 1870 while the United States Congress was in session, Victoria set up an office in Washington, DC. By entertaining and networking in the capitol city, Woodhull connected with Congressman Benjamin Butler of Massachusetts who was one of the most powerful men in the United States Congress. Butler had previously served in the Civil War as a major general in the Union Army and, at that time, was one of the Radical Republicans leading the reconstruction of the Southern states to support more racial equality. Woodhull developed a close relationship with the Congressman while his wife and children were away on an extended visit to Europe. Rumors that their relationship was physically intimate were published in the newspaper.[238]

Working with Butler, Woodhull was given the opportunity to present an opinion paper on woman suffrage to the Congressional Judicial Committee in January 1871. From the start of her presidential campaign, Woodhull had been promoting a constitutional interpretation called "the new departure." Her speech to Congress explained this position. She believed that because the law did not specifically forbid women from voting, women only needed to claim their existing suffrage rights as citizens. No new woman suffrage laws were necessary. The majority of the congressional committee rejected this legal interpretation, but Woodhull continued to promote it—encouraging women to go to polling places and demand to be allowed to vote. Woodhull's victory in becoming the first woman to speak before Congress catapulted her to immediate national fame as a leader of the women's rights movement.

The sudden success of this independent newcomer stunned the women who had worked for decades to build the movement. They had failed in their attempts to get an official hearing by Congress. But what really got the attention of the women's rights leadership was the fact that Woodhull's Congressional speech happened to coincide with a women's rights convention held in Washington, DC. Of course, the women wanted to attend the hearing to witness this significant event. But the next question was whether and how to include Woodhull in their organization.

Isabella Beecher Hooker had meticulously planned every detail of the National Woman Suffrage Association (NWSA) Convention in Washington, DC—to the point that it was dubbed "The Hooker Convention"—only to have to decide at the last minute whether to invite Woodhull to speak at her convention. Bringing this unknown newcomer into the mix would endanger Hooker's carefully laid plans. Hooker had only recently taken over the leadership of the NWSA from Susan B. Anthony and Elizabeth Cady Stanton, who were ready to let someone else do the hard organizational work. As a member of the prominent and respected Beecher family — a daughter of the famous Christian evangelist, Reverend Lyman Beecher — Hooker's goal in joining and leading the NWSA was to encourage a tone of dignity and respectability, in hopes of reuniting the women's rights movement.[239]

The movement had recently split into two separate competing factions over the issues of black suffrage, political party affiliation, conflicting approaches, personal grudges, and other differences. Previously, antislavery activists and women's rights activists had always worked together. After the Civil War ended, they worked on a national equal rights campaign for "universal suffrage" with the expectation that both women and blacks could win the right to vote simultaneously with the support of the Republican Party. But as political priorities were being debated, antislavery leader Wendell Philips famously stated in a speech that "this is the Negro's hour," insisting that blacks get the vote first. Philips believed that women needed to wait.[240]

Wendell Philips had been a strong, early advocate of women's rights. In fact, Wendell Philips helped to launch the movement in 1848 when his antislavery organization hired Lucy Stone to be a lecturer alongside himself and William Lloyd Garrison. Philips encouraged Stone to speak on women's rights on her days off, and so she became America's first professional women's rights leader. According to Stanton, Stone was "the first person by whom the heart of the American public was deeply stirred on the woman question." Lucy Stone inspired Anthony and many others to take up the work. After the Civil War, Philips advocated for "Negro's hour" because he saw the right of suffrage as an issue of life and death for the newly freed black slaves, whereas from his perspective whatever injustices there were for women were not life threatening and so not as urgent. He implored all reformers to focus on achieving black suffrage first.[241]

But Anthony and Stanton rejected the logic and leadership of Philips. They were concerned that newly enfranchised black men would be even more reluctant to give women the vote than white men. They were determined at all costs that white women get the vote first, even to the point of actively working against black suffrage. They abandoned the coalition and formed their own organization to promote woman suffrage only, under the slogan "educated suffrage."

Anthony campaigned with Democrat George Francis Train in Kansas where voters were considering separate suffrage measures for blacks and women. Train was an eccentric international businessman and railroad real estate tycoon whose later world travel adventures would inspire the Jules Verne classic novel *Around the World in 80 Days*. But at the time of the Kansas suffrage campaign, he was most famous for his racial bigotry — especially his use of the derogatory term "nigger." Train funded and edited Anthony and Stanton's newspaper, *Revolution*, and injected it with racially divisive content. To the antislavery leaders as well as the majority of women's rights leaders, Anthony and Stanton's tactics were despicable and unforgivable. Lucy Stone and other leading figures distanced themselves from the NWSA and blamed Anthony for the failure of the Kansas suffrage ballot measures for both women and blacks.[242]

Lucy Stone took a more diplomatic approach to woman suffrage than Anthony and Stanton. Her Boston-based American Woman Suffrage Association (AWSA) fully supported black suffrage with the expectation that woman suffrage would soon follow. As a counterbalance to Anthony and Stanton's controversial and divisive *Revolution*, Stone founded her own newspaper *Woman's Journal* to explore women's rights issues with a tone of dignity and respectability. While financial failure forced the closure of *Revolution* after just a few years, subscriptions for *Woman's Journal* increased and sustained the newspaper for a run of fifty years, putting Stone once again in the position of highest prominence within the movement.

Stone focused her extensive grassroots organization on winning woman suffrage at the local and state level. By the early 1870s women had full voting rights in Wyoming and Utah, and full or partial woman suffrage laws were being considered in many other states, including Vermont, Michigan, and Minnesota. The momentum for woman suffrage was building, and a tipping point of success seemed to be imminent. To keep efforts on track, Stone continued her strategy of marginalizing and excluding Anthony and Stanton. Isabella Beecher Hooker, however, believed success for woman suffrage would be more certain if the two factions of the women's movement could be reunited.[243]

Hooker preferred the diplomatic approach used by Lucy Stone and the AWSA, but she joined the NWSA because she believed she could work within the organization to encourage a similar tone of dignity and respectability. Bringing the New York faction in line with the Boston faction would be a first step toward unification. In support of that goal, Hooker succeeded in diplomatically excluding the always-controversial Stanton from the January 1871 Hooker Convention, and she set a strict agenda of safe topics. All controversial topics relating to marriage law, divorce, and birth control were forbidden.

Inviting Woodhull to the convention at the last minute would be risky. It would endanger all of the carefully laid plans for respectability. There was no way to know if Woodhull would follow Hooker's direction for tone and content. But whatever hesitation Hooker had toward Woodhull was erased after she witnessed the groundbreaking speech to the congressional committee. Woodhull made a powerful first impression. Hooker became fascinated with Woodhull—with her peculiar dress, the man's hat she wore, and the way she spoke in front of the audience. Isabella Beecher Hooker also had a strong interest in Spiritualism. At the last minute, Hooker decided to invite Woodhull to join the convention as a speaker.[244]

Woodhull stole the show.

A *New York Tribune* reporter described Woodhull's appearance at the convention:

> All the past efforts of Miss Anthony and Mrs. Stanton sink to insignificance beside the ingenious lobbying of the new

leader and her daring declaration. . . . Mrs. Victoria C. Woodhull and her sister were the chief ornaments of the Convention.

The New York Herald came to a similar conclusion about Woodhull's new role in the women's rights movement:

She seems to be the head and front of the movement now, having pushed the others aside, who never could manage to stir up public enthusiasm and enlist prominent politicians in the cause as Mrs. Woodhull has done.

Victoria's stardom at the Hooker Convention created a close association between Woodhull and Hooker in the minds of Americans, which would have a lasting impact on the women's rights movement—and on Hooker's good name.[245]

At the May 1871 NWSA Convention in New York, Woodhull was held up throughout the day as the quintessential example of female success and was such a prominent speaker that the meeting was dubbed "The Woodhull Convention." Stanton had returned to her leadership role in the NWSA, and she was ready to address a broad range of controversial women's issues, from divorce to birth control. Stanton put Woodhull into the keynote speaker role. Woodhull used the NWSA platform to declare war on the institution of marriage:

But why do I war upon marriage? I reply frankly: First, because it stands directly in the way of any improvement in the race, insisting upon conditions under which improvement is impossible; and second, because it is, as I verily believe, the most terrible curse from which humanity now suffers, entailing more misery, sickness, and premature death than all other causes combined. It is at once the bane of happiness to the present, and the demon of prophetic miseries to the future—miseries now concealed beneath its deceptive exterior, gilded over by priestcraft and law, to be inwrought in the constitutions of coming generations to mildew and poison their lives.[246]

Woodhull compared the institution of marriage to legalized rape, sexual slavery, no better than prostitution, forcing women to bear unwanted children by men they hated. Her reception at the NWSA was mixed. Some leaders refused to sit near her on stage. Others saw Woodhull as hyperbolic in her rhetoric, but an exciting speaker because of her fearlessness in discussing sensitive issues. Her desire to free women from total financial dependence on a husband was something most women's rights leaders could agree on.

Stanton generally agreed with Woodhull's views and was her strongest supporter within the NWSA. Stanton saw a beneficial effect for the movement in allowing Woodhull a platform to publicly express her views. In defense of Woodhull, after the convention, Stanton wrote to longtime women's rights leader Lucretia Mott with a touch of the glow of someone who had just discovered the anticipated evangel of womanhood:

> Victoria Woodhull stands before us today one of the ablest speakers and writers of the century: sound and radical, alike in political, religious, and social principles. Her face, form, manners, and conversation all indicate the triumph of the moral, intellectual, spiritual, over the sensuous in her nature. The process and localities of her education are little to us, but the grand result is everything.[247]

Not long after the May 1871 Woodhull Convention Woodhull's public image became tainted with scandal and associated with the term "free love." In a publicized civil court case between feuding Claflin family members, Woodhull's mother made frequent references to free love in her testimony. Most notably, referring to Woodhull's household, Annie declared that "there is the worst gang of communists and free lovers in that house that ever lived." She specifically mentioned Canning Woodhull and the well-known free-love advocate Stephen Pearl Andrews, who had recently become Woodhull's speech writer and newspaper editor.[248]

Woodhull's private life came under public scrutiny. The legitimacy of both her divorce from Canning Woodhull and her marriage with James Harvey Blood were questioned. People were shocked by the thought of a woman living with two husbands at the same time and possibly having other lovers too. "Free Love!" was one of the attention-getting newspaper headlines on the scandalous revelations. Ever since the opening of the stock brokerage, images and articles on Woodhull had been in the news regularly, especially in the racy sports newspapers that catered to young men. She was frequently portrayed in illustrations as having exaggerated masculine traits and in situations that subtly suggested her sexual availability. But now her publicity took a more obviously negative turn. Reputations and public careers were ruined through association with free love.[249]

Despite the negative news coverage, Anthony, Stanton, and Hooker continued to welcome Woodhull's leadership in the NWSA. They even defended her, perceiving a double standard in society on sexual morality. When male public figures visited brothels or had adulterous affairs the newspapers turned a blind eye, but when women were in any way associated with sex scandals, they were vilified and their reputations ruined. Out of objection to this double standard, NWSA leaders publicly supported Woodhull. Another reason for their staunch support was the fact that Woodhull had pledged to contribute $10,000 to the cash-starved NWSA. Also the NWSA had been having trouble getting publicity since the split, and Woodhull's participation brought a much-needed boost of attention, even if it included controversy.[250]

In a response letter in the *New York Times*, Woodhull clarified that her ex-husband was someone "incapable of self-support," whom she had taken into her home as a charity case with the approval and cooperation of her current husband. This justification might have addressed the public concern if she had just stopped there. But, she continued on to openly make the case for free love for the first time:

I believe in Spiritualism; I advocate free love in the highest, purest sense, as the only cure for the immorality, the deep damnation by which men corrupt and disfigure God's most holy institution of sexual relations.

She accused Christian clergy of hypocrisy. She was being vilified by a male-dominated "self-appointed orthodoxy" that did not practice what they preached. She refused to be held up as an example of immorality. Instead, she challenged the criticism:

[L]et him who is without sin cast his stone. . . . I know that many of my self-appointed judges and critics are deeply tainted with the vices they condemn.[251]

Woodhull continued to work toward building a political coalition of suffragists, spiritualists, and socialists with remarkable initial success. She attended a national convention for Spiritualists and was elected president of the organization. To win the support of industrial workers she organized a New York section of Karl Marx's political organization, the International Workingman's Association. She was hopeful that her message of social freedom could unite these different interest groups behind her leadership. With enough support, she could get her name onto state ballots as a candidate for the 1872 presidential election—a campaign goal which was just as difficult for independent and third-party candidates in the 1870s as it is today.[252]

On November 20, 1871, in Steinway Hall, the largest auditorium in New York City, she delivered a speech called "The Principles of Social Freedom Involving the Question of Free Love, Marriage, Divorce, and Prostitution." Her fliers had advertised these principles as "God's first, last, and best law." On this late autumn evening of drenching rain, over three thousand people came for the event. The hall was packed—"seats, aisles, and galleries"—and hundreds were turned away. Later, she promoted this speech as "the first distinct announcement of the doctrines upon which the new social order will be founded—perfect individual sexual freedom, to be regulated by education instead of law."[253]

Woodhull, reading her address from printed pages, began with what the *New York Tribune* called "a rather tedious sketch of the progress of individual freedom, the battle for which began in the sixteenth century." Her two-hour speech was a carefully worded argument for her views that legal restrictions on sexuality constituted tyranny and oppression. Throughout, she promoted women's rights, the spiritualist doctrine of affinities, no-fault divorce, and legalized prostitution. The essence of her position is summarized in this part of her speech:

> It must be concluded, then, if individuals have the Constitutional right to pursue happiness in their *own* way, that all compelling laws of marriage and divorce are despotic, being *remnants* of the barbaric ages in which they were originated, and *utterly unfitted* for an age so *advanced* upon that, and so *enlightened* in the general principles of freedom and equality, as is this.[254]

Woodhull challenged the American sense of morality rooted in Puritan Christianity by condemning the prevailing system of marriage as evil. She argued that sexuality should be a private matter conducted by individuals without any interference from others. She took Elizabeth Cady Stanton's model of marriage as a private business contract completely beyond the law into the spiritual realm, declaring love to be higher than law. She pitched her affinities-influenced spiritual marriage to the audience:

> Two persons, a male and a female, meet, and are drawn together by a mutual attraction—a natural feeling unconsciously arising within their natures of which neither has any control—which is denominated love. This is a matter that concerns these two, and no other living soul has any human right to say aye, yes or no, since it is a matter in which none except the two have any right to be involved, and from which it is the duty of these two to exclude every other person, since no one can love for another or determine why another loves. . . . They are sexually united, . . . which

is to be married by nature, and to be thus married is to be united by God. . . . Suppose after this marriage has continued an indefinite time, the unity between them departs, could they any more prevent it than they can prevent the love? It came without their bidding, may it not also *go* without their bidding? And if it go, does not the marriage cease, and should any third persons or parties, either as individuals or government, attempt to compel the continuance of a unity wherein none of the elements of the union remain?[255]

The *New York Times* reported on the strong reaction of the audience:

The novelty of the doctrines enunciated, and the still greater novelty of their expression by a lady, excited this highest amount of curiosity, and though not wishing to interrupt the continuance of the lecture, the audience was twice compelled to condemn the theories advanced in loud and continued hissing.[256]

The biggest heckler in the audience that night was Woodhull's youngest sister, Utica Claflin Brooker, who shouted from her box seat near the platform. The *New York Times* recounted Utica's "violent interruption" of the lecture with "vehement denunciations of the principles advocated" by Woodhull:

as she boldly stood to repudiate the sentiments of her sister, a perfect storm of cheers and counter-demonstrations greeted her appearance. For fully ten minutes the utmost confusion prevailed.[257]

A police officer tried to remove Utica from the hall to keep order, but it only created more confusion as members of the audience defended Utica and encouraged her to give a speech. Finally Utica yelled out, "How would you like to come into this world without knowing who your father was?" To which Woodhull responded that it is "not such a terrible thing after all to be born illegitimately. . . . [S]ome of the noblest and best men in the country . . . were illegitimate children."[258]

Woodhull continued with rapid speech toward her conclusion that no harm would come of repealing all laws governing marriage. She was convinced that free love would ultimately triumph — it would be an integral part of the religion of the future.

Someone in the audience shouted out the question, "Are you a free lover?" Woodhull responded with what may be the most famous statement of her whole career. "Yes, I am a free lover!" Loud hisses were heard from the audience. Woodhull eventually continued:

> I have an inalienable, constitutional, and natural right to love whom I may, to love as long or as short a period as I can, to change that love everyday I please! And with that right neither you nor any law you can frame have any right to interfere. And I have the further right to demand a free and unrestricted exercise of that right, and it is your duty not only to accord it, but, as a community, to see that I am protected in it.[259]

Woodhull immediately took her social freedom lecture on tour to other American cities and towns. Her support team developed a campaign approach that she used for the next several years. James Harvey Blood referred to it as running "the machine." It was a system of publicity both before and after her lectures, reprinting the positive portions of reviews in the *Woodhull & Claflin Weekly*, and then using the newspaper to further promote Woodhull as a lecturer.[260]

Woodhull concluded her extraordinarily eventful year of 1871 with one of her most noted accomplishments — second only to running for president. The *Woodhull & Claflin Weekly* published *The Communist Manifesto* by Karl Marx and Friedrich Engels. Because this was the first time that famous document had ever been printed in America, this was the country's first formal introduction to the political philosophy of socialism. Not published as a curiosity or educational exercise, but as part of her political platform, the socialist call to abolish marriage and the family fit with Woodhull's campaign to portray marriage as the worst form of slavery. Her newspaper also published interviews of Karl Marx and reports on socialist developments in Europe. In lectures Woodhull painted a picture of a country divided economically between the "Lower Million" and the "Upper Ten." She railed against Vanderbilt and others in the "Upper Ten," and she called for revolution. The appeal for Communism was summarized in this now famous line:

> Workers of the world, unite! You have nothing to lose but your chains![261]

Moral Science

Mary Baker Eddy certainly could have been among the ranks of civic leaders working for one of the many reform movements of post-Civil War America, such as black suffrage, woman suffrage, or temperance. Born into the political class from which most of America's female leaders came, she had always followed the news closely and had strong political opinions. At the time of her injury from falling on the ice, Eddy was on her way to a meeting for a democratic organization in which she was an elected presiding officer. Her regular contributions to newspapers and magazines might have led to a famous career as a journalist or editor. She had even given several public lectures on various topics. One person who knew her in this period said Eddy reminded him of women's rights leader Lucretia Mott in the way she "seemed to fill the room with her presence and the ideas she expressed compelled our attention."[262]

In 1864 she had expressed to her friend Dr. Quimby a desire for some high calling for her life: "I can love only a good, honorable, and brave career; no other can suit me." From the time of her falling-apple moment in 1866, she saw her mission to reestablish Christianity's "lost element of healing" as the ultimate cause. It promised to cure every human problem by establishing the highest concept of the rights of man. Eddy would soon write this statement in *Science and Health*:

> A few sentences of the science of being, understood, would enable man to grasp the standard of liberty. Citizens of the world, accept their glorious import and gain your freedom! This is your divine right.[263]

In July 1869 Eddy completed the manuscript that she used as a classroom textbook for her students. Eventually renamed "Recapitulation" and added to *Science and Health,* at this time it was called *The Science of Man, By Which the Sick are Healed, Embracing*

Questions and Answers in Moral Science. In 1870 near Boston in Lynn, Massachusetts, she launched the educational system that would eventually become known as Christian Science class instruction. Her students formed a close community around her. Most of these students were confident enough in their practice of Eddy's healing system that they were immediately willing to treat patients. This type of healer would eventually become known as a Christian Science practitioner.[264]

As Eddy's relationship with her first small group of students developed, her practical healing methods took on the dimension of spiritual teachings with a focus on personal character. The students began to realize why she called her healing system "Moral Science." As student Samuel "Putney" Bancroft explained it:

> Mrs. Eddy did not claim to be a teacher of a religion, however, but of a method of healing the sick without the use of medicine. That was what induced us to study with her. The object of some was to regain health; of others, to commercialize the knowledge acquired. They considered it a good business proposition. Her religious views, while not concealed, were not capitalized. Later, we learned that our success or failure in healing depended on the purity of our lives, as well as on the instructions she gave us.[265]

Richard Kennedy was the first of this group of students to sign on with Eddy. He had first made her acquaintance and had become interested in her ideas on spirituality and healing when they lived in the same boarding house in 1868. They kept in touch until Eddy was ready to put her theories and methods to a more extensive test and Kennedy was ready to commit to going into the healing practice. In February 1870 Eddy and Kennedy formed a partnership and in May they established their practice in Lynn, Massachusetts, in a boarding house. Kennedy would be the face to the public and Eddy would teach him, help him, and handle the more difficult cases. In the beginning, Kennedy would meet with the patients while Eddy did the healing treatment from an adjacent room. After a few months they needed an additional room in the building as a waiting area for patients. Their partnership was successful, both in the healing practice and as a thriving business. Eddy's share of the revenues was almost $2000 for the first year—ten times the amount her husband had promised to give her in alimony payments.[266]

Eddy admired Kennedy, but she expressed this word of caution to him in a letter:

> Richard, this is a very spiritual life that Mind Science exacts, and the world offers many alluring temptations. You know but little of them as yet. If you follow me you must cross swords with the world. Are you spiritually-minded enough to take up my work and stand by it?

In the end, the answer was no. Richard Kennedy would not stand by his teacher. In fact, not one of these early students continued their association with Mary Baker Eddy longer than a few years. They went their own way, and some of them became her worst enemies. There were so many accusations, conflicts, lawsuits, and even criminal charges among this early group of students, that Eddy's fledgling movement earned the label "notorious" by one Lynn newspaper.[267]

Many of these rebellious students continued to believe Eddy's teachings were true, valuable, and practical. They had paid a premium for her teaching, as her standard class tuition was $300 when a typical Lynn factory worker earned $1000 a year and some paid full tuition. Not only did most students believe her teaching was worth the price, but one notably hostile student years later described the value as "beyond any money consideration." Nearly all the students were at least somewhat successful in their healing practice. Even when rebellious students were spreading rumors, making accusations in the newspapers, or fighting her in lawsuits, they still valued their own transforming healing experiences, and most of them fully intended to continue in the healing practice they learned from Eddy.[268]

Exposure to Eddy's healing treatment was so life-changing these students felt as though they had been reborn into a brighter world of overflowing good. The problem for the students was how to maintain this elevated state of mind. Eddy believed the practice of Moral Science required living a pure life, which included chastity. Anything less would work against the healer's success. Eddy taught in her class:

> A student of Moral Science . . . must be a pure and undefiled Christian, in order to make the most rapid progress in healing.[269]

The failure of this early group of students to heed their teacher's instructions on the Christian aspect of her healing system may have been the influence of Spiritualism. Eddy never had any interest in Spiritualism. In the 1860s she had lived in boarding houses that sometimes hosted séances, but she considered Spiritualism to be the opposite of her own Bible-based beliefs. However, the people most interested in her healing work and her spiritual insights at this time were Spiritualists. Her devout Christian friends, family, and acquaintances were uncomfortable with the whole idea of spiritual healing, even when they saw or experienced her successful healing work for themselves.[270]

Eddy found Spiritualists to be "liberal, kind-hearted people" who were "quite ready to accept new ideas." Knowing of their receptivity to new ideas, and needing students willing to test her theories, the very first advertisement Eddy placed for her instruction in healing without medicine in 1868 was in *Banner of Light*, a Boston-based Spiritualist magazine. Consequently, most of her first students and the first willing to try the public practice were coming to her from Spiritualism. But along with open minds, Eddy also found Spiritualists to have "loose morals."[271]

One problem among her first group of students was the love triangles that developed among them over the next several years. Biographer Gillian Gill found evidence suggesting that Richard Kennedy had a long-term adulterous affair with Addie

Spofford. Wallace Wright may have also briefly tried to pursue a love interest with Mrs. Spofford. Addie Spofford separated from her husband, and he later took a class from Eddy. He quickly became a leader among the students and developed a close relationship with Eddy. Still legally married to Addie, he became infatuated with his teacher and made unwelcome advances. Later, Mr. Spofford moved in with a new girlfriend—years before he and his wife Addie divorced. Spofford eventually married his girlfriend, but in the meantime, living together unmarried was both immoral and illegal. Called "lewd cohabitation" in the criminal code, it was a "crime against public morals and decency." He was expelled from the student association for failing to perform his duties and for immorality.[272]

Eddy's earliest teaching for her Moral Science emphasized the healer's personal morals as crucial to success in healing. This meant no smoking, no drinking, and no sexual misconduct. Her manuscript explained:

> You cannot destroy error, by error: if you are profane swearers, if you are adulterers, if you are thieves, if you are murderers, these errors must be given up if you would heal with truth.[273]

Another contentious issue Eddy confronted was physical contact with patients. Alternative healers in that era, including clairvoyant mediums, magnetic doctors, and mesmerists or hypnotists, all commonly used some form of manipulation, massage, or rubbing of the patient as part of the treatment. The earliest of these healers rubbed the head and abdomen of patients, raising concerns of potential sexual abuses of the technique, especially because the patients were also given hypnotic suggestions by the doctor. Quimby, the magnetic doctor who had worked with Eddy in the early 1860s, typically wet his hands with magnetized water and vigorously rubbed his patient's head on the theory that the water conducted vital electric energy to the patient. As his practice evolved, Quimby reduced his use of manipulation in favor of verbal and mental suggestions.[274]

Eddy never used any kind of physical manipulation in her healing work, but she did allow Richard Kennedy and her earliest students to rub the heads of their patients. Eddy expected them to phase out rubbing as their confidence as healers increased. But as Richard Kennedy's confidence increased, he did not give up his practice of rubbing. In fact, Eddy concluded that the rubbing treatments promoted a dependent "habit more pernicious than opium-eating."[275]

Kennedy was young, handsome, charismatic, and sociable, and his rubbing treatments were popular with women. He may have been manipulating the emotions of his patients along with their bodies for his own dishonest and possibly lustful purposes. This was not Mary Baker Eddy's vision for her Moral Science. Eddy privately accused Kennedy of committing sins in secret, but no further communications between Eddy and Kennedy were preserved. Biographer Gillian Gill has brought forward evidence that suggests his sins were of a sexual nature. Gill has speculated that besides possible sexual exploits with women, Kennedy may have begun exploring homosexuality. If so, there was very good reason for keeping the issue secret. Although sodomy laws were rarely enforced, homosexual acts—the "crime against nature"—carried a penalty in Massachusetts of up to ten years in prison.

Whatever Kennedy's sins were, Eddy took them very seriously. She described her approach to reformation of sin at that time in *Science and Health*:

> In warfare with error, you attack with intent to kill, and the wounded or cornered beast bites you if he can; the sin you assail turns on you and succeeds in getting the world to condemn you, that it may justify itself. It being found necessary to uncover sin to destroy it, you must tell a sinner what his sins are before you can do him good, and if he hates you for it, it is because he is unwilling to reform.[276]

When Eddy forbade her students from rubbing or having any physical contact as treatment, several of her students refused to obey, with Kennedy chief among them. He openly rebelled against his teacher. It became clear — and Kennedy later openly admitted — that he never really understood Eddy's healing method. As the conflict between teacher and student escalated, Eddy came to think of Kennedy as evil personified. She bemoaned having placed her great cause in "the hands of *lust* and *lies*." Eddy made this public statement that biographer Gillian Gill believed was referring to Kennedy:

> spurning a Christian life, and exulting in the absence of moral restraint . . . it became a secret passion of his to produce a state of mind destructive to health, happiness, or morals.[277]

After many years of conflict, Kennedy broke off all contact with Eddy and her students. He continued in his own lucrative practice in Boston for the next thirty years, but it is not known what his practice was. He did not practice Moral Science or Christian Science. The only label he ever gave himself was "Masseuse."[278]

Eddy believed Kennedy was responsible for rumors around town that she practiced and promoted free love. Kennedy could have intentionally spread false rumors to tarnish Eddy's reputation out of spite. Or he could have just encouraged people's own suspicions when they leapt to their own conclusions, which would have been easy for Lynn residents to do. Alternative healing was generally associated with Spiritualism, and Spiritualism was generally associated with free love. Eddy was working to distinguish her Moral Science from Spiritualism, but at the same time Lynn spiritualists were claiming Eddy as one of their own, insisting that Eddy was "a medium, controlled by a departed spirit of great power." However the free-love rumors came to be, they were persistent enough that years later the owner of the boarding house where Kennedy and Eddy lived and worked was questioned about their relationship. She vouched for Eddy's proper behavior:

Dr. Kennedy had his apartment and Mrs. Eddy had hers. I never saw anything that indicated anything wrong.[279]

Only one of Eddy's students from this early period did not later turn against her. Samuel "Putney" Bancroft simply drifted away when he married and started a family. Bancroft had taken a course of instruction from Eddy in the fall of 1870 and successfully treated a few patients. His teacher urged him to go into the professional practice. He wrote to her that he could not practice healing full-time because he was engaged to be married. Her response to him in an April 1871 letter expressed concern about his motive for marriage:

Dear Student, Your brief letter lies before me, and I have no objection to your decision because I know experience is the best teacher, if this experience be not bought too dearly . . . You say "love has triumphed over wisdom." This cannot be, for love and wisdom are one, but you might have said, sense has overruled the soul for a brief time; erelong the case will be changed and you will wish this had not been the case. I fear you will inherit this truth through the discipline of affliction.[280]

Bancroft went ahead with his marriage, and a few years later he did go into the professional healing practice in Cambridge, Massachusetts. But he gave it up after only a couple of months when his first child was born. In Eddy's response letter to him, she took the opportunity to explain her thoughts to Bancroft on why he and these other early students were not succeeding long term in the healing practice:

Why is this all? Simply because they have not started with right motives. They tell me they have, and I try then to help them, but there is nothing hid that shall not be revealed in this, sooner or later. Their success in healing tells more than all else. They love more the ties of the flesh than those of

Spirit, and always hold on to the former, if they conflict with the latter. I am not censuring anyone, I am only explaining for your good what hinders your success . . . Do not let it be thought you left because you were driven out. Call it your family, as it was in reality. Had you not laid up first your treasures in earthly things you would have been free to work on under difficulties.[281]

She hoped her students would consider the practice of healing to be the most important thing in their lives, as she did. But they did not. The first student to launch a public attack on Eddy was Wallace Wright. He wrote a series of letters to the local newspaper with various accusations against Eddy, objections to her emphasis on morality, and explanations of why he would no longer practice her healing system:

While I do not question the right of it, it teaches a deprivation of social enjoyment if we would attain the highest round in the ladder of Science.[282]

While Eddy was responding to the attack in the newspapers, it became clear to her that to fully defend herself and her unique system of healing without medicine, she needed to fully explain it in a book. In February 1872 in the last of her responses to Wright in the *Lynn Transcript*, she announced her forthcoming book:

I am preparing a work on Moral and Physical Science, that I shall submit to the public as soon as it is completed.[283]

Eddy immediately began the long process of writing *Science and Health*. The overall content would be a description of the treatment methods she used and the theory behind her system. But the book would also include a defense of the Puritan view of marriage and an attack on Spiritualism. And most significantly, the book would announce a new name for her healing system that better reflected its Christian foundation: Christian Science.

Shortly after Eddy forbade rubbing and announced her book, Richard Kennedy tore up the business contract he had with her. Their relationship rapidly deteriorated and by May 1872 their two-year business partnership was irreconcilably ended. Kennedy became Eddy's nemesis. He and the other early students almost destroyed the Christian Science movement before it could even begin to move. Eddy later wrote extensively and publicly about her perception of Richard Kennedy:

> From the time we dissolved partnership with the aforesaid mesmerist, because of his depravity, he avowed his intention to injure us, and we have the testimony who have heard him say that he would follow us to the grave for that purpose.[284]

Will Marriage Survive? (1872 to 1875)

I intend that this article shall burst like a bomb-shell into the ranks of the moralistic social camp. I am engaged in offering, and in some sense conducting, a social revolution on the marriage question. . . . I came slowly, deliberately, and reluctantly to the adoption of this method of warfare.

Victoria Claflin Woodhull

The broad-cast power of evil so conspicuous to-day, is the materialism of the age struggling against the spiritual era, that advances. . . . The mental chemicalization that has brought infidelity to the surface, will as surely throw it off, and marriage will settle down purer after the scum is expelled.

Mary Baker Eddy

Woodhull's Bomb

"What sort of brazen tramp of a woman" would want to run for President? one man asked rhetorically. "Would it be any kind of a woman that we should want to see at the head of our government?" The respectable male characters in Harriet Beecher Stowe's 1871 novel shuddered at the whole notion of subjecting any woman to the mudslinging of a campaign for president of the United States of America.[285]

Even before Woodhull launched her social freedom lecture tour, Christian defenders of marriage began attacking Victoria and her campaign. Most notably, Stowe's story addressed in parable form "the most stirring and exciting topics of the day, where all that relates to the joint interests of man and woman has been thrown into the arena as an open question." When she showed "the embarrassment of the young champion of progressive principles, in meeting the excesses of modern reformers," readers would notice that one of the fictional female characters, Audacia Dangyereyes, had remarkable similarities to Victoria and Tennie.[286]

In her introduction, Stowe announced that it was no coincidence that she chose the popular magazine *Christian Union* for first publication of her story as a serial. Stowe openly challenged "Miss Anthony and Mrs. Stanton, and all the prophetesses of our day" to notice how the title of her story, *My Wife and I*, described "the oldest and most venerable form of Christian union on record." Her title expressed the Christian humility and benevolence of the husband in always putting his wife first, in word and deed. She bemoaned how "this ancient and respectable firm has been attacked as a piece of old fogyism, and various substitutes for it proposed," including socialistic communities and partnerships made temporary by easy divorce.[287]

In Stowe's story, the respectable members of New York society were shocked by their unpleasant encounters with Audacia

Dangyereyes, who swore "like a pirate" and disregarded all standards of etiquette and respectability. Audacia entered the story by barging into Harry Henderson's apartment uninvited and refusing to leave until he subscribed to her newspaper. In her main soliloquy she asserted that woman's rights extended to the right to do anything that men do, whether men liked it or not, including the right to drink and smoke if she wanted to, and even to pursue a man to "have a good time." She wore a Woodhull-style man's hat, sat in a provocatively unladylike position, and made advances of physical affection toward Harry.

> "Now, I'm a woman that not only dares say, but I dare *do*. . . I know you don't like this, I can see you don't, but it's only because you are a slave to old prejudices. But I'm going to *make* you like me in spite of yourself."

After she left the room, Harry discussed his reaction with his friend Jim:

> "Mercy upon us! Jim, who and what is this creature?"

> "Oh, one of the harbingers of the new millennium," said Jim. "Won't it be jolly when all the girls are like her? But we shall have to keep our doors locked then."[288]

Harry Henderson, the male hero of the story, had been an outspoken supporter of women's rights, but after his encounter with Audacia, he was on the defensive for his position.

> "Well, it was woman *as* woman that I was speaking of, and not this kind of creature. If I believed that granting larger liberty and wider opportunities was going to change the women we reverence to things like these, you would never find me advocating it."

In the story Audacia was taken to court for blackmail and swindling. She routinely bullied men into subscribing to her newspaper, *The Emancipated Woman*, which Harry described:

> I found [it] to be an exposition of all the wildest principles of French communism. It consisted of attacks directed about

equally against Christianity, marriage, the family state, and all human laws and standing order, whatsoever. . . . It was a paper that a man who reverenced his mother and sisters could scarcely read alone in his apartment without blushing with indignation and vexation. . . . Society assumed the aspect of a pack of breeding animals, and all its laws and limitations were to return to the mere animal basis. It was particularly annoying to me that this paper, with all its coarseness and grossness, set itself up to be the head leader of Women's Rights; and to give its harsh clamors as the voice of woman.[289]

The male characters of the story celebrated a womanly influence that is "quiet, calm, warming, purifying, and uniting," and is best expressed in woman's role as queen of her own domestic sphere. These men were open to women getting involved in civics through a slow evolution, but only if they brought to the public sphere those noble female qualities of purity that men so admired. Otherwise, "the quagmire of politics, foul enough now, will become putrid."[290]

Harriet Beecher Stowe, a respected voice of the moderately progressive view, had spoken. Woodhull was ridiculous and the women's rights leaders from respectable families were fools for associating with her.

Woodhull received other unfavorable publicity. Political cartoonist Thomas Nast caricatured Woodhull as "Mrs. Satan." Others in the press dubbed her "The High Priestess of Free Love."

All the negative publicity raised concerns within Woodhull's political alliance that she would discredit their causes. Although Woodhull drew large crowds to socialist events, the leadership of the American International Workingman's Association was concerned about her involvement with the labor movement. Karl Marx believed in abolishing marriage, but it was low on his list of priorities. He tended to believe that once socialist policies were adopted by governments, people would naturally abandon marriage. Marx showed no respect for Woodhull and supported her expulsion from his organization. Even the Spiritualists were deeply divided over having Woodhull as their figurehead, although she was able to retain her position as president of their national association.[291]

Woodhull's campaign created the strongest reaction within the women's rights movement. Woodhull intentionally encouraged a connection in the public thought between her social freedom campaign and woman suffrage because it gave her credibility. But many longtime woman suffrage leaders became concerned about the impact Woodhull was having on their cause. The women's rights movement had always been surrounded with controversy and criticism, but this was different. Ida Husted Harper, an early historian of the movement who lived through the events herself, explained that Woodhull "precipitated a storm of criticism compared to which all those that had gone before were as a summer shower to a Missouri cyclone." By early 1872 this storm of criticism was starting to form. The following newspaper headline referred to Woodhull's first "Principles of Social Freedom" lecture in New York City:

> Died of Free Love, Nov 25th in Steinway Hall, the Woman Suffrage Movement[292]

This particular headline may have tolled the death knell prematurely, but in fact the terms "woman suffrage" and "free love" were becoming increasingly associated in the newspapers and in the minds of the American people.

Lucy Stone of the Boston AWSA led an effort to defend woman suffrage against Woodhull's campaign. Because Stone is best known today for using her own wedding as a public protest against marriage laws, one could easily assume that she would agree with Woodhull's radical views on marriage. But Stone's protest was not against marriage itself, only against the legal concept of "coverture," which suspended a woman's legal existence during marriage. Having worked tirelessly for decades to build the movement into something respectable, Stone was strongly motivated to protect its image.

Woodhull hired people to distribute pamphlets at important woman suffrage events in Philadelphia and Washington. Stone hired people at those same events to collect up Woodhull's pamphlets and destroy them. Stone's close associate Mary Livermore added to her national tour repertoire a lecture called "Marriage vs. Free Love," in which she refuted Woodhull's claim that woman suffrage and free love were identical. Livermore advocated for an equal partnership and enduring love between a man and a woman in marriage and denounced the present "social epidemic of moral looseness" and "mire of sensualism." In *Woman's Journal*, Stone promoted a similar message in favor of the "sanctity and permanence of marriage" and against "social evil."[293]

But despite Stone's best efforts, she still believed that "the Free Love incubus" within the women's rights movement had caused "incalculable harm to the cause of woman suffrage." Many people became convinced that supporting woman suffrage meant advocating free love. Membership in woman suffrage organizations declined dramatically in what one leader called "the Free Love panic." Pending woman suffrage bills in state legislatures were put on hold. Lecture hall owners refused to rent their facilities for woman suffrage lectures. There was an increase of hostility to the women's rights movement in general, and the wives of prominent men organized antiwoman suffrage efforts to lobby against women getting the vote. Woodhull was held up as proof of the potential corrupting effect of woman suffrage.[294]

While this was a tumultuous period in the women's rights movement, it was the next phase of Woodhull's campaign that most resembled a Missouri cyclone—and ultimately ensured that free love and woman suffrage would be associated in the minds of Americans for the next twenty years.

Woodhull's career, public image, and finances were all in rapid decline. On top of that, after being evicted from her rental home, she found it difficult to find a landlord willing to rent to her. But rather than give up her campaign, she chose to take her war on marriage to a higher level. She sought vindication for herself by trying to associate the most respected members of society with free love. She took a few shots at various public officials and clergymen, and then focused her full effort on the Reverend Henry Ward Beecher, whom Woodhull referred to as "the American Pope."[295]

The Reverend Henry Ward Beecher was one of the most influential men in America. He was the most prominent American minister of the nineteenth century — even more famous than his father, Reverend Lyman Beecher — and a pioneer of the contemporary mega-church. Beecher's Plymouth Church was a Congregational church with an innovative 2,800-seat auditorium-style building designed specifically for Beecher's popular evangelical ministry. It was located in Brooklyn, New York, which was then known as the "city of churches" — a quiet pocket of New England culture separated by the East River from New York City. Fleets of ferries referred to as "Beecher's Boats" brought crowds of New Yorkers across the water to hear the great preacher's sermons. Henry Ward Beecher was leading American Christianity away from strict theology toward a warmer, more welcoming "Gospel of Love." He encouraged innovations in music and congregational singing and floral arrangements. He was an engaging and entertaining speaker, bringing colorful stories, humor, and even impersonations into his sermons. People commonly stated as an accepted fact that Beecher was the best orator in the English-speaking world. He lectured nationally, had a syndicated newspaper column, and wrote popular books on Christian topics, such as *The Life of Jesus, The Christ*, which had just been published in 1871.[296]

Besides his church innovations, Beecher had the extraordinary ability to get involved in highly controversial political issues, push the boundaries of social acceptability, and come out relatively unscathed. He had the greatest impact on the issue of the abolition of African slavery. Henry's sister Harriet Beecher Stowe is often given credit for changing how millions of Americans felt about African slavery prior to the Civil War through her 1852 novel *Uncle Tom's Cabin*—the nineteenth century's best-selling book after the Bible. But Harriet's literary masterwork was inspired in the late 1840s by Henry's career as an activist minister. He was a central participant in the "Underground Railroad," which helped escaped slaves find safety and freedom. He organized economic boycotts against New York businesses involved with slavery. During the violent conflict over whether Kansas would be a free state or a slave state, he raised money to send the free-state supporters guns and ammunition. Most significantly, he transformed the cause of the abolition of slavery from the dangerous lunatic fringe to a socially acceptable political position in the Northern states.

Henry Ward Beecher was able to change the opinions of Americans about slavery by tapping into their strong feelings about marriage and sexuality. Americans who had accepted involuntary servitude as a necessary evil changed their positions when confronted by the realities of the sexual abuse of women, the debasement of motherhood, and the tearing apart of families, which was also very much a part of the institution of slavery. Beecher accomplished this change of heart by holding mock slave auctions as fundraisers to purchase the freedom of young mixed-race women who were going to be used as breeding stock for hard labor slaves.

Beecher's emotionally charged theatrics at Plymouth Church fundraisers were so popular and successful that he became a powerful force in religion and politics. In 1860 when presidential candidate Abraham Lincoln decided to support abolition of slavery, he announced his position during a visit to Beecher's Plymouth Church. During the war Lincoln sent Beecher on a European lecture tour to rally support for the Union cause. At the ceremonial end of the American Civil War in April 1865, after the Union Army captured the last stronghold of the Confederate Army, President Lincoln invited Beecher to give the rededication sermon at Fort Sumter. So, after the Civil War, it was politically significant when Beecher announced his support of woman suffrage.

Considering Beecher's powerful support of women's rights, it might have seemed irrational for Woodhull to target him as an enemy, especially since he was also the half-brother of her faithful friend Isabella Beecher Hooker. But Beecher was firmly committed to preaching the importance of fidelity to monogamous marriage—what he referred to as "the New England doctrine." He used the power of his pulpit to preach against Woodhull's social freedom campaign. Even more aggravating to Woodhull, Beecher was the editor of the magazine *Christian Union*, which had published Stowe's story *My Wife and I*.[297]

Woodhull wanted to transform the issue of social freedom from the dangerous lunatic fringe to an acceptable political position—just as Beecher had done with the issue of the abolition of slavery. Ultimately Woodhull decided a public attack on the prominent reverend was the best way to accomplish this. She wanted to expose his hypocrisy, rebrand him as the "king of free love," and make his "Gospel of Love" connote something sexual. She publicly explained her motives:

> It is not, therefore, Mr. Beecher as the individual that I pursue, but Mr. Beecher as the representative man; Mr. Beecher as a power in the world; and Mr. Beecher as my auxiliary in a great war for freedom, or Mr. Beecher as a violent enemy and a powerful hindrance to all that I am bent on accomplishing.[298]

Woodhull's opportunity for attack came when she heard a rumor about Beecher's close personal relationship with Elizabeth Tilton.

A warm, charismatic, and personable man, Reverend Beecher had friendly relationships with many people in his congregation, including women. He was in the habit of writing, ministering, and socializing outside his own home because his wife Eunice had become a bitter and unpleasant person after tragically losing five of her nine children to illness. Beecher had an especially close friendship with Theodore and Elizabeth Tilton, often doing his writing at their home. Theodore Tilton was a well-known member of Plymouth Church and the editor of a popular Christian magazine. Beecher had been Tilton's hero and role model for many years, and more recently he had become a mentor and professional associate. Tilton's wife, Elizabeth, often read Beecher's manuscripts and made suggestions for improvements. Occasionally, she was alone in the house with Beecher.

During a social visit with her close friends Susan B. Anthony and Elizabeth Cady Stanton, Mrs. Tilton claimed to have had an affair with Henry Ward Beecher. Stanton later passed the information on to Woodhull, who immediately put this juicy bit of gossip to use. In what some may call blackmail, but she began asking Beecher for favors. Woodhull made it clear that if he did not oblige her, she would publish the gossip. Beecher ignored her requests. Woodhull retaliated with escalating ferocity.

Woodhull asked Beecher to lend his credibility to her by giving an introduction at her "Principles of Social Freedom" lecture at Steinway Hall. When he refused, she took the gossip to the New York City newspapers, but none would print it. So she made vague public threats toward unnamed prominent clergy in her own *Woodhull & Claflin Weekly*:

> My judges preach against "free love" openly, and practice it secretly. . . . I shall make it my business to analyze some of these lives, and will take my chances in the matter of libel suits.

On October 28, 1872, just after the Plymouth Church "Silver Jubilee," a huge celebration of Beecher's 25th year of preaching at that church, Woodhull struck a more forceful blow against the Reverend. The *Woodhull & Claflin Weekly* included an article describing in exaggerated detail the Beecher-Tilton affair and cover-up, citing sources Isabella Beecher Hooker and Elizabeth Cady Stanton. Woodhull explained her motivations:

> I intend that this article shall burst like a bomb-shell into the ranks of the moralistic social camp. I am engaged in offering, and in some sense conducting, a social revolution on

the marriage question. . . . I came slowly, deliberately, and reluctantly to the adoption of this method of warfare.

She launched her offensive by printing 150,000 copies of the incendiary Beecher-Tilton scandal issue. It was red hot. The initial 10-cent price for the issue shot up to $2.50, and once the paper sold out, readers rented and resold their copies for as much as twenty dollars each. Woodhull's bombshell was a blockbuster.[299]

The immediate repercussion to Woodhull was that she and her sister and husband landed in jail a few days later. Police deputy Anthony Comstock, a member of Plymouth Church, in retaliation for the attack on his beloved minister filed criminal charges of sending obscenity through the US mail. He wanted to silence Woodhull, but as an unintended consequence, respectable New York newspapers, which had previously refused to print the Beecher gossip, now briefly mentioned it when they reported on the arrest of Woodhull—giving the scandal a newsworthiness it did not have before the arrest.

Because of the timing of Woodhull's arrest, she was not able to vote for herself on Election Day 1872. The previous Election Day in 1871, Woodhull had led a group of women to a New York polling place and insisted on being allowed to vote under the "new departure" legal interpretation that she had been promoting. Because Woodhull was already in jail on Election Day 1872, she was not with Susan B. Anthony and sixteen other women who were arrested for "knowingly voting without having a lawful right to vote." Anthony turned her arrest into a campaign for woman suffrage. Woodhull turned her arrest into more ammunition for her attack on Beecher.[300]

After being released from jail, Woodhull took her Beecher-Tilton scandal story on a national lecture tour, and the *Woodhull & Claflin Weekly* newspaper reprinted the scandal issue several more times. The bombshell was a reliable fundraiser for Woodhull. The explosion expanded over the next two years, and in August 1874, when Theodore Tilton filed a lawsuit against the great Reverend for alienating the affections of his wife — the civil court equivalent of an adultery charge — it consumed the whole nation.

When Woodhull first began making blackmail threats against Beecher, Theodore Tilton befriended her. He hoped to gain her trust and persuade her to keep the story quiet. During the summer of 1871, Tilton and Woodhull spent evenings together gazing at the stars from the roof of her home, swimming and boating at public beaches, and writing a biography of Woodhull together. But Tilton's strategy had the opposite effect of his original intention. Instead of Woodhull becoming converted to Christian values through their friendship, it seems that Tilton became sympathetic to free-love philosophy — which began showing up in subtle ways in his Christian magazine. He even published the Woodhull biography, which helped her win the presidency of the Spiritualist association, using his own publishing company — at great professional risk. Also, it seems the two friends developed a close intimate relationship. Woodhull publically claimed (and then later publically denied) that Tilton slept in her arms every night for six months. Most significantly, Tilton's personal loyalties shifted from Beecher to Woodhull. And when Theodore Tilton filed the lawsuit against Beecher, it served Woodhull's purposes at Tilton's own expense.

The trial began January 11, 1875, and included six months of testimony and summaries. Hailed as the trial of the century, it was the longest, most expensive, and best publicized trial in American history at that time. The trial was a showcase of famous witnesses orchestrated by the most prominent attorneys with a parade of celebrities making guest appearances in the gallery of the courtroom. Including standing room and bleacher-style benches in the upstairs gallery, the courtroom could accommodate an audience of five hundred spectators. The courtroom was packed full every day, and hundreds were regularly turned away.

About sixty journalists from around the country sat in a special media section in the courtroom throughout the trial. According to biographer Debby Applegate, there were more newspaper headlines for the Beecher-Tilton affair than for the entire American Civil War. Newspapers sold as many as four hundred thousand copies of special issues on the trial. Throughout the legal process, Beecher was also on trial in the court of national public opinion. News stories and editorials, transcripts of court testimony, and analysis of evidence were published daily throughout the nation. Newspapers took sides and debated whether or not Beecher was guilty of adultery. The *New York Herald* commented on the significance of the event to the American people:

> We can recall no one event since the murder of Lincoln that has so moved the people as this question whether Henry Ward Beecher is the basest of men.[301]

There was no question that Henry Ward Beecher and Elizabeth Tilton had an unusually close friendship. The purpose of the trial was to determine whether there had been actual "criminal intimacy." In the process, Theodore Tilton and Beecher each accused the other of having adopted the philosophy and practice of free love. Woodhull was frequently mentioned in the court testimony and nearly everyone associated with her was called to testify, but she was never called as a witness. However, near the end of the trial Woodhull received a subpoena to deliver some of her personal letters. She caused such a dramatic stir by the way she delivered them to the courtroom that the *New York Tribune* devoted nearly a half page to her surprise appearance, describing it as the biggest sensation since the trial began.[302]

In late June after testimony was done, the jury deliberated for eight long days in the summer heat, but could not agree on a verdict. Finally, on July 2, 1875, the judge declared a mistrial. Journalists and the American people following the trial were left with their own speculations as to Beecher's guilt or innocence.

For all practical purposes, Theodore Tilton lost his case and much more. He was ruined financially, his marriage ended in divorce, he was excommunicated from Plymouth Church, and his reputation as a Christian author, editor, and leader was destroyed. Tilton finished out his life in Europe in self-imposed exile.

Beecher, on the other hand, came out of the trial somewhat vindicated. His wife, Eunice, faithfully stood by him throughout the trial. The Plymouth Church congregation, unwavering in support of their minister, held a fundraiser to pay the huge fees for Beecher's legal defense team, and then they raised his annual salary to $100,000. Beecher's career, personal finances, and public image recovered, although his political influence waned.[303]

The Beecher-Tilton trial damaged woman suffrage, as both Beecher and Tilton had been outspoken supporters of the movement. Before the trial Henry Ward Beecher had served as president of the Boston-based AWSA and Theodore Tilton had served as president of the New York-based NWSA. Having these two respected male figureheads fighting in court over adultery and free love only further tainted the cause of woman suffrage. Anthony and Stanton and every other woman involved had their images as public figures tarnished through their association with the scandal and trial. Isabella Beecher Hooker was disowned by the Beecher family and snubbed by friends and neighbors because of her support of Woodhull.

It could have been worse for the women's rights movement. In the midst of the storm when Woodhull needed money, she blackmailed her fellow suffragists—as she put it, "to shut the mouths of a clique of loose and loud-tongued women who were continually stabbing" her. Woodhull sent them a proof print of a *Woodhull & Claflin Weekly* scandal issue that if it had been printed, would have exposed rumors of their extramarital love interests. But unlike Reverend Beecher, the women's rights leaders paid Woodhull's price for silence. They would not risk further damaging their personal reputations and the image of their movement. All of this NWSA-related scandal only strengthened Lucy Stone's resolve not even to consider reuniting the two factions of the women's rights movement.[304]

Another public figure entangled in Woodhull's campaign was Frederick Douglas, the famous black civil rights leader who had been an early advocate of woman suffrage. Just as the free-love storm was beginning, Woodhull announced Douglas as her vice-president running mate for her presidential campaign. Of course, making a claim does not make it true. Douglas had never met or corresponded with Woodhull, had no connection with the NWSA, and had never agreed to be part of Woodhull's presidential campaign. Woodhull's claim, however, got some publicity as news commentators and political cartoonists made fun of the notion of a white woman and a black man running for the highest office. Shortly after this negative publicity in association with Woodhull, Douglas' home in Rochester was burned down in what he called a "Ku Klux spirit."[305]

The contentious division within the American Association of Spiritualists, caused by Woodhull's involvement over several years, resulted in the decline and doom of that newly created organization. By the time Woodhull resigned her presidency in 1875, rather than try to revive the national organization, the members chose instead to dissolve it and revert to informal local networks.[306]

As determined as ever, Woodhull continued the fight with another national lecture tour.

Eddy's Text Book

In February 1872, as the tornado of controversy was forming within the American women's rights movement, Mary Baker Eddy began writing her book *Science and Health*. For the first few months, issues with rebellious students kept her from writing full time, but by June she had written sixty pages. One of her students, with whom she lived for several months, described her perseverance:

> I have known her when nearly crushed with sorrow, but she wrote on. I have known her when friend after friend deserted her, but she wrote on. I have seen student after student bring ridicule and reproach upon her, but still she wrote on.[307]

By the end of 1872, she had settled into the rhythm of what was roughly a three-year period of writing. Living off the savings she had accumulated in 1870 and 1871 from teaching and her partnership with Kennedy, she withdrew from society to focus on writing. To keep her expenses low, she lived in temporary rooms at boarding houses or in the homes of her students. According to biographer Irving Tomlinson, her ideas came to her in the early morning, she would start writing at dawn, and she always quit by sunset. In December she wrote to one of her first students about her writing progress:

> I have a very nice time this winter everything so quiet pleasant scientific and comfortable. I have a better opportunity to write than ever before. . . . I have never since my first perceptions of God in science gained the understanding I have this year and been able to so sift the tares from the wheat.[308]

Eddy's theories of healing were based on her new insight into the message of the Bible. The Bible was her reference book, and she had just acquired *Cruden's Bible Concordance* as a study aid. According to Robert Peel, she also read the Reverend Henry Ward Beecher's 1871 book *The Life of Jesus, The Christ*. As she often did, Eddy wrote notes in the margins, marking passages that spoke to her. In Beecher's writings Eddy found a similar sentiment to her own desire to explain Christian healing to a scientific age:

> Truths remain the same; but every age has its own style of thought. Although this difference is not so great as is the difference between one language and another, it is yet so great as to require restatement or, as it were translation. . . . It is the business of preachers to re-adapt truth, from age to age, to men's ever-renewing wants.[309]

In the fall of 1873, Eddy completed her first draft of *Science and Health* – a book she would later call "hopelessly original." Around that same time she divorced her husband Daniel Patterson, which gave her the legal right to use the name Mary Baker Glover for her authorship. She had begun using the name Mrs. Glover again in recent years, but now it was official. The legal change also eliminated any possibility that Patterson could ever claim ownership of her book. In the next thirty-five years, she would write other books, found organizations, and do many other noteworthy accomplishments, but she would always see *Science and Health* as her most important work, and it was worthy of whatever protection she could give it. This was a first sign of the copyright savvy that would become characteristic of Eddy.[310]

Over the next year, she worked to get the book published. She went to several different publishers, she revised and rearranged her manuscript several times, but was still rejected. In July 1874 she finally gave up on publishers and instead found a willing printer. She had to pay the full cost. In September 1874 she delivered the manuscript to the printer, but the next year was full of unexpected delays and problems. So during the year when America was transfixed by the trial of the most prominent leader of American Christianity, the printing of *Science and Health* was on hold.[311]

One of the delays was caused by the printer taking the liberty to revise Eddy's manuscript. The printer was a Spiritualist and Eddy took "a hard thrust at Spiritualism," as one Boston book reviewer later put it. The printer revised the text as he made the metal plates used for printing. To make corrections, she had to replace individual letters and words within the entire page already laid out. This was no small task, as the printer had changed thousands of words throughout the book. But as an experienced poet, she was up to the creative challenge. Working to rescue her book until "tired to death," she was able to restore her meaning. Even so, the first edition of *Science and Health* was disappointingly less than perfect.[312]

However, during the year of delay, wonderful things were happening for Eddy. After many years of renting rooms in other people's houses, she was finally able to have a permanent home of her own in Lynn at 8 Broad Street. Her remaining savings were enough for a down payment, and income from tenants covered the mortgage payments. She slept in the tiny attic room, and began teaching students again in the front room on the main floor. That summer she and her students held their first public worship services in Lynn, with Eddy as their preacher. Between sixty and one hundred people attended. A favorable review in the newspaper described her preaching as "solemn, earnest, and eloquent." One of her students recalled this period as a very happy time for Eddy. Her great cause was moving forward regardless of the delay printing her book.[313]

Along with these early successes, Eddy was learning to face opposition to her ideas. Spiritualists came to the public worship services and heckled Eddy as she spoke. After only five Sundays, she thought it best to discontinue public preaching for a while. On July 4, 1875, for the final Sunday of her preaching series, she addressed the underlying issue of contention with a sermon called "Moral Science and Mesmerism Contrasted."[314]

At this same time, she felt impelled to add more to *Science and Health* to clarify her disagreements with Richard Kennedy and other students. Working at her desk under the skylight in the attic room in her new home, she added sixteen pages to the final chapter "Healing the Sick." The new content was on ignorant and malicious malpractice, specifically explaining why mesmerism and manipulation of patients was not part of her healing system. The essence of this content would comprise a chapter in later editions called "Animal Magnetism Unmasked." As soon as she completed the extra pages and left home to deliver it to her printer in Boston, she unexpectedly crossed paths with him at the train station. He had started printing the book and had come for the final pages without any communication between them. The printing was completed at the end of October 1875.[315]

The author later called her book "my babe! . . . that will forever testify of itself, and its mother." Mary Baker Eddy's book is known today as *Science and Health with Key to the Scriptures*, the seven hundred-page final edition that has sold millions of copies in multiple languages. Between 1875 and 1910, as Eddy became a stronger spiritual leader, a more experienced teacher, and a better writer, she published hundreds of revised editions. The result was a more gracious, poetic, and uplifting tone in the final edition. She also added the "Key to the Scriptures," including a glossary of Bible terms, plus one hundred pages of "Fruitage" — testimonies of healing from readers. Other revisions include renamed and rearranged chapters, refinement of her terms and concepts, and the addition of marginal headings. But much of the original 456-page book was retained through all the changes.[316]

The quotes from *Science and Health* used in this chapter are from the 1875 edition. Many of these were later modified (refer to the endnotes for the equivalent citations in the final edition) or removed from the book.

The most obvious way the 1875 edition of *Science and Health* "crossed swords with free-love" — as Eddy later claimed — was through the chapter called "Marriage." One could easily wonder why marriage is even relevant to the topic of curing sickness without medicine. But throughout her book Eddy included statements that revealed her emphasis on Christian morality as a prerequisite for practicing Christian healing. She saw marriage as the "school of virtue." In the "Preface" of the book, she made her position clear:

> those who would learn this science without a high moral standard will fail to understand it until they go up higher.[317]

To Eddy, Spiritualism was the opposite of her own belief system. Considering the conflicting viewpoints on marriage between Puritan Christianity and Spiritualism, it is significant that her chapter on marriage is followed (in the final edition) by a chapter denouncing Spiritualism. In the first edition of *Science and Health*, the chapter on Spiritualism is called "Imposition and Demonstration."[318]

Eddy traced her criticism of Spiritualism and its moral implications back to its origins with the Fox sisters:

> The Rochester rappings inaugurated a mockery destructive to order and good morals. . . . its rites and ceremonies that choose darkness rather than light, and above all its loose morals, do not entitle spiritualism to the standing it has gained in society.[319]

Eddy bemoaned the lowering of moral standards caused by the Spiritualism movement:

> To-day sin offers a premium; let down the bars of morality, and you are society's favorite; put them up higher than society can leap, and you bring opprobrium on the bartender. Woman especially should hold the standard that rebukes vice, and saith to virtue, join us, and though we battle beneath stripes, we will fall in our armor, or lay it down on the field of victory.[320]

Throughout her book, Eddy made it clear that although she appreciated some Spiritualist individuals, she had no respect for Spiritualism, or any other "isms:"

the majority of what is termed mediumship, is simply imposition, not even clairvoyance, or mind-reading, but a catch-penny fraud.[321]

The chapter denouncing Spiritualism discussed issues of life and death, identity and relationship, science and superstition. Only by Christian transformation, Eddy predicted — through the recognition of one God, the one eternal Spirit — would mortal life be replaced with eternal life.

Following the chapter on Spiritualism, Eddy discussed spirit and matter and creation, before coming to the topics of prayer and atonement. Eddy emphasized that sin must be overcome through repentance and reformation before the salvation of oneness with God can be experienced. In Eddy's view, God only forgives sins that have been completely given up. From this discussion of atonement Eddy transitioned to the chapter "Marriage" with this statement that suggested the hot news topic of the day:

But for these false views regarding the forgiveness of sin, ministers and laymen would never break the commandment, "Thou shalt not commit adultery," and then talk of their love for God, and Christian experience.[322]

Overall, the first edition chapter on marriage is remarkably similar to the final edition. This is significant considering the dramatic changes that were going on in American culture through that thirty-five year period, and the rapidly expanding role of women in Eddy's movement and society. Questions and issues relating to marriage and sexuality would come up again and again throughout Eddy's career, but she made surprisingly few changes to this chapter.

"Marriage" begins with the launch of Jesus' ministry, when receiving baptism by John seemed to be a necessary step in his

Christly career. John was reluctant, but Jesus asked John to allow the baptism, saying "suffer it to be so now, for thus it becometh us to fulfill all righteousness" (Matt. 3:15). Eddy applied this same logic to marriage. She saw marriage as a concession in human experience, but not the ultimate state. She explained:

> The time cometh when marriage will be a union of hearts; and again, the time cometh when there will be no marrying or giving in marriage, but we shall be as the angels; the Soul rejoicing in its own mate wherein the masculine Wisdom and feminine Love are embraced in the understanding.[323]

But Eddy's view of marriage as temporary in the grand scheme of spiritual development by no means meant she had any agreement with the proponents of free love. Instead, Eddy elevated the Puritan view of marriage.

Fellow rural New Hampshire resident Noah Webster, who in 1824 published the first dictionary of American English, wrote this definition of marriage:

> Marriage is a contract both civil and religious, by which the parties engage to live together in mutual affection and fidelity, till death shall separate them. Marriage was instituted by God himself for the purpose of preventing the promiscuous intercourse of the sexes, for promoting domestic felicity, and for securing the maintenance and education of children.[324]

Early in the chapter of "Marriage," Eddy gave this definition with similar elements:

> Marriage is the only legal and moral form among the higher species, for generation. . . . Marriage should improve the species, become a barrier to vice, a protection to woman, a strength to man, and a center for the affections.[325]

Immediately after defining marriage, Eddy gave her view of the importance of fidelity to marriage, to society as a whole, and to the salvation of each individual:

Infidelity to the marriage covenant is the social scourge of all peoples; the pestilence that wasteth and walketh at noon-day. The commandment, "Thou shalt not commit adultery," is not less imperative, than "Thou shalt not kill." Virtue is the basis of civilization and progress; without it there is no true foundation to society, and it were utterly impossible to attain the Science of Life.[326]

In later editions Eddy changed the text to emphasize the importance of chastity to civilization and progress. Next, Eddy addressed the topic of free love, which was so much in the news during the years she was writing *Science and Health*:

Owing to the shocking depravity of mankind, chastity is looked at suspiciously; it requires more moral courage for woman to meet the low estimates in society of virtue, than to help lift its standard from the dust. The last infirmity of error that would fasten itself on society, to see it hop and hobble under a new burden of guilt, is named "free love"; wherein "they declare their sin as Sodom, and hide it not," but the boldness of depravity will show its deformity.[327]

Eddy had a strong interest in women's rights. During the writing of *Science and Health*, as busy as she was, she took time to attend a lecture in Lynn by women's rights leader Mary Livermore. In "Marriage," Eddy began a discussion on women's rights issues by saying they were being "discussed on grounds that seem to us not the most important." Then Eddy took political positions on a whole list of the hot-button issues of the day. She supported women's property rights, including the right to own real estate, make banking transactions, collect wages, and enter into contracts. She also supported child custody rights for women who had been abandoned by their husbands. With these statements Eddy agreed with the broadest spectrum of women's rights leaders in their objection to the then-prevailing legal concept of Blackstone's "coverture," which suspended a woman's individual legal existence during marriage even when separated from her husband.[328]

On the topic of woman suffrage, Eddy would not have supported the aggressive activist tactics being used by women's rights leaders to demand the use of ballots at polling places on Election Day. By 1875 the "new departure" legal interpretation had made its way to the US Supreme Court where it was declared invalid. Eddy clearly supported woman suffrage, but only if it would not cause "difficulties of a greater magnitude." Eddy's suffrage position took a patient approach focused on general improvement of society and nobler motives for legislation. This put Eddy's women's rights leadership on the spectrum somewhere between the diplomatic approach of Lucy Stone and the higher education advocacy of Catherine Beecher.[329]

Most notably missing in Eddy's discussion on women's rights issues was any appeal for changing divorce law. Eddy did not support the idea of marriage as an indissoluble bond; she believed God's "Wisdom will ultimately separate what it hath not joined together." But she advised couples not to separate "if there is no moral demand for this." She used the analogy of a captain sailing a ship through stormy waters, advising the reader to stay with the ship until either it sinks or the storm clears. She saw adversity and sorrow in relationships as propelling spiritual progress and a deeper trust in God—the furnace that reveals the image of God.[330]

Eddy saw the need for a stronger, more spiritual foundation for the institution of marriage. America was leading the world with its rising divorce rate (as it has continued to do since that time) and for this it had gained a reputation of notoriety among western nations. Eddy believed the increasing divorce rate was an unpleasant reaction to humanity's demand for "a higher affection." In this regard, her view was similar to that of Margaret Fuller who, in *Woman in the Nineteenth Century*, had predicted a "slight temporary fermentation" happening with the emergence of the ideal of woman. Eddy foresaw a hopeful outcome:

The broad-cast power of evil so conspicuous to-day, is the materialism of the age struggling against the spiritual era, that advances. . . . The mental chemicalization that has brought infidelity to the surface, will as surely throw it off, and marriage will settle down purer after the scum is expelled.[331]

In later editions of her book, Eddy added that it is the beautiful and good in character that weld "indissolubly the links of affection."[332]

Eddy concluded the chapter with this wise warning to those considering marriage and choosing a partner:

be not in haste to take the vow "until death do us part," but consider well its obligations, responsibilities, and relations to all your future happiness; "judge before friendship, then confide till death."[333]

The warning included a quote from "Night Thoughts" by eighteenth-century English poet Edward Young. This famous poem was common reading for New England school students and was one of Eddy's favorites. This excerpt expresses the Puritan model of marriage as friendship.[334]

But since friends grow not thick on ev'ry bough,
Nor ev'ry friend unrotten at the core;
First on thy friend delib'rate with thyself;
Pause, ponder, sift; not eager in the choice,
Nor jealous of the chosen: fixing, fix:
Judge before friendship, then confide till death.
Well for thy friend, but nobler far for thee.

Despite the profound disappointments Eddy experienced in her first two marriages, it is clear throughout the chapter that she placed a high value on the institution. She used the chapter "Marriage" to engage with prospective students even before *Science and Health* was published. In January 1875 she wrote to her student Putney Bancroft who was engaged in the public healing practice at the time:

> What do you say to my introducing myself to my hearers with the chapter on Marriage that has some women's rights in it, and is a finished, almost perfect thing, then, turning from my notes, addressing them briefly on Science, sufficient to interest them in its cures, so as to refer them to Dr. Bancroft.[335]

The chapter "Marriage" in the first edition was followed by a chapter called "Physiology," and then finally the much-awaited chapter "Healing the Sick," which specifically described her system of healing without medicine. A sincere reader could heal any disease by rejecting materialistic thinking and recognizing God's ever-present spiritual power. Just in case the reader had not yet gotten the message on the importance of the moral foundation of her healing system, within the chapter "Healing the Sick," she included more reminders, such as this one:

> The greatest hindrance this science can meet will arise from backsliding students, those claiming to practice it who do not adhere to its moral obligations, who have not yet realized until the fountain is purer, the stream will be turbid; mind must be right or its action on others will be inharmonious.[336]

A significant element of the first edition of *Science and Health* was the introduction of the term "Christian Science." Mary Baker Eddy was not the first person to use this term. Presbyterian minister Samuel Miller had used the term in 1803 in his encyclopedia of new areas of study. Describing efforts by Christian theologians in the late 1700s to apply scientific principles and reasoning to the religion of Christ, Miller pronounced the period to be "the age of Christian Science," and predicted that the nineteenth century would bring its fulfillment. Presbyterian-founded Oberlin College, known as the first college to admit blacks and women, claimed in early advertisements in the 1830s that the institution was "beginning to diffuse the cheering beams of Christian Science." Several published works in America and England in the mid-1800s made reference to Christian Science, but the term had not been fully defined or explored. Eddy may not have been aware of these sporadic uses, but the term already expressed advancing Christian thought.[337]

Eddy waited to use the term until the last two words of the last sentence of her book. By doing this, Eddy defined Christian Science as she understood it with her entire book, dramatically revealing the term in the conclusion only after the reader had been thoroughly introduced to the topic. She had already privately explained to her students how potentially provocative the term might be:

> In the nineteenth century I affix for all time the word, *Science*, to Christianity, and *error* to personal sense; and call the world to battle on this issue.[338]

Eddy's title *Science and Health* matched a phrase from the early English Bible translation by John Wycliffe, translated in the later King James Version as "knowledge of salvation" (Luke 1:77). Eddy believed the ideas in her book would lift humanity into health and happiness, and conquer destructive human passions and wrong desires. Even as she was writing her book, Eddy was hopeful of its impact on the world. She wrote within it:

> We have faith this book will do its work, though not fully understood, in the nineteenth century.[339]

The first edition of *Science and Health* had a print run of one thousand copies, and it was sent to and read by some influential people—newspaper book reviewers, ministers, and philosophers—with a range of reactions. The transcendentalist lecturer Bronson Alcott shared his comments about this "remarkable volume":

> In times like ours, so sunk in sensualism, one hails with joy any voice speaking an assured word for God and Immortality; and the joy is heightened the more if the words are of

woman's divining. . . . The popular Spiritualism finds no favor from her divining spirit.[340]

Bronson Alcott was intrigued enough by *Science and Health* to pay a visit to Lynn to meet the author. After his visit, Alcott wrote in his journal that he found Eddy to be "a Christian in the truest sense." He contrasted Eddy's "wholesome views" with "the sorceries of current spiritualism, fast running its polluting social race into detestation." A similar sentiment was expressed in a favorable newspaper review by the *Springfield Republican:*

> The Doctrines of this book are high and pure, and it seems wholly free from those vile theories about love and marriage which have been so prevalent among the Spiritualists.[341]

Most significantly, a copy of the first edition of *Science and Health* found its way into the personal book collection of the Reverend Henry Ward Beecher. According to Beecher's granddaughter Margaret Beecher White, he spoke of it as "one of the most wonderful books ever written." This was publicized years later at the height of Mary Baker Eddy's career in a 1908 *Cosmopolitan Magazine* article called "Beecher and Christian Science" written by White, who became a Christian Science practitioner. In the article, she described the close friendly relationship she had with her famous grandfather. She claimed that *Science and Health* subtly influenced Beecher's sermons from that point forward.[342]

Two Worlds Collide (1876)

Did the lecture of Victoria Woodhull meet the taste and indicate the tone of character of those who attended it? Must we admit there are in our very midst men and women claiming respectability who could be made even to listen to the most detestable and loathsome inculcations of vice from one who outrages decency, insults human nature and disgraces the name of woman?

Mary Baker Eddy

It is to just such gratuitous abuse as this that I owe the shadow that has fallen upon my name — due not to anything I have said or done. Mr. Editor, you know well enough that "the most detestable and loathsome inculcations of vice" formed no part of that lecture. . . . You know better; and the people who listened, who are joined with me in this attack, know that the pen that writes it lies.

Victoria Claflin Woodhull

Eddy's Centennial Celebration

The centennial of the signing of the Declaration of Independence was a momentous occasion for the people of America — the celebration of the century. Since the time of the founding of the United States of America, the fourth of July had become "the great anniversary festival," solemnized with picnics, patriotic music, public prayers, parades, military gun salutes, bonfires, decorative lighting, and fireworks — just as the "Champion of Independence" John Adams had predicted in 1776. The day had recently been designated an official "Independence Day" national holiday, and in 1876 this commemoration of the American Revolution was taken to a whole new level — a climax in a momentous buildup of what historian Robert Peel called "a delirium of patriotic fervor." Perhaps it was refreshing — even inspiring and unifying — to have a yearlong patriotic celebration after having been through the divisiveness and demoralization of the Beecher-Tilton trial the previous year.[343]

The City of Philadelphia hosted the first World's Fair held in America, with thirty-seven countries participating. The international exposition had an American centennial theme and it was originally planned to have its grand opening on the anniversary of the historic battle of Lexington and Concord, which had since been dubbed by American poet Ralph Waldo Emerson, "the shot heard round the world." Nearly ten million visitors from America and Europe and beyond came to see the famous Liberty Bell and an impressive showcase of American architecture, history, culture, industry, and invention.[344]

Americans received a grand lesson in history and civics as, all over the country, community leaders gave speeches reflecting on the founding of the American Republic and the significance of its proven success. On July 4 in the Boston Music Hall decorated for the occasion, the reading of the Declaration of Independence was followed by a speech by former Congressman

Robert C. Winthrop. Since retiring from public office, Winthrop had revived the "city on a hill" imagery in his book on his direct ancestor, colonial Massachusetts governor John Winthrop, whose likeness had just been committed to stone for the National Statuary Hall at the US Capitol Building. At this Independence Day celebration Robert Winthrop cheered, "A century of self-government completed!" He welcomed the dawn of "The American Age" and announced a joint French-American effort to build a gigantic statue at the mouth of an American commercial harbor to represent "Liberty enlightening the world!" —a monument that would come to be known as the "Statue of Liberty." Winthrop expressed his own awestruck sentiment of the occasion:

> Yet what can I say? What can anyone say, here or elsewhere, to-day, which shall satisfy the expectations of others, or meet his own sense of the demands of such an occasion? For myself, certainly, the longer I have contemplated it, — the more deeply I have reflected on it, —so much the more hopeless I have become of finding myself able to give any adequate expression to its full significance, its real sublimity and grandeur. . . . Emotions like those which ought to fill, and which do fill, all our hearts, call for the swelling tones of a multitude, the cheers of a mighty crowd, and refuse to be uttered by a single human voice. The strongest phrases seem feeble and powerless.[345]

On America's centennial, Mary Baker Eddy was not in Boston listening to Winthrop's speech. She was not in front of Independence Hall at the Philadelphia World's Fair with Susan B. Anthony and other NWSA leaders staging an activist demonstration in support of woman suffrage. Eddy was doing something she believed was far more important. She was at home in Lynn with her small group of students having discussions and drawing up documents. On that day, those seven created their first formal organization: The Christian Science Association.[346]

Associations of Christian Science students would always be an important part of Eddy's multifaceted religious organization, and Independence Day would have an extra significance to Christian Scientists. Twenty-one years later, 2,500 dedicated students of Christian Science celebrated Independence Day by making a pilgrimage to Concord, New Hampshire, to Mary Baker Eddy's home, which was decorated for the occasion with one solitary American flag. There, in the backyard, they heard their leader deliver a brief speech to "commemorate not only our nation's civil and religious freedom, but a greater even, the liberty of the sons of God, the inalienable rights and radiant reality of Christianity," followed by a lineup of government and religious officials, who spoke on related themes.[347]

Eddy's 1876 Independence Day focus was very much in agreement with a book reviewer from *The Boston Investigator* who wrote that if the claims in *Science and Health* were true, that by simply reading the book one could be cured of any ailment, then certainly that is "better than going to Philadelphia to see the Centennial show." Eddy quietly celebrated that significant day by starting a revolution based on the "self-evident Truth" of Christian Science. Her revolution was about declaring independence from the brutal tyranny of sickness, sin, and death. In the first edition of *Science and Health*, Eddy spoke of the declarations of God through Scripture "that man has dominion over [the] earth" and "that man was made [in] the image and likeness" of God. Eventually, she made a connection to the spirit of 1776 in her book:

> Like our nation, Christian Science has its Declaration of Independence. God has endowed man with inalienable rights, among which are self-government, reason, and conscience. Man is properly self-governed only when he is guided rightly and governed by his Maker, divine Truth and Love.[348]

For the record, Mary Baker Eddy did go to the Centennial Exhibition later that year, and even she was as overwhelmed with patriotic sentiments as Winthrop claimed to be at the Boston Music Hall on Independence Day. "Having returned so gushing," she used her "pen as a safety-valve" to describe the astounding and startling exhibition to the readers of the *Lynn Transcript* newspaper. But she followed up her report a week later by soberly clarifying her view in a poem, which has since been retitled "Communion Hymn," that it is the word of God which makes man free.[349]

> Felt ye the power of the Word?
> 'Twas the Truth that made us free,
> And was found by you and me
> In the life and the love of our Lord.

Earlier in the centennial year, Eddy shared a poem called "Woman's Rights" with Lynn newspaper readers, which revealed what she considered the most important right.

WOMAN'S RIGHTS

> Grave on her monumental pile:
> She won from vice, by virtue's smile,
> Her dazzling crown, her sceptered throne,
> Affection's wreath, a happy home;
>
> The right to worship deep and pure,
> To bless the orphan, feed the poor;
> Last at the cross to mourn her Lord,
> First at the tomb to hear his word:
>
> To fold an angel's wings below;
> And hover o'er the couch of woe;
> To nurse the Bethlehem babe so sweet,
> The right to sit at Jesus' feet;
>
> To form the bud for bursting bloom,
> The hoary head with joy to crown;
> In short, the right to work and pray,

"To point to heaven and lead the way."

Eddy had already published her poem "Woman's Rights" in New Hampshire in 1853. Around the same time, a Congregational Church not far from Seneca Falls, New York, made women's rights history by ordaining Antoinette Brown Blackwell to be their minister. Eddy published her poem a second time in Maine in the mid-1860s while she was studying with Dr. Quimby. Eddy would republish the poem several more times in her own periodicals and books. Clearly, to Eddy, the message of the poem was both important and enduring.[350]

The idea of woman as a Christian religious leader was a radical and controversial notion throughout the nineteenth century. The conclusion of Eddy's poem—"In short, the right to work and pray, 'to point to heaven and lead the way,'"—suggests that the women's rights issue that was most important to Mary Baker Eddy was the right to serve in the holy profession of the Christian ministry—in short, the right to use the title "Reverend."

Around the same time the Christian Science organization was formed, Eddy was trying to establish the name Christian Science with the public and clearly distinguish it from Spiritualism. She had settled into her new home and had put a sign out front that read "Christian Scientists' Home." In her parlor, she met with patients and students regularly and taught classes, steadily expanding her community of followers.

Much to her chagrin, the local gossip about her took a turn for the worse. She was accused of dyeing her hair, using makeup, having loose morals, and promoting free love, along with practicing witchcraft and mediumship. Eddy tried to make light of the accusations with her good sense of humor, wryly commenting to a close acquaintance, "of course I believe in free love, I love everyone." But still the false accusations bothered her. Coincidentally, it was around that same time that Victoria Claflin Woodhull planned a New England lecture tour that would include an event in Lynn. The high priestess of free love was coming to town.[351]

Woodhull's Boston Lectures

By the end of September 1876, Victoria Claflin Woodhull had given lectures all over the country, including in the South and the farthest western states, but New England was her most difficult region, because it was the most hostile to her message. For her "Principles of Social Freedom" lecture in Boston in early 1872, the press reports focused on the hisses of the hostile audience. Several months later, Woodhull had chosen a Spiritualist convention in Boston to launch on attack on Reverend Henry Ward Beecher. In that Boston speech, besides the shocking content, Woodhull herself admitted to using "some naughty words." The Boston press, refusing to publish what she said, simply called her speech "obnoxious" libelous slander of a well-respected clergyman. Since that time, community opposition had made it difficult for Woodhull to lecture there.[352]

At the end of 1872 after her month in jail on obscenity charges, Woodhull tried to attack Beecher through another lecture at the Boston Music Hall, but the lecture was cancelled because of pressure from politically connected people with loyalties to Beecher, including Harriet Beecher Stowe and the governor of Massachusetts. Woodhull gave her speech "The Naked Truth" in New York City, and at the end of the speech she was arrested and put in jail again by police deputy Anthony Comstock. She made another attempt to speak in Boston's Tremont Temple a few months later, but was again prevented by community opposition. Her labor movement event was moved to a smaller, less prominent hall. Still another New England lecture tour planned for late 1873 was scaled back due to pressure from local authorities—although newspapers reported she was simply postponing until the lawsuits filed against her were not so pressing.[353]

During these combative years, Woodhull was essentially blacklisted—ignored by most newspapers, except for the extensive negative publicity relating to the Beecher-Tilton scandal. But by 1876, for her lecture tour for "The Human Body, The Temple of God," her team had become much more sophisticated in how they managed her image and publicity.

Woodhull had a complete makeover of her stage costume. She no longer made bold fashion statements as part of her pioneering image. Her hair had grown long again and she wore conventionally feminine outfits. As a further image change, she often held a Bible in her hand as she lectured. Even so, because of her notorious reputation, the name Woodhull had become synonymous with licentiousness. Through experiences with local hostility in Boston and elsewhere, Woodhull's lecture and publicity team had developed techniques for using the opposition to draw crowds to her events and encourage people to reconsider their preconceptions.[354]

Woodhull's team contracted the lecture halls, negotiated ticket prices, arranged hotels and transportation, long before Victoria arrived. They would begin promoting the lecture in an intentionally provocative way. Community leaders and Christian ministers would sound the alarm of warning to their church members, demanding a boycott of the event. Woodhull's public relations team would respond in the newspaper with righteous indignation. Raising doubts about the validity of the criticism, they challenged news reporters and curiosity seekers to come hear Woodhull speak, to judge for themselves whether her reputation was true or not.

One technique they developed was to hold two lectures in the same area. The first lecture would be presented in the most inoffensive and respectable way. This unexpectedly noncontroversial presentation by itself was newsworthy! The local news reporters would announce their surprise at how ladylike they found Woodhull to be and would give a favorable review of the lecture—which the Woodhull team used for promotion. Those attending were encouraged to come again and bring others. When the locals came out to fill the hall for the second lecture,

Woodhull might present audiences with more challenging and controversial topics.[355]

Through extensive experience on the lecture circuit, giving talks day after day and by drawing on the theatrical skills of her early acting career, Woodhull developed highly effective techniques for creating a strong emotional connection with audiences. She would start out timid and hesitant, with a soft shaky voice. Once she had gained the sympathy of the audience, her performance would build strength, still giving the impression of sincere spontaneity. Finally, she would build up to the fiery passion that so surprised and impressed her audiences. As one reporter described it, "when she paces the platform and stamps out her terrific sentences, the audience are electrified up to the highest pitch." From her 1873 lecture in Lynn on the apparently benign topic of politics and finance, the *Lynn Record* provided a vivid description of her stage presence:

> For the benefit of those who have never seen the woman who has been the subject of so much newspaper comment and tea table gossip, we will say that she is neither very tall nor very short; neither is she a venus, but she is a woman of fair height and proportions, and, although not handsome, is good looking, and when fired up by the telling points of her discourse the blood mounts quickly to her cheeks, coming and going in rapid succession, and it is then that her audience instinctively feel that a woman of extraordinary ability is addressing them. That she is gifted with remarkable talents, we think no one who listened to her on Tuesday evening will deny. Her manner of presenting her subjects to her hearers is logical, thoroughly systematic, in many respects quite original, often electrifying, sometimes astounding, now soaring to lofty oratorical heights, then gracefully descending to plain, unvarnished facts, sending a thrill of conviction home to the minds of the listeners; but it is when speaking without notes that she is most brilliant, and is best appreciated by the audience.[356]

Another journalist from the *St. Louis Republican* described the bond Woodhull was able to make with her audiences during her lecture tour in early February 1876:

> Men and ladies were to be seen brushing tears from their eyes as the pathos of this strange woman went home to their hearts, linking them together in that chain of common sympathy whose weird spell no individual present could successfully resist if they would.[357]

Not all of the press reports were so positive, as an example, this report a week later in a Tennessee newspaper:

> The South has always been free from the corrupting isms that affect Northern cities, and Southern men and women have an especial horror of the doctrines of the Free Lovers, the fruits of which have recently been made manifest in the great Beecher-Tilton scandal. We are to be no longer exempt from temptation, however — Victoria Woodhull, the high priestess of the loathsome creed, is traveling South, and has visited St. Louis, Memphis, and Nashville. . . . Like Satan, she quotes Scripture when it suits her purpose. She tells some shameful truths on our boasted Christian civilization, and good people are bound to endorse what she says, while at the same time they will loath and despise her remedy for the same.[358]

Tennie came along on Woodhull's 1876 lecture tours as part of the promotional team. Tennie and Victoria both met with local news reporters prior to lecture events to ensure the most positive coverage possible. Tennie collected lecture reviews and sent them to other newspapers for republishing in preparation for the next lecture destination. A news quote of Elizabeth Cady Stanton praising Woodhull for her extraordinary trailblazing accomplishments for woman's cause was reprinted in newspapers throughout the country, sometimes appearing alongside news about Woodhull's lecture tour.

Between July and September the news reports on Woodhull focused on her divorce suit against her second husband, James

Harvey Blood, on grounds of adultery. The commentators often noted the irony that Blood was being sued for simply practicing what Woodhull preached. They also expressed puzzlement over how a spiritually adopted husband could be legally divorced in court. Newspapers all over the country reprinted a *Cincinnati Enquirer* article that reported on the divorce suit, the closure of the *Woodhull & Claflin Weekly* newspaper, Woodhull's declining mental and physical health, and the imminent downfall of her public career. She responded with an indignant letter to the *New York Sun* tabloid, which editors entitled, "Mrs. Woodhull Aroused."[359]

In late September 1876, following this flurry of news coverage, Woodhull arrived in Boston for an extended stay. A reporter from the *Boston Daily Globe* came to Woodhull's elegant reception room at her hotel for an interview. The reporter was received by the charming Miss Tennie, who talked about Woodhull's successes on her recent lecture tour and showed the reporter hundreds of newspapers from all around the country. The reporter read lecture reviews from several major cities that "commended" Woodhull's lecture "in very high terms."

"It is only in Boston that Mrs. Woodhull has been denied a hearing," Tennie told the reporter. "Why should she not be heard in her own defense, that she may refute the lies and slanders heaped upon her? Fair play and justice, especially towards a woman, ought to give her the opportunity."

Then Woodhull entered the room. The reporter described his first impression of her as "a most courteous lady, of thoroughly refined appearance." In a "pleasant" interview with the reporter, Woodhull explained that she had been misrepresented and wrongly persecuted, and now she wanted to clear her name for the sake of her children by lecturing in Boston.

"Yes, I propose to lecture in the Boston Theatre next Sunday evening," Woodhull shared with the reporter. "Mr. Beecher and Mr. Tilton have been given opportunities to lecture here, while I have always been denied the right. It is wholly due to the efforts of villifiers and blackmailers that the impression has been made that my lecture is one not fit to be delivered before a decent audience. . . . I have been subjected to the most outrageous charges."

The reporter pleaded Woodhull's case to the Boston public on the front page of the *Boston Daily Globe*:

VICTORIA WOODHULL

Why Should She Not Have the Opportunity of Speaking in Boston?

Her Lectures Not What Her Enemies Have Charged

Mrs. Victoria C. Woodhull, who has spoken in nearly every city in the country except Boston, but who has here been steadily refused permission to lecture, is once more in town. . . . Many citizens, at the last time she was refused an opportunity to speak in Boston, expressed the opinion that the action of the city authorities was wholly arbitrary and unwarranted. Nothing in the reports which had been made of Mrs. Woodhull's lectures from time to time indicated that there was anything improper or immoral in what she said. There was, therefore, a good deal of sympathy felt for Mrs. Woodhull in regard to this course of the city authorities, even among those who would be the last to accept her views; and the charge of unfair treatment, as made by the noted agitator, was conceded by many to be well founded.[360]

Woodhull may have been denied permission because Henry Ward Beecher would also be in Boston to give lectures and sermons within the next couple of weeks. This was not the first time Woodhull had appeared in a city to lecture while Beecher was also there. In fact, Beecher, Theodore Tilton, and Woodhull had all coincidentally just given lectures in Ontario, Canada, where the *Daily Free Press* noted that this "free-love trio" were all profiting from the great interest in them due to the highly-publicized adultery trial. It was an especially sensitive time for Beecher, because he was facing a new lawsuit from another well-known member of Plymouth Church. The Congregational Association of New York and Brooklyn had put out a final call for accusations against Beecher: come forward now before they closed their internal investigations forever. Considering Woodhull's history of launching attacks against Beecher during Boston appearances, civic leaders might have been reluctant to allow Woodhull a local platform at this time.[361]

The next day, the *Boston Daily Globe* reported that Woodhull was still being denied use of the largest halls in Boston. The Boston Theatre, the Globe Theatre, Tremont Temple, Boston Music Hall, and Howard Athenaeum all refused her. A second "plea for free speech" was made by a "very indignant" Woodhull friend in a letter to the editor:

> Many will ask, What does Mrs. Woodhull want? She wants to do here in the . . . Athens of America, the cradle of free thought and free speech, the nursery of advanced ideas that benefit the human race, what she has done in every city in the land before the best and most intelligent people of the country: she desires to discuss a principle by which the future happiness of the human race shall be benefitted mentally, physically, and morally. She desires to tell the people of Boston why the American race is degenerating.[362]

However, it seems the people of Boston did not rise up as "an army for the right of free speech" as the indignant writer requested. But Woodhull was able to speak that Sunday evening at the newly built Paine Memorial Hall, which the *Boston Daily Globe* called a "temple to free thought."

The hall was named after Thomas Paine who was most famous for *Common Sense,* his wildly popular 1776 work which argued against hereditary monarchy and energized support for the American War of Independence, and for *Rights of Man,* his

1791 work which inspired the French Revolution. But Paine also later wrote an unpopular 1794 work called *The Age of Reason*, which argued for a religious revolution rejecting all churches and refuting all scriptural authority in favor of individual reasoning on morals, the question of deity, and afterlife. Paine was speaking from the Deist theological viewpoint, which he shared with Thomas Jefferson and Benjamin Franklin. Deists appreciated the ethical and moral system taught by Jesus in the Bible but rejected the stories of miracles as mere mythology. By 1876, Paine had become a philosophical figurehead for the Free Thought movement, which took Paine's revolution even further. Paine Memorial Hall had been built to support the activities of these "freethinkers."[363]

One of the first big events held at Paine Hall was a social freedom convention where members of the newly established New England Free Love League passed a resolution that legal marriage should be abolished. One speaker praised Victoria Woodhull as the first woman to "strike a blow for woman's freedom." The management of this hall was more than willing to rent to Woodhull for a lecture.[364]

On Sunday evening, October 1, Woodhull delivered her lecture "The Human Body, the Temple of God" to a crowded hall. She wore a "tasteful and becoming" dark brown silk velvet dress trimmed with black lace, with white neck collar and cuffs. She wore no jewelry, only her trademark white rose pinned to her dress. She walked up to the lecture platform with a Bible in her hand and began by reading from First Corinthians. "Know ye not that ye are the temple of God, and that the spirit of God dwelleth in you? If any man defile the temple of God, him shall God destroy; for the temple of God is holy, which temple ye are" (1 Cor. 3: 16, 17). The newspaper reported:

> In beginning the exposition of this text, she quoted the remark made by Tom Paine nearly 100 years ago, when he said in Philadelphia, "What we want is independence, and I want revolution." What she wanted was revolution; she wanted revolution in the existent condition of things social.

She wanted the mothers of this country to know and understand their position; she wanted them intelligent; she wanted them to appreciate the great responsibility of maternity. She wanted all to understand the great truth of the chapter she had read, that man was the temple of God.[365]

In her speech, she reviewed the history of human civilizations and argued that they had all failed because they did not support this great truth.

Woodhull had long promoted the idea of sexuality as "God's most holy institution." Along with trying to convince audiences that Reverend Beecher's powerful sermons were due to an unusually strong sex drive, Woodhull had promoted new sexual interpretations of Bible stories and claimed that sexual activity is critical to sustaining the life of an individual. Her lecture title, "The Human Body, The Temple of God" suggested her view of sexual intercourse as a form of worship. Woodhull preached:

> The passions, instead of being regarded as we have been taught to regard them, as merely satanic or malign forces to be repressed or enslaved, will be recognized for what they are: as the *voice of God* in the soul.[366]

At this point in her social freedom campaign, Woodhull focused on the reproductive aspect of sex. She saw women as cocreators with God, having a great responsibility for the improvement of the race. Woodhull wanted to put women in total control of their own reproduction, through sex education, birth control, and a societal shift in culture and economics. She wanted to free women from dependence on a husband and instead support reproduction only between two healthy adults who feel a passionate love for each other. She told audiences the heartbreaking story of her ill-conceived son Byron who spoke only strange sounds, had a vacant look in his eyes, and would never be able to take care of himself. Woodhull's ultimate goal was for no unwanted or unhealthy children to ever be born. A new approach to conditions surrounding conception would mean "no more sickness, no more poverty, no more crime." Woodhull would uplift humanity through better breeding. In her view, five thousand years of Mosaic law and two thousand years of Christian monogamy had proved ineffective in improving the human species. It was time for a new approach.[367]

From early on in her lecturing she had presented social freedom as merely a transitional step in moving society toward "stirpiculture," the selective breeding of humans in the same way that domestic animals are bred. Stirpiculture was an innovation of John Humphrey Noyes and was part of his social experiment at the Oneida community. Around the same time that Woodhull first began her national campaign, Noyes stopped using the term "free love" in favor of "complex marriage" because it better described the marriage-like commitment of community members to each other and to their communal children. In fact, love at the Oneida community was not very free at all. Sexual activity was highly regulated by a committee of elders to prevent exclusive relationships from developing, to reward and punish individuals, and to implement committee-approved selective breeding. Likewise, Woodhull now focused on promoting a scientific approach to the propagation of the human species. The social vice that most concerned Woodhull was poor breeding practices in which children inherited an inclination towards crime, illness, physical defects, and mental weakness. Woodhull put the responsibility on individual women and their daughters to decide whether to reproduce and to educate themselves on how to produce improved offspring.

As was typical for Woodhull's lectures, she commented on the phenomenon of far more men than women being in attendance at the lecture. She encouraged the men to bring their wives and daughters anywhere they went themselves, including to go hear Mrs. Woodhull. "The intelligent, cultured lady need not fear to go anywhere," Woodhull assured her audience. She commented on negative gossip about her:

> When she learned what was thought of her in Boston, she cried out in amazement. She wondered what kind of vulgar

minds the people had anyway; whether they had no culture, no intelligence. She would not dare or think of giving utterance to the coarse and vulgar thoughts this pureminded people had conjured up beneath their modesty.[368]

In response to insults that had been "hurled in her face" that she would "break up the marital relations," Woodhull admitted that "Yes, . . . she would [break up] the present system of licensed debauchery, but not the glorious, healthful system of God's free love."

> You hear people say, "Oh, Mrs. Woodhull is a free-lover." When you hear this you can answer, "So was Jesus Christ. Did not he love humanity? Did he not wander here and there to lift up and love the poor harlot and outcast?" . . . I teach the pure free love of God toward humanity. When that free love permeates humanity we shall become a great and grand human family. Let your preachers teach this from the pulpits; let us try to love our neighbors as we do ourselves. . . . Universal love and universal knowledge should prevail; then men and women will become great. This has been my mission.[369]

Near the end of the lecture, a small child dressed in white came to the stage and crowned Woodhull with a ring of roses while her "zealous friends" in the audience applauded enthusiastically. Finally, she concluded the lecture with a hopeful wish:

> She prophesied a glorious redemption for both man and woman, asked for the sympathy and prayers of the audience in her work, and spoke feelingly of her incarceration in New York for uttering just the sentiment she had uttered in this lecture. In conclusion she thanked the audience for their attention and sympathy, and stated that the crown of flowers given her she dedicated not to her body but to the principles she advocated; and she hoped that the crown of freedom would rest upon the people of Boston.

The *Boston Daily Globe* review the next day reported that Woodhull was "respectable in appearance, and, with one or two individual exceptions, acted in a respectable manner." The lecture content was "far more sensible and less racy than some who attended anticipated." The headline declared that the Woodhull lecture was "not so 'awfully shocking' after all."[370]

With the somewhat positive reviews in hand, Woodhull's lecture team continued to work on gaining access to one of the large halls in Boston. Meanwhile, Woodhull headed out for lectures in the Boston vicinity, including in the nearby town of Lynn. For publicity for the lecture in Lynn, the Woodhull promotional team took a shock approach to advertising:

A STARTLING LECTURE
WILL BE DELIVERED BY
VICTORIA C WOODHULL!
Same lecture as in Boston last Sunday evening
when the hall was so crowded that 3000
who applied for admission were unable
to get into the hall

It is certainly possible that people were turned away from the Paine Memorial Hall lecture considering the front-page publicity she received and the fact that the hall seated only eight hundred. But despite the hype, there was no problem with crowding on Thursday, October 5 at the Lynn Music Hall, perhaps because the advertisement came out only one day before the event. Attendance was moderate. The *Lynn Transcript* review was brief, focusing on the newsworthiness of the lack of shock to the audience:

> Mrs. Victoria C. Woodhull lectured in Music Hall on Thursday evening, taking for her subject "The Human Body the Temple of God." There was nothing objectionable in the lecture, but on the contrary much truth and sound sense, presented in an eloquent and forcible manner.[371]

The *Lynn Semi-Weekly Reporter* gave a much longer review of the lecture:

Mrs. Woodhull's language and manner were unexceptionable, and none who listened to her could deny the correctness of the general positions which she assumed. She claimed that she had been a martyr to the truth, but that her sufferings had been in a righteous cause which would yet triumph. Already, she said, there had been a great advance, and those who two or three years ago had listened to her with averted ears were now ready to acknowledge that she had spoken the truth. She claimed that she had been misunderstood in many things; that she advocated free love only as one who loved all mankind and desired to benefit the race by ridding the world of vice, which ignorance and deep-rooted prejudice had engendered and continued to foster. Mrs. Woodhull spoke for an hour with great rapidity, frequently repeating herself in her apparent earnestness and desire to impress upon her hearers the truth of what she was saying. She was listened to with close attention, and at times was warmly applauded. Her manner was that of one who was thoroughly convinced that she had a mission to perform and was determined to do her duty, come what might. In closing she asked the prayers of all her hearers that she might have strength and wisdom to perform her work faithfully, looking for her reward in a world redeemed from vice and made pure through a knowledge of the truth.[372]

The reviews could hardly have been more favorable if they had been written by someone from Woodhull's publicity team.

Mary Baker Eddy (then known as Mrs. Glover) — always the avid newspaper reader — could not stand by silently while Victoria Claflin Woodhull received such high praise. She pulled out her pen to write a response letter to the editor of the *Lynn Transcript*. Eddy's criticism focused on the fact that Lynn had not rallied to prohibit the lecture in the recent tradition of nearby Boston. Her letter published on October 14 was more of a commentary on the hosting townspeople of Lynn than on the notorious Woodhull:

Lynn Morals and Woodhull

The increase of arts and sciences and the radiation of honest history point out the march of civilization and a nation's prosperity; but its theatricals and lectures are said to indicate its taste.

If this axiom applies strictly, what we wish to learn at this time is, Did the lecture of Victoria Woodhull meet the taste and indicate the tone of character of those who attended it? Must we admit there are in our very midst men and women claiming respectability who could be made even to listen to the most detestable and loathsome inculcations of vice from one who outrages decency, insults human nature and disgraces the name of woman? That she should be allowed a public hall in which to disclaim her abominations almost discourages humanity in its ennobling efforts. Was the fate of Sodom a fable? No, it was the inevitable result of its sins; and we should entertain no hope of escaping its doom if we should deserve its punishment. It can but surprise us, to say the least, that there exists in the enlightened mind such ignorance of morals. Did the gray-haired father take his son to the sacrifice and never reflect on the danger, morally, that son thereby incurred? Or did the mother accompany her modest daughter to the scene of sacrifice gilded with the rhetoric of vice, and return home to pray "lead us not into temptation?"

A purer, more happifying and ennobling social system awaits us, or a degradation it would be painful to contemplate. For one, we honor the Puritan faith and fidelity of our mothers and fathers in the relations of husband, wife, or parent, and say let well enough alone. And if the present age has departed, as it surely has, from the good old landmarks, let the haste be to return to the Father's house, and not to a brothel, or to the sermons of a Lorett on these subjects.

The effect of such a lecture as was delivered on Thursday evening at Music Hall is not understood. Doubt it as you may, no mind listened to it and went away not disgusted with it, that was not injured by it, and some great chord thrilled that will echo the names of the damned.

The ancient "Babylon" that has "become drunk with the blood of the saints" knoweth her power for a season. If the wretched spectaculars of our theaters, the spurious novels from our public libraries, the lectures from the "Hulls" of humanity, and the cloaks that cover professions, were only annihilated, once and forever, I should like to remain on *terra firma* a century longer; but in the present state of things "I would not live always," or care to wait a century for the hope to be fulfilled. Let it not be forgotten that the prostration of virtue is the downfall of individual and national honor and enlightenment.

Mary Baker Glover

Lynn newspaper readers had heard from Eddy before on moral issues. In 1871 she had written a letter to the editor to show support for Reverend Joseph Cook's exposure of deplorable moral conditions at the Lynn factories where men and women worked together in close quarters. She applauded him for "the truly Christian stand" he had taken against crimes "least rebuked, and therefore the more fearful and devastating." She supported him in insistence on purity, and concluded with a reference to ancient Sodom. But this letter about Woodhull's visit had a sharper edge. Eddy seemed most concerned about the potentially contagious effect on anyone listening to the lecture. The danger lay in an audience member being influenced by Woodhull's erroneous views and so tempted not to abide by Christian morality.[373]

Eddy's recommended "return to the Father's house" suggests the Bible story of the Prodigal Son, who, after he "wasted his substance with riotous living" (Luke 15:13), had a change of heart and returned in humility to his father. Eddy's rejection of "the sermons of a Lorett" suggests a condemnation of alternative lifestyles that encouraged sexuality outside of marriage, even extramarital sex. A "lorette" was the name for a type of young woman in the 1840s who lived near a church called Notre-Dame-de-Lorette in a newer part of Paris, which was built with wealth from industrialists and stock market investors. The standard of living of these independent working women was significantly improved by their sexual relationships with wealthy (presumably married) men.[374]

In the biblical reference to "ancient 'Babylon' that has 'become drunk with the blood of the saints'" (Rev. 17:6), Eddy brought into her letter to the editor deeply significant imagery. In the concluding book of the Bible called Revelation, St. John recorded his inspired vision of the word of God, which he explained through symbols. Eddy would later call Revelation "the acme," or culmination, of Divine "Science as the Bible reveals it." The vision includes two representations of womanhood. One is a "great wonder in heaven," a woman so radiant it was as though she were "clothed with the sun," who gave birth to a man child destined "to rule all nations with a rod of iron." (Rev. 12:1, 5). The other is "the great whore" of ancient Babylon, "mother of harlots and abominations of the earth" (Rev. 17: 1, 5). In the book there is a war in heaven, a battle called Armageddon, then angels announce that Babylon is fallen. A triumphant chorus of "mighty thunderings, saying, Alleluia, for the Lord God omnipotent reigneth!" is followed by "the marriage of the lamb and his wife" (Rev. 19: 6, 7)—which Eddy interpreted as the "true sense of Love," bringing deliverance from "the sum total of human misery."[375]

Many Americans in that era read through the entire Bible regularly, in the enduring habit started by the early Puritans, and so the imagery of Revelation was widely known. When Eddy made the reference to ancient Babylon in her letter, she was condemning hypocrisy, lustful thinking, and disregard for the Mosaic Decalogue. Eddy was not suggesting that Victoria Woodhull was the great whore, as if specifically prophesied by St. John nearly two thousand years earlier. The woman "clothed with the sun" and the Babylonish woman in the vision were each a "type," a timeless universal aspect of the human experience—a distinction made clear in recent work by authors Steven Gottschalk and George Denninger. Eddy would also refer to ancient Babylon in the future when confronting free-love thought within her own church. She would later write using language full of imagery and phrasing from Revelation:

> The hour is come; the bride (Word) is adorned, and lo, the bridegroom cometh! . . . The doom of the Babylonish woman, referred to in Revelation, is being fulfilled. This woman, "drunken with the blood of the saints, and with the blood of the martyrs of Jesus," "drunk with the wine of her fornication," would enter even the church,—the body of Christ, Truth; and, retaining the heart of the harlot and the purpose of the destroying angel, would pour wormwood into the waters—the disturbed human mind—to drown the strong swimmer struggling for the shore,—aiming for Truth,—and if possible, to poison such as drink of the living water. . . . And a voice was heard, saying, "Come out of her, my people" (hearken not to her lies), "that ye receive not of her plagues . . . ." That which the Revelator saw in spiritual vision will be accomplished. The Babylonish woman is fallen, and who should mourn over the widowhood of lust, of her that "is become the habitation of devils, and the hold of every foul spirit, and a cage of every unclean . . . bird"?[376]

Eddy's letter to the editor of the *Lynn Transcript* concluded with a warning about the "downfall of individual and national honor and enlightenment." She used the language of the American Republic and the wisdom of the founders so recently reviewed in the centennial celebrations. In his famous 1796 farewell address, President George Washington had sternly warned of grave dangers to the Republic if the nation ever allowed a decline in religion, virtue, and morality, which he believed to be the "great pillars" of happiness, security, liberty, and prosperity as well as the spring from which a free government comes. Eddy was essentially heeding Washington's admonition:

Who that is a sincere friend to it can look with indifference upon attempts to shake the foundation of the fabric?

A week later on October 21, 1876, a response letter was published in the *Lynn Transcript* from someone who made a special point of referring to Woodhull multiple times as a Mrs. Perhaps the writer noticed that Eddy had followed the form of Woodhull critics who refused to use the customary term of Mrs. when referring to Woodhull, sometimes referring to her instead as "the Woodhull." The reader signed the letter as Junius, a common pseudonym used for political protest since the late 1700s. This Junius could very well have been Stephen Pearl Andrews, Woodhull's primary public relations writer. The long response letter had a tone of righteous indignation, epitomized by one of Woodhull's earlier public statements:

> It is hard to bear the criticism of vulgar minds, who can see in social freedom nothing but licentiousness and debauchery.[377]

In the *Lynn Transcript* response letter, Junius compared Eddy to Mrs. Grundy, a humorously dreaded fictional character who enforced the conventions of proper behavior through tyrannical controls of social pressure, as expressed by the then-well-known rhetorical question, "What would Mrs. Grundy think?" Junius called Eddy's criticisms a "flight of Lilliputian arrows," making a satiric jab inspired by the fantasy novel *Gulliver's Travels* and suggesting small-minded petty criticism. Junius also ridiculed Eddy for having the audacity to sign her letter to the editor with her real name!

Junius criticized Eddy for being "so strongly [e]ntrenched in the righteousness of her own judgment" and claimed that Eddy's characterization of the Woodhull lecture was "indicative of entire ignorance of the subject upon which she so flippantly writes." After consulting with several respectable people who had attended the Lynn lecture, Junius "failed to see any grounds for this serious charge" made by Eddy.

On the contrary, they commended the lecture very highly, believing that a great necessity exists for just such frank discussions, and seeing no reason why any one interested in the good of humanity should not approve of them and wish for them a more extensive auditory. Such were some of the sentiments expressed by these hearers, and we think it may fairly be claimed by all, as unprejudiced, that the discourse constituted a strong appeal in favor of a pure, right life. Wrong-doing received her severest denunciations. And certain it is that many of the best truths she uttered have been published by eminent public teachers before her . . . and should be understood by every mother in the land.

Junius was "thoroughly impressed with the idea that the human body is the temple of God." The formation of human beings in a better way by improving the conditions of conception was "exalted and important" work. It was Eddy who had the unenlightened mind and a hidden bad motive. Junius concluded the response letter with this:

> This is not the language of one who loves his kind. A true Christian philosophy should not lead us to pass our time in lugubrious meditations upon the low condition of a generally ill-conceived humanity, "echoing the moans of the damned," but to a more cheerful and serene view of the race as God's people marching steadily, but surely, in His wisdom, towards a better state of existence. This, it seems to us, is the better way. Do what you can, trusting in God.
>
> "Junius"

Oneida stirpiculture selective breeding, or something like it, was Junius' view of "God's people marching steadily, but surely, in His wisdom, towards a better state of existence." In future writings Woodhull further explained the philosophy of her concept:

> The religion of the future, which will be founded on the great truth that the human body is the Temple of God, will

awaken mankind to the awful responsibility of creating His image when unfit to do so . . . . The ignorance which surrounds the awful procreative problem makes mankind abject slaves. How long ere the piercing rays of science shall dissipate the mists of prejudice and superstition, leaving us to see, and inciting us to aspire after, that altitude of perfection which, when attained, will make us indeed a race of gods?[378]

In the Bible, it was an evil serpent who tempted Adam and Eve to disobey God's commands with the promise "ye shall be as gods" (Gen. 3:5). By attacking Woodhull in the *Lynn Transcript*, Eddy was crossing swords with what opposed her biblical view of man as made in the image and likeness of God (Gen. 1:26). Eddy had been teaching and preaching in Lynn that as one becomes conscious of man's true divine nature, morals improve, sickness is healed, and even undesirable "hereditary taints" are eradicated. Science would improve humanity, but Eddy promoted science to mean overcoming material limitation while respecting the law of Moses—an improved practice of Christianity. Eddy's idea of better conception of children required the continuation of marriage and Christian values, as she had recently stated in *Science and Health*:

> The good we possess should have ascendancy over the evil, and the spiritual over the animal, or happiness is never reached. This would improve progeny, diminish crime, give higher aims to ambition, and prepare the way for science. The offspring of such parents would inherit more intellect, better balanced minds, and sounder constitutions . . . . The most important education of the infant is to keep it mentally free from impurity, and let mind develop the body harmoniously . . . . Because progeny needs to be improved, let marriage continue, and permit no breakdown of law whereby a worse state of society is produced, than at present.[379]

A week after Junius' letter was published, on October 28, a more hard-hitting response to Eddy's article "Lynn Morals and Woodhull" was published in the *Lynn Transcript*. This letter was from Woodhull herself:

Letter from Mrs. Woodhull

To the Editor of the Transcript: —Some one has taken the trouble to send me your paper containing an article which, since it has appeared in the *Transcript*, I cannot permit to pass unnoticed. So far as its author is concerned, I scorn to descend to notice her. A woman who will basely attempt to pervert facts and to vilify another, as this one has, is beneath contempt. But your publication of such an attack is quite a different matter. How you could have permitted such a waspish exhibition in your columns, is beyond my conception of journalism. The representatives of the *Transcript* attended my lecture at Lynn, and they know that such a fulmination is not a criticism of it, but a malicious personal attack upon me. Indeed, it does not pretend to be anything else, because there is not a single sentiment to which I gave expression mentioned. It is simply a tirade, the character of which would have been evident had it been made in connection with almost any part of what I said. It is to just such gratuitous abuse as this that I owe the shadow that has fallen upon my name—due not to anything I have said or done.

Mr. Editor, you know well enough that "the most detestable and loathsome inculcations of vice" formed no part of that lecture. You know that I pleaded for a purity of which, it is to be deplored, the people have too little comprehension; for a purity of which, perhaps, it is impossible for this woman to conceive, and that I denounced social vice in every form. . . . Did I advocate these evils? No! You know better; and the people who listened, who are joined with me in this attack, know that the pen that writes it lies, and the person who held that pen, if she knew of what she was writing, knew it was false . . . . Every gray-haired father and fond mother, who listened to me in Lynn, knows that what I there said is true; and, the *Transcript* article to the contrary notwithstanding, every such person went away from Music Hall that night thanking God that at last some one had risen who is not afraid to speak out boldly about these things. And you, Mr. Editor, know in your heart that this is true.

I defy the production of a single utterance that fell from my lips that night that was calculated to exert a deleterious influence upon anybody. And yet the *Transcript* permits it to be said in its columns that I "declaimed abominations."

No one more than myself desires honest criticism; or honors those who, by not understanding what I am aiming at, seek enlightenment. Had the *Transcript* article been an honorable criticism of anything that I said, which the writer might have felt had an evil tendency or that was not strictly true, I should have been glad to reply in an altogether different way; but to such wholesale denunciations there is but one method of treatment. Their authors require to be shown that the time is gone by when they can murder my reputation with impunity; that they deserve to held responsible to the law of libel: to be arrested, tried, convicted and imprisoned for their malicious falsehoods; and that it is only the thought of meddling with such characters that protects them.

Victoria C. Woodhull

In late October, in between Junius' and Woodhulls' letters to the *Lynn Transcript*, Woodhull was fighting a similar public relations battle on a grander scale in Boston. After Reverend Henry Ward Beecher had given his lectures in Boston and returned home to Brooklyn, New York, Woodhull was allowed to rent Boston Theatre for a second lecture. But Mrs. Elizabeth Winthrop, the wife of Boston centennial celebration keynote speaker, Congressman Robert Winthrop, countered Woodhull's message with a lecture in the Boston Tremont Temple called "A Reply to Mrs. Woodhull."[380]

Woodhull responded in her Boston Theatre lecture with her own centennial speech, called "Review of a Century," in which she asserted that the grand ideals of human rights of the American Revolution were far from being achieved. The US Constitution had been made "a fraud and a cheat" and America's so-called republican form of government was really a tyranny of rule by money. Woodhull argued against corporate banking in favor of government banks. If she had the power to do so, she told the audience, she would make charging interest on financial loans a crime, as it is in the Bible, and make idleness and starvation impossible in this land of plenty by providing jobs and food for everyone. She concluded the lecture with "a few words illustrating her well-known views on the marriage question" and a reminder to women of their duty in "regenerating the land."[381]

It was a presidential election year and Boston voters would soon be heading to the polls. The close, highly contested presidential race focused on issues relating to the years-long economic depression, monetary policy, and management of debt related to the Civil War. Reverend Beecher's recent Boston lectures, "Ministry of Wealth" and "Hard Times," supported the political platform of Republican candidate Rutherford Hayes, who promoted a return to stable gold-backed currency and repayment of all debt. Beecher preached that there is no sin in wealth and comfort, and that all Americans should embrace hard work and frugality, and "look for Divine aid in times of trouble." Woodhull's statements directly contradicted Beecher's political position.[382]

The review in the Boston Daily Globe, entitled "Victoria Woodhull's Farewell," noted that this would be Woodhull's last lecture before sailing to Europe—presumably for an extended lecture tour. But the Woodhull & Claflin machine was breaking down. Having closed the stock brokerage firm and newspaper, divorced James Harvey Blood, and resigned from the presidency of the American Association of Spiritualists, she was making big changes in her life. Victoria was ready for something new.

A New Chapter in Life (1877 and Beyond)

Marriage should signify a union of hearts . . . . Until it is learned that God is the Father of all, marriage will continue. Let not mortals permit a disregard of law which might lead to a worse state of society than now exists.

Mary Baker Eddy

I now openly avow, with all the earnestness of righteous indignation, that during no part of my life did I favor Free Love even tacitly . . . . I regarded it with loathing when once I got a slight idea of its character and the deep infamy to which it led.

Victoria Claflin Woodhull

Union of Hearts

Toward the end of 1876, there were big changes going on in Mary Baker Eddy's life. Her small community of students was growing in number, and they were selling copies of *Science and Health*. People far beyond Lynn, Massachusetts, were writing to Eddy to request Christian Science treatment for their diseases. She had enjoyed a peaceful happiness in 1875, but now she was beginning to feel the stress of leading a movement in uncharted territory, and she had a foreboding anticipation of reaction against her book. She was already sensing a new level of dissention and discord within her growing community of students. The next few years were perhaps the most difficult period of her whole career. She was just about to begin what biographer Robert Peel called her "years of trial." She described her feelings to her most trusted and successful student at the time, Daniel "Harry" Spofford:

> The mercury of my mind is rising as the world's temperature of thought heats and the little book 'sweet in the mouth' but severe and glorious in its proof, is about to go forth . . . . But my student, in my lonely chamber I read the coming storm. I feel it gathering.[383]

The biggest change in her life was her third and most pleasant marriage, in which she most experienced her ideal of "a union of the affections that tends to lift mortals higher." She did not want to ever marry again and told her students so, but in a sudden and unexpected turn of events she married the man she would call "my loved precious one" and who would be her strongest support in the trials to come.[384]

In the maturity of her mid- to late-50s, Eddy had as many marriage prospects as she had ever had. Samuel Putnam Bancroft claimed that she was "sought in marriage by several" men around this time. People who knew Mary Baker Eddy consistently remarked on how attractive she was as a woman. She had a joyful lightness about her, an expressive face, a musical voice, a witty sense of humor, and a gracious sophistication. Her posture was perfect, her figure slim but shapely, and her appearance "striking." She was always fashionably and neatly dressed and "never a hair out of place." Bancroft described her face:

> Her features were regular, and finely moulded. The most noticeable were the eyes, large and deep-set, dark blue and piercing, sad, very sad, at times, yet kind and tender.[385]

Besides being attractive, people who knew her consistently remarked that she seemed to be many years younger than she really was — ten, twenty, even thirty years younger. Considering her attractive qualities and youthful appearance, perhaps it should be no surprise that she attracted some younger men.[386]

One of her suitors was Edward Hitchings, who contributed to the printing of *Science and Health*. Hitchings was a local real estate agent who had been given the assignment of finding Eddy a home. Before purchasing her house in Lynn, she wanted to relocate to Cambridge to establish her organization near Harvard College and other prestigious institutions of higher learning, which she expected would find her healing science of great interest. But according to Bancroft, Hitchings never worked on the relocation project because he did not want her to leave Lynn. He wanted to marry her.[387]

Another marriage suitor was her student Harry Spofford, who was twenty years younger. Spofford had taken a class with Eddy in May 1875 after separating from his wife Addie. He became immediately successful in his healing practice and also became a trusted assistant to his teacher. In the spring of 1876, Spofford became a tenant in Eddy's house and worked on the sales of *Science and Health*. Living and working closely with his teacher, Spofford developed a strong personal attraction to her. Not long after moving in, Spofford sued his wife for divorce on grounds of adultery. His divorce was not granted. His unwelcome attraction to Mary only increased until it became a problem. According to a Spofford family story, he asked her to marry him at gunpoint. Whatever happened between them near the end of the year 1876, it was upsetting to Mary, and it was the beginning of the end of their professional relationship.[388]

In a note to Spofford immediately after the incident, along with her demand *"quit thinking of me,"* she instructed her legally married student to read this paragraph from *Science and Health:*

> Sin is thought before it is deed, and you must master it in the first, or it conquers you in the second instance. Jesus said, to look with foul desire on forbidden objects, breaks a moral precept; hence, the stress he laid on the character of a man that is hidden from our perception . . . . When malicious purposes, evil thoughts, or lusts, go forth from one mind, they seek others, and will lodge in them unless repelled by virtue and a higher motive for being.[389]

Their relationship was further strained by the introduction of a new rival for the role of most trusted and successful student. Asa Gilbert Eddy was the new rising star. From the time Gilbert took a class, he made rapid strides in his healing practice. He first learned about this new healing method through his friend Mrs. Godfrey, whom Mary had healed of a dangerously infected wound several years earlier. Mrs. Godfrey encouraged Gilbert to try the treatment for his heart trouble and to study the method. He was a perfect candidate for a student of Christian Science because he had grown up in the Puritan-influenced culture of rural New England, and his mother, who was an independent thinker, always open to new ideas, had experienced healing through a form of Spiritualism. Gilbert investigated Spiritualism, but rejected it and became a member of a Baptist church. Even so, Gilbert was open to the idea of nonmedical healing and was willing to try Christian Science.[390]

After experiencing dramatic improvement in his heart condition, Gilbert took a three-week class in March 1876, for which he paid $150. Afterwards, he quit his job as a sewing machine salesman, moved to Lynn, and became the first person to advertise his services as a "Christian Scientist." His business card declared, "No Medicine, Mediumship, or Mesmerism." Within the circle of students, he was called "Doctor" Eddy—the customary title for any type of professional healing practitioner. To integrate this successful newcomer into the Christian Science Association and improve the organization's effectiveness, Mary reassigned duties. Dr. Spofford was asked to oversee sales of *Science and Health* full-time and to send the patients from his healing practice to Dr. Eddy.[391]

There was no early indication of marriage potential between Mary and Gilbert. He was about eleven years younger than she, and at first Gilbert was just another enthusiastic and dedicated student. But on one especially challenging day for Mary, she saw a new side of Gilbert that she found attractive. In fact, it seems she was smitten on that day in July 1876. In a letter to her cousin Hattie Baker, she described this unexpected development in their relationship:

> The day after my return home I had a violent seizure. . . .
> Mrs. B ran for Dr. Eddy, he came when I was unconscious
> and immediately broke the spell! I was astonished at his
> skill, he was calm, clear, and strong, and so kind! I fell in
> love with him. Never before had I seen his real character, so
> tender and yet so controlling.[392]

Mary's description of the qualities she admired in Gilbert was remarkably similar to her description of the ideal male qualities she had recently described in the chapter "Marriage" in *Science and Health:*

> A union of the masculine and feminine mind seems requisite for completeness; the former reaches a higher tone from communion with the latter; and the latter gains courage and strength from the former; therefore, these different individualities meet and demand each other, and their true harmony is oneness of Soul. Woman should be loving, pure, and strong. Man, tender, intellectual, controlling; the attraction

between the sexes will be perpetual only as it is pure and true, and like the seasons, brings its sweet changes and renewal.[393]

By the end of 1876, Asa Gilbert Eddy won Mary's affections "on the ground alone of his great goodness and strength of character." While Gilbert was much newer to the practice of Christian Science than Spofford and the other students — he was relatively inexperienced and untested — Mary saw in him "latent noble qualities of head and heart." She was confident that with her influence he had great potential as a spiritual healer and teacher. She appreciated his thoughtful approach to working with her, his quiet strength, and especially his unwavering support. A member of the Godfrey family who, as a child, had known Gilbert made this description of his general demeanor:

> There was always a sweet smile on his face and his eyes were so gentle you could not imagine him hurting anything in the world.

Yet even with Gilbert's quiet thoughtfulness, his humility and patience, his gentlemanly manners and calm temperament, he held a strength in reserve that one student compared to Napoleon's Imperial Guard.[394]

On the same day that she rebuffed Spofford's aggressive proposal, Mary spoke privately with Gilbert. She had set clear boundaries with Spofford, but she wondered if she could ever allow a male student to live in her household again. Around that same time, Mary was being harassed by men who were following her around and ringing her doorbell late at night. It was a serious enough problem that the police were called. Besides the threat to personal safety, the ongoing nuisance had a financial impact, as she was having trouble keeping her rental rooms occupied. When Gilbert heard about it, he suggested she marry him so he would have the right to live in the house to protect her.

Her first response to his proposal was, "No, I must rely wholly on God. This is my mission." But Mary spent that evening in prayer, feeling that she must completely trust God in this decision. As she slept that night, she had a dream that was meaningful to her, which she later told to one of her students:

> She seemed to be standing on one side of a beautiful field of wheat. As she was rejoicing in its promise, dark swinish forms seemed to move underneath it; their uprooting instincts were destroying thought. She could not cross the field as intended. Terror and abhorrence chained her to the spot. Then on the other side of the field she saw Gilbert Eddy's manly form. 'Come on, Mary,' he said, 'I will help you.' And she awoke, feeling she could marry him not for her own sake but to *save the cause*.[395]

Spofford was the first to hear the big news and was enlisted to help obtain a clergyman while Gilbert applied for the marriage license. The next day, on Monday, January 1, 1877, a friendly Unitarian clergyman conducted the wedding ceremony in the parlor of the house. The wedding was "a quiet affair" with her students and a few friends attending. So after considering Gilbert's proposal of marriage for one day, followed by a one-day engagement period, the author of the statement in *Science and Health* "be not in haste to take the vow 'until death do us part'" was married to Asa Gilbert Eddy. With such complete clarity that this was the right course of action, there was no reason to wait. She took the name Mary Baker Eddy by which she would become world famous. It was the start of a new year, and a new chapter in her life, very much in line with this passage from the first edition chapter "Marriage" in *Science and Health:*

> A bridal altar is the verge of a new existence; wherein the old is fading out of the experience, to admit the new.[396]

The marriage was a complete shock to the members of the Christian Science Association. According to one student, many disapproved. It took a while for the tight-knit group to adjust to the unexpected change. At the end of the month, the students organized a surprise party as a wedding reception for the newlyweds, which provided an opportunity for Mrs. Eddy to answer questions on her reasons for the marriage. She made it clear that her life focus on the cause of Christian Science was unchanged. Her marriage to Gilbert was a "union of affection and high purposes." She explained that she had made the decision to marry Gilbert "with a view to promote this cause and to find in union there is strength, to bring another into my department of labor, and last though not least to unite my life to one whom I know will bless it." She had expressed similar sentiment in the chapter "Marriage" in *Science and Health*:

> To happify existence by constant intercourse with those adapted to elevate it is the true motive for marriage; wedlock gives pinions to joy, or trails its drooping wings in dust. . . . Unselfish ambition, nobler motives for existence, increased harmony, happiness and usefulness, because the different elements of mind meet and mingle, finding in union there is strength—is the true marriage. Let there be moral freedom in wedlock.[397]

As happy as things seemed to be among the group at the Eddy wedding reception, it was not long before the storm of contention broke. There had already been feelings of dismay, grumblings of resentment, and whisperings of dissatisfaction. Finally, George Barry fired the first shot of the student rebellions.

Barry was a young man who had been a devoted student, friend, and helper to his teacher since taking a class with her. He had had such a feeling of being born again that he counted his age by the number of years since the class. By the time he was "five years old," he behaved like a son to Mary. In fact, he was the first student to ask to be able to call her "Mother." He had given her this sweet poem:

O, mother mine, God grant I ne'er forget,
Whatever be my grief or what my joy,
The unmeasured, unextinguishable debt
I owe to thee, but find my sweet employ

Ever through thy remaining days to be
To thee as faithful as thou wast to me.[398]

George Barry had helped finance the printing cost for *Science and Health,* and he had been one of the students most involved in selling the book to the public. But he resented the reassignment of duties when Gilbert joined the group and Spofford was put in charge of sales of the book. As the spiritual community grew, the change in the group dynamic and the increasing competition for the teacher's attention was too much for him. Barry kept his resentment to himself during the fall of 1876, hoping things would return to the way they had been. But shortly after the Eddy wedding, his antagonism erupted with a March 1877 lawsuit demanding compensation of $2,700 for services he had provided to his teacher over the previous five years. When the lawsuit was settled more than two years later, George received a few hundred dollars.[399]

Spofford was the next trusted student to rebel. Just before the wedding, there had been complicated emotional reactions between student and teacher. Mary had accused Spofford of trying to make her into a personal idol. In reaction, he felt a "momentary hatred" for her. He intended to continue in the Christian Science Association, but he became increasingly critical of his teacher's leadership. He soon decided that she was "incapable as a leader" and "unworthy to be the standard bearer of Christian Science." He wanted to replace her as leader. By the end of 1877, Spofford was expelled from the Christian Science Association for breaking his agreement to sell *Science and Health* and for immorality — possibly due to having moved in with a new girlfriend before his divorce was final. Perhaps this situation influenced the requirement in the church organization formed in 1879 for the pastor to be "strictly moral, and an earnest and devoted follower of Christ."[400]

The conflicts with Barry and Spofford were just the beginning of the turmoil to come in the next several years. Other students rebelled and always lurking on the periphery was Richard

Kennedy, described by Barry as being "like a snake in the grass, spitting his poison venom into them he would slay." Lawsuits and criminal charges, printing problems and copyright infringements, rumors and rebellions, "sleepless nights, and harrowing days" became the new norm for Mary Baker Eddy.[401]

But even as the storm raged, Mary found peace and comfort in her marriage with Gilbert. He was exactly the sort of support she needed. The Eddy marriage was a consistently harmonious relationship during this tumultuous, confusing, and challenging period. Clara Choate, a student who lived in the Eddy household, provided this glimpse into Mary and Gilbert's marriage:

> The highest friendship seemed ever to exist between them. . . . Dr. Eddy was careless in nothing but his own comfort. Mrs. Eddy often reminded him of his unselfishness. She would tell him not to neglect eating and sleeping properly and to walk in the park near by. She objected to his assiduous attention to the Cause or to herself. She felt it conveyed too great care of affairs. Yet amid all this I have heard Mrs. Eddy talk to the Doctor this way, 'Now Gilbert dear have you had your breakfast? You must not undertake this business only in proper time and a right frame of mind. You know evil is only too glad to put a wedge to disturb us and little things tell where we stand.' Dr. Eddy enjoyed this loving solicitation and with beaming face he would deferentially reply, 'Now Mary, you think too much of me and not enough of yourself; how is it with you? Do you feel equal to the undertaking?' Mrs. Eddy would then answer in her sincere loving way, 'Gilbert, you know what God has appointed me to do. He will give me the strength, wisdom and ways of performing it.' . . . I do not feel I can overestimate the helpfulness of Dr. Eddy any more than I can the spiritual achievements of Mrs. Eddy.[402]

Unlike Spofford, Gilbert Eddy had no ambitions of pushing Mary aside to take over the role of leadership of the Christian Science Association. While Gilbert had strong opinions of his own, according to Choate, he "invariably deferred to Mrs. Eddy's superior judgment, and would then abide by her conclusions." He faithfully followed her instructions in everything he did. As one interesting example, when he applied for their marriage license, he refused to give the age of the bride or groom because he had taken to heart his teachers' admonition to think of himself as an ageless spiritual being, and so to "never record ages." Not knowing what to do without the information for the paperwork, the government clerk simply wrote forty as the age for both.[403]

With her husband's support, Mrs. Eddy could her focus on writing. Sometimes Mr. Eddy acted as a mediator between teacher and students when conflicts arose. Gilbert also became the gatekeeper who controlled visitor access to the chief executive of the rapidly growing Christian Science organization. Gilbert conducted business on his wife's behalf, accompanied his wife on her errands, managed their household, and even did housework.

Domestic chores were easy and natural for Gilbert because of his unusual family background. His mother had taught domestic skills to her five sons as well as her two daughters. Gilbert's unconventional mother was a "lively talker and filled with new-fangled ideas." She enjoyed traveling around town conducting business while her industrious husband worked the farm in the summer and built wooden containers in the winter. The children took care of the housework.

Of all the Eddy children, Gilbert was especially strong in domestic skills because he was the son who stayed at home to take care of his parents. Consequently, he inherited the family farm after his parents died. But rather than continue living on the farm, he rented it out, went to work in the textile industry, and later went into sewing machine sales. Living on his own as a bachelor, he continued to do his own housework to keep his expenses down. Between his experience living on the family farm, caring for his parents, and working with textiles, he was known to be as good at cooking, cleaning, and ironing as any woman. Gilbert had no qualms about using these skills during his marriage to help out when needed. The Eddys chose to do their own housework for their modestly furnished home, rather than hire domestic servants—saving money and avoiding privacy problems. Gilbert's upbringing prepared him perfectly for his marriage.[404]

While Gilbert's family dynamic was quite different from the more traditional Baker family, Gilbert shared Mary's general religious and cultural heritage. He grew up less than one hundred miles away from Mary in a similar rural New England town of Londonderry, Vermont. Like Mary, his family heritage was deeply rooted in Puritan Christianity with seven generations in America—all in New England. Gilbert's father, Asa Eddy, descended from a prominent reform-minded English clergyman whose son John Eddy was among the earliest pilgrims. Arriving at Plymouth Colony in 1630 at the start of the Great Migration, John Eddy was one of the two "gentlemen" aboard the ship *Handmaid,* along with sixty other passengers. This ancestor became involved in the colony government. Gilbert's mother, Betsy Smith Eddy, had similarly deep roots in Puritan culture, with several early American ministers among her ancestors.

By taking the surname Eddy through marriage, Mary Baker made this Puritan name famous throughout the world. Working together as a team, Mr. and Mrs. Eddy would take the Christian Science movement to the national level in just a few years. Gilbert and Mary were an unconventional married couple by nineteenth-century standards, redefining gender roles in their own marriage and elevating the role of woman in religion and society. Yet, together they exemplified the Puritan ideal of marriage as "two sweet friends." Their life expressed this description of marriage from *Science and Health*:

> fulfilling the different demands of separate spheres, their sympathies may blend to comfort, cheer and sustain each other, thus hallowing the copartnership of interests and affection wheron the heart leans and is at peace.[405]

Becoming a Lady

The big changes that were going on in Victoria Claflin Woodhull's life toward the end of 1876 put her on course to a completely different lifestyle. Ironically, she would fully embrace that social institution against which she had so long railed.

Just after New Year's Day, unexpected events took place that altered Woodhull's plans for her voyage to Europe. On January 4, 1877, Cornelius Vanderbilt died, leaving his extraordinary $105 million estate almost entirely to his son William. Facing legal challenges over the will from his siblings who wanted an even split, William offered $100,000 to Victoria and Tennie to guarantee their unavailability for the court proceedings. The sisters accepted the offer and moved permanently to London where the Vanderbilt heir graciously purchased a house for them.

Victoria looked forward to the opportunity for a fresh start. She fabricated an alternative personal history for herself and her family, complete with forged documents. Instead of Woodhull, she used the name Woodhall—a good respectable English name. Shortly after arriving in England, Victoria gave a series of lectures in London on the scientific propagation of the human race, starting with "The Human Body, the Temple of God." At one of these lectures, Victoria met her husband-to-be. A wealthy bachelor named John Biddulph Martin became fascinated with her. He was from a prominent English family that owned the oldest bank in England. Victoria worked hard to present an image of dignity and respectability to John and the Martin family, whom Victoria described as representing "the very soul of conservatism."[406]

But when John and Victoria became engaged to be married, Victoria's past was exposed. Martin family members did some research on their potential daughter-in-law which quickly revealed her true name and her notorious past. Even in England the name Woodhull was synonymous with free love and licentiousness. The Beecher-Tilton scandal and her role in it continued to reverberate in the news. American woman suffrage activists sternly warned their English counterparts to avoid all contact with Woodhull.

It took some effort working through reputation issues for Victoria's relationship with John to develop into marriage. She convinced him that she had been misunderstood and mistreated by American journalists. She claimed that Stephen Pearl Andrews had printed filthy writings under her name without her approval or knowledge. She accused her previous husband James Harvey Blood of failing to protect her and being unfaithful to her. To put her claims on record, she printed an issue of a newspaper called *Woodhall & Claflin's Journal* in which she denounced her former close associates and denied that she ever supported "free-lovism."

Victoria's relationship with John continued, but John kept it secret. After several years of sleeping together, Victoria tried some unconventional tactics in an effort to formalize the relationship. She purchased her own engagement ring. She asked a mutual acquaintance to put social pressure on him. She even threatened a lawsuit against him. After these attempts failed, she just started referring to him as her husband and to herself as his wife. Finally, in 1883, he agreed to marry her—to make her happy. They married legally in a traditional church wedding. Victoria took her husband's name, becoming Mrs. John Biddulph Martin.

The Martin family did not approve of John's choice for a wife, and they did not attend the wedding. Martin family members considered mounting a legal challenge to the marriage as having been based on fraudulent information. But ultimately, they decided against it because the publicity would only leave John to "appear as the dupe of a clever harlot." Instead, the Martins accepted her as part of the family, although Victoria generally chose not to attend family gatherings at the palatial country estate of her formidable in-laws.[407]

But Martin family dynamics were the least of Victoria and John's worries. After the public announcement of their marriage, they received a steady flow of accusations and blackmail threats from people who knew of Victoria's notorious past. Having a normal social life or being involved in civic activities was sometimes difficult for the newlyweds. Their marriage was happiest when they spent time together in the privacy of their mansion in London's prestigious Hyde Park neighborhood or traveled abroad, as they did frequently.

However, the Martins successfully hosted a party each year on the fourth of July, which they called "Interdependence Day." A closer political relationship between England and America was a cause that Victoria would promote for decades. Also, Victoria engaged in civic life by publishing a magazine called *The Humanitarian,* which explored issues relating to the scientific improvement of humanity.[408]

After many years of living a quiet life in London, Victoria longed for the excitement and glamour of the public career she had once known. In 1892 she returned to America to make another run for president of the United States against incumbent Grover Cleveland. Supporters all over the country were glad to have their heroine return, and were willing to help nominate Victoria as an independent political party candidate. She made plans for an extensive American campaign tour in the fall of 1893. Her new lecture topics "The Scientific Propagation of the Human Race" and "The Rapid Multiplication of the Unfit" addressed topics her respectable husband could support:

> We no longer look upon man as something apart in the universe, as a being specially created and consecrated. We recognize our animal origin. . . . How inconsistent are they who discuss openly the breeding of choice animals, but blush at the mere mention that these same laws govern their own breeding! . . . If we desire to stamp out constitutional defects, and to have a superior race of men, the radical remedy is to exclude the unfit from breeding. Hence,

how such exclusion can best be accomplished becomes the all important problem.[409]

The Martins rented Carnegie Music Hall in New York City for her first stop on the lecture tour. Victoria was still a celebrity in America, and she could still draw an audience. But with her new persona as a respectable English matron, Victoria did not excite her listeners as she once had done. Perhaps through practice she could have learned new techniques for connecting with her audience. But her public presence in America stirred up press coverage of embarrassing stories from her past, accusations, threats of blackmail, and a warrant for her arrest. After the first lecture in New York City, the Martins canceled the rest of the campaign tour and immediately sailed back to England. Victoria's career as a lecturer and presidential candidate was over.

When the Martins returned to England, they launched a new campaign to protect Victoria's reputation. John sued the British Museum for libel because the reading room of the museum owned a book on the Beecher-Tilton trial that included information about Victoria's role in the scandal. The museum had already removed the book from circulation at Mr. Martin's request, but this highly publicized libel trial in London provided an opportunity to put on public record the fact that Mrs. Martin was a refined lady who would never even consider being involved in any way in anything improper or scandalous. John and Victoria also modified and republished newspaper illustrations of Victoria from the early 1870s to make her look more respectable in them—lengthening her skirts, making her features more feminine, and changing the backgrounds to suggest more wholesome surrounding imagery. John spared no expense or effort in the cause of defending his wife's honor. Even so, in one of her last communications to her husband, Victoria's words suggest lingering issues:

Oh could we but live our life over again those who have made us suffer so intensely might attempt in vain to disturb the tranquility of our hearts.[410]

In March 1897 John Martin died from illness while away on a wilderness expedition abroad. Coincidently, his father Richard Martin also died from illness three days earlier. Because the elder Martin died first, Victoria inherited both her husband's entire estate and his full portion of his father's estate. This inheritance made Victoria the largest shareholder in the Martin bank. Whatever disrespectful attitudes Martin family members and others may have still held for Victoria certainly would have changed overnight due to her new personal economic status.

In her 1876 Boston lecture, Victoria had proposed a revolution in banking—an end to private ownership of banks and an end to charging interest on loans. Victoria finally had it within her power to make such radical change. But instead, in her senior years Victoria shifted into a lifestyle of leisure and philanthropy.

She stopped publishing *The Humanitarian* and retired to her fifteen hundred-acre country manor where she lived for most of her remaining thirty years. But even while Victoria enjoyed her retirement, her previous work on *The Humanitarian* continued to influence civic leaders in Europe and America. She had become acquainted with many prominent and influential people, including artists and writers, diplomats and lawyers, and all types of English nobility, including Queen Victoria's daughter Helena and the Prince of Wales (the future King Edward VII). Bestselling author and futurist visionary H. G. Wells had been a subscriber to "her monthly organ of propaganda," as he described it, wherein "popular preachers, popular bishops, and popular anthropologists vied with titled ladies of liberal outlook." In his early 1900s magazine articles in *Cosmopolitan Magazine* and his popular non-fiction book *Mankind in the Making*, Wells proposed a new political doctrine for a government where the intentional evolution of the human race would motivate all public policies. He agreed with Woodhull that "to prevent the multiplication of people below a certain standard, and to encourage the multiplication of exceptionally superior people, was the only real and permanent way of mending the ills of the world." Wells praised Woodhull for having "battled bravely" in this cause. He paired her with Charles Darwin's cousin Francis Galton, who coined the term "eugenics" for a more developed philosophy of scientific propagation of the human species. In the early 1900s eugenics was rapidly gaining in acceptance as a field of research and policy. During that optimistic time, Victoria Woodhull Martin was frequently given credit as its first important promoter. Her primary philanthropic legacy would be an endowment to the Royal Institution of Great Britain science organization for eugenics research.[411]

In the last phase in her life, Victoria kept a cool distance from acquaintances, refusing to shake hands or let visitors come closer than six feet to avoid exposure to germs. She spent most of her time with her adult daughter Zula Maude and her son Byron, who still needed constant care because of his developmental deficiencies. Victoria forbade her daughter Zula Maude from ever marrying, giving as a reason the fear that any children she bore might be unhealthy like Byron. Zula Maude became a companion to her mother and then a caretaker for Byron. Despite the time she now had to spend with family, one relative Victoria rarely saw was her sister Tennie.[412]

After arriving in London in 1877, Tennessee Claflin became the mistress of Francis Cook, an elderly wealthy businessman. When Cook's wife died, he married Tennie. Less than a year later, Francis earned a title of nobility through his wealth, and so Tennie took the title and prestige of Lady Cook.

Victoria and Tennie had married two of the wealthiest men in England, but tensions arose between them around the start of their marriages, and they never again had the closeness of their earlier years. Even years later after their husbands had both died, the two sisters never really reconnected, although they had regular correspondence through letters. Neither sister seemed to be able to find the time to visit the other's palatial estate. Like Victoria, Tennie was enjoying her own rich inheritance, privileged lifestyle, private family life, and reputation of respectability. The sisters had both left their notoriety behind and along with it all remnants of any partnership.[413]

Throughout her life in England, Victoria was always consistent in presenting herself as the proper lady she had wanted to be when she published this disclaimer:

> I now openly avow, with all the earnestness of righteous indignation, that during no part of my life did I favor Free Love even tacitly . . . . I regarded it with loathing when once I got a slight idea of its character and the deep infamy to which it led.[414]

Postscript

The truth is that I am too many years ahead of this age and the exalted views and objects of humanitarianism can scarcely be grasped as yet by the unenlightened mind of the average man.

Victoria Claflin Woodhull

In the present or future, some extra throe of error may conjure up a new-style conjugality, which, ad libitum, severs the marriage covenant, puts virtue in the shambles, and coolly notifies the public of broken vows. Springing up from the ashes of free-love, this nondescript phoenix, in the face and eyes of common law, common sense, and common honesty, may appear in the role of a superfine conjugality; but, having no Truth, it will have no past, present, or future.

Mary Baker Eddy

After Victoria Claflin Woodhull left America, the battle for the soul of marriage continued. There is much more remaining of the story of how Mary Baker Eddy crossed swords with free love, but it will need to be told in depth and detail in another book. This one will end with an overview of what happened next—a preview of the story that remains to be told.

There was a broad backlash against free love throughout America, known as the social purity movement. Oneida's next generation rejected free love in favor of monogamous legal marriage, and they converted from a socialist commune to a private corporation, which is known today for the manufacture of silverware. Plural marriage was outlawed in Utah after being legal for fifty years. Spiritualism rapidly declined in popularity after receiving a deathblow. And the women's rights movement reunified and eventually achieved woman suffrage throughout America.

As Mary Baker Eddy's movement grew into a recognized established religion, she continued to defend the Puritan-influenced view of marriage and to promote Christian morality as a necessary discipline for the spiritual path called Christian Science. Ironically, as soon as Eddy gained prominence at the national level, leaders of other Christian denominations accused Eddy of promoting free love! And so a new battlefront opened up in Eddy's war. But this time she had her own army at her command. She instructed her soldiers to use her writings on marriage in newspapers across the country to clear up the misunderstanding.[415]

As people abandoned Spiritualism and joined the Christian Science movement, Eddy fought against free love within her organization to ensure that her church would support marriage as a legal and religious institution. Like the heroes of her youth, the Reverend Mary Baker Eddy spared no denunciation for the alternative views on marriage and morality that came into American culture through Spiritualism. She established rules that required the marriages of members of her church to be recognized by law and conducted by Christian clergy.[416]

Eddy worked to elevate the view of women in society and to develop new female leadership within her organization, The Church of Christ, Scientist. Her church supported "equal rights and privileges, equality of the sexes, rotation in office." By the end of Eddy's career, there were more than 4,800 Christian Science practitioners and teachers throughout the world. Nearly nine out of ten of these full-time professionals were women. Her church organization had expanded to include more than eleven hundred congregations in the United States alone, plus congregations in twenty-two other countries in North and South America, Europe, Asia, Africa, and Australia. Eddy put women into the pulpit in all of these churches, since she required a "First Reader" and "Second Reader" to deliver a sermon from the Bible and *Science and Health* to the congregation, and she encouraged these two elected positions to be filled by a man and a woman. As one writer and lecturer stated, Eddy "placed woman by the side of man in the pulpit as co-worker and co-equal." Throughout the world in 1910, six out of ten of the more prominent First Readers were women. Even when a man held the leading role—as was often the case at the largest urban churches—he preached words written by a woman: Mary Baker Eddy. Previously, only a few Christian denominations had women preachers and ministers, and it was still rare. Eddy boosted women's prominence within Christianity considerably.[417]

As the nineteenth century progressed, there were more and more interactions between the Christian Science movement and other American leaders. Some of the historic figures included in this story made noteworthy statements about Eddy, and many were specifically mentioned in Eddy's later published writings or in the Christian Science periodicals. These periodicals frequently reported on the progress of woman suffrage, and Eddy even allowed Lucy Stone's daughter Alice Stone Blackwell to make a political appeal for woman suffrage in the *Christian Science Journal*.[418]

Susan B. Anthony ended up taking the twelve-day intensive course called Christian Science class instruction from Laura

Lathrop, one of Eddy's students. Although Anthony did not embrace the Christian Science religion, she owned a copy of *Science and Health* for many years. Her previous support of Woodhull had so changed that Anthony's multivolume historical record of the women's rights movement, *The History of Woman Suffrage*, only mentioned Victoria Woodhull once and omitted her name from the index.[419]

Brigham Young's nephew Bicknell chose a monogamous marriage, converted to Christian Science, and then held several important official positions in the Christian Science church. Henry Ward Beecher's granddaughter and Isabella Beecher Hooker's daughter became pillars of the Christian Science church in New York City.[420]

When Henry Ward Beecher died in 1887, Eddy publicly paid tribute to America's most famous preacher:

> We stand on a far-reaching battlefield, amidst fallen heroes. The brave Beecher has passed on, and the advancing ideas of the nineteenth century have lost a prop. His was a steady aim, and a broad battleaxe, raised against the worst forms of tyranny and oppression. A nation mourns him, and the proper function of society is to remember virtue and forget vice. The great cause of humanity has lost a friend in Rev. Henry Ward Beecher.[421]

At the very peak of Mary Baker Eddy's fame, in an interview with journalist Arthur Brisbane, Eddy again spoke in praise of Beecher for his work on behalf of the African slave. Beecher's fame in America continued long after his death, and his influence can be seen in Eddy's Christian denomination. Many of the larger Christian Science churches were built in a similar scale and style as Beecher's Plymouth Church — with an auditorium-style sanctuary designed for good visibility and acoustics and without the center aisle of more traditional church design. A hymn tune with the title "Beecher," composed by the Plymouth Church organist and named in honor of the great Reverend was included in the Christian Science Hymnal. While there were many famous Beechers, the foremost Beecher was known to be Henry Ward. Of special note is the frequent inclusion of Henry Ward Beecher quotes and other mentions in the early Christian Science periodicals. One reprinted article grouped Beecher with Martin Luther, Abraham Lincoln, St. Paul, and Jesus. Another reminded readers of Beecher's advocacy for woman suffrage.[422]

This story would not be complete without a brief explanation of why the public exchange between Mary Baker Eddy and Victoria Claflin Woodhull is generally unknown even among the most studious of Eddy's followers. The final editions of Eddy's books include little about the free-love movement. Eddy continuously revised *Science and Health* to improve and clarify it and, in the process of editing, many of the quotes on free love and the social influence of Spiritualism that were used in *Crossing Swords* were later removed or significantly changed. Likewise, some of her strongest statements denouncing free-love, which were published in the Christian Science periodicals, were not included in the *Prose Works* compilation of her miscellaneous writings. For the past century, the newspaper article Eddy wrote in 1876 condemning Woodhull's views was buried in obscurity along with Woodhull's public career.[423]

Woodhull has recently been revived as a historic figure by biographers who have rediscovered her dramatic life story and reconnected her with the history of women's rights. Now that women are starting to be seen as viable candidates for president of the United States, Woodhull is being freshly presented as a trailblazing pioneer and visionary who was misunderstood and mistreated in her own era, just as she herself believed. During a press interview on Election Day in 1892, after her second failed run for president, she stated:

> The truth is that I am too many years ahead of this age and the exalted views and objects of humanitarianism can scarcely be grasped as yet by the unenlightened mind of the average man.[424]

By the early twentieth century, Victoria's free-love campaign was moving into the realm of distant memory. However, in the final editions of Eddy's published writings, she included a warning of some "new-style conjugality . . . Springing up from the ashes of free-love" in the future. In "the whole warfare of sensuality" her book *Science and Health* would continue to lay the axe at the root of materialism. As for the development of the Christian Science movement, like any mother, Eddy wanted to focus on her beloved child's growth and forget the pangs of delivery. She spared her readers even knowing about the battle she had fought so many years before:

> I have tried to remove the pioneer signs and ensigns of war, and to retain at this date the privileged armaments of peace. With armor on, I continue the march, command and countermand; meantime interluding with loving thought this afterpiece of battle. Supported, cheered, I take my pen and pruning-hook, to "learn war no more," and with strong wing to lift my readers above the smoke of conflict into light and liberty.[425]

Acknowledgements

A huge thank you to my dear husband for supporting me throughout the process of writing *Crossing Swords*. I worked alone for three years, often struggling with the results of my research and wrestling with my fears of how it would be received. He consistently encouraged me and during critical phases protected me from distractions. He never doubted that I was doing a great work.

I am profoundly grateful to the people in my life (you know who you are!) who read my manuscript at various stages and offered honest feedback. I received exactly what I needed to hear. I cherish every comment of criticism and encouragement. Each one of you helped me make *Crossing Swords* the best it could be.

I also want to acknowledge the backers of my crowd-funding campaign through Kickstarter. My backers not only contributed to the costs of publishing this book, but also gave me a needed boost of confidence as I launched the advance publicity. The seventy copies pre-ordered through the campaign will always be a very special reminder of support to me.

Bibliography

Anderson, Robert Charles. *The Winthrop Fleet: Massachusetts Bay Company Immigrants to New England, 1629-1630*. Boston: New England Historic Genealogical Society, 2012.

Applegate, Debby. *The Most Famous Man in America: The Biography of Henry Ward Beecher*. New York: Doubleday, 2006.

Armstrong, John. *Love, Life, and Goethe: Lessons of the Imagination from the Great German Poet*. New York: Farrar, Straus and Giroux, 2006.

Aronson, Marc. *John Wintrhop, Oliver Cromwell, and the Land of Promise*. New York: Clarion Books, 2004.

Bancroft, Samuel Putnam. *Mrs. Eddy As I Knew Her in 1870*. Boston: G.H. Ellis Press, 1923. Reprint, Santa Clarita, CA: The Bookmark, undated.

Banks, Charles Edward. *The Winthrop Fleet of 1630: An Account of the Vessels, the Voyage, the Passengers, and their English Homes from Original Authorities*. Baltimore: Genealogical Publishing Co. Inc., 1989.

Bargmann, Linda. *In Mrs. Eddy's Day*. St. Louis: Linda Bargmann, 2005.

Beecher, Henry Ward. *The Life of Jesus, the Christ*. New York, 1871.

Benz, Ernst. *Emanuel Swedenborg: Visionary Savant in the Age of Reason*. Translated by Nicholas Goodrick-Clarke. West Chester, PA: Swedenborg Foundation, 2002.

Braude, Ann. *Radical Spirits: Spiritualism and Women's Rights in Nineteenth-Century America*. Boston: Beacon Press, 1989.

Brisbane, Arthur. *What Mrs. Eddy Said to Arthur Brisbane*. New York: M. E. Paige, 1930.

Brody, Miriam. *Victoria Woodhull: Free Spirit for Women's Rights*. New York: Oxford University Press, 2003.

Carpenter, Gilbert C., Jr., ed. *Items By and About Mary Baker Eddy . . . Culled From the Press (1845 to 1888)*. Reprint, Santa Clarita, CA: The Bookmark, undated.

Carpenter, Gilbert C., Jr., and Gilbert C. Carpenter, Sr., eds. *Miscellaneous Documents Relating to Christian Science and its Discoverer and Founder Mary Baker Eddy*. Reprint, Santa Clarita, CA: The Bookmark, undated.

Clark, Clifford E., Jr., *Henry Ward Beecher: Spokesman for Middle-Class America*. Champaign: University of Illinois Press, 1978.

Clinton, Catherine. *The Other Civil War: American Women in the Nineteenth Century*. New York: Hill and Wang, 1984.

Coontz, Stephanie. *Marriage, A History: How Love Conquered Marriage*. New York: Viking, 2005.

Corrigan, John, and Lynn S. Neal, eds. *Religious Intolerance in America: A Documentary History*. Chapel Hill: University of North Carolina Press, 2010.

Cullen-DuPont, Kathryn, ed. *American Women Activists' Writings: An Anthology, 1637-2002*. New York: Cooper Square Press, 2002.

Denninger, George. *Revelation: The Prophecy and Fulfillment of Man*. St. Louis: Publishing Good, 2012.

Eddy, Mary Baker. *Church Manual of The First Church of Christ, Scientist, in Boston, Massachusetts*. 1895. Boston: The First Church of Christ, Scientist, 1910.

—— *The First Church of Christ, Scientist and Miscellany*. In *Prose Works Other Than Science and Health With Key to the Scriptures*. Boston: The First Church of Christ, Scientist, 1925.

—— *Footprints Fadeless*. In *Speaking for Herself, Autobiographical Reflections*. Boston: The Writings of Mary Baker Eddy, 2002.

—— *Message to the Mother Church: Boston, Massachusetts, June 1901*. In *Prose Works Other Than Science and Health With Key to the Scriptures*. Boston: The First Church of Christ, Scientist, 1925.

—— *Miscellaneous Writings*. 1897. In *Prose Works Other Than Science and Health With Key to the Scriptures*. Boston: The First Church of Christ, Scientist, 1925.

—— *No & Yes*. 1892 (first edition 1887). In *Prose Works Other Than Science and Health With Key to the Scriptures*. Boston: The First Church of Christ, Scientist, 1925.

—— *Retrospection and Introspection*. 1899 (first edition 1891). In *Prose Works Other Than Science and Health With Key to the Scriptures*. Boston: The First Church of Christ, Scientist, 1925.

—— *Science and Health with Key to the Scriptures*. Final edition. Boston: The First Church of Christ, Scientist, 1910.

Ellis, John B. [pseudonym]. *Free Love and Its Votaries, or American Socialism Unmasked*. San Francisco, 1870.

Epstein, Barbara Leslie. *The Politics of Domesticity: Women, Evangelism, and Temperance in Nineteenth-Century America*. Middletown, CT: Wesleyan University Press, 1981.

Eskridge, William N., Jr., *Dishonorable Passions: Sodomy Laws in America, 1861 – 2003*. New York: Viking, 2008.

Ferguson, Isabel, and Heather Vogel Frederick. *A World More Bright: The Life of Mary Baker Eddy*. Boston: Christian Science Publishing Society, 2013.

Friedman, Lawrence M. *A History of American Law*. New York: Touchstone, 2007.

Frisken, Amanda. *Victoria Woodhull's Sexual Revolution: Political Theater and the Popular Press in Nineteenth-Century America*. Philadelphia: University of Pennsylvania Press, 2004.

Fuller, S. Margaret. *Woman in the Nineteenth Century*. London, 1850.

Gabriel, Mary. *Notorious Victoria: The Life of Victoria Woodhull Uncensored*. Chapel Hill, NC: Algonquin Books, 1998.

Gamble, Richard M. *In Search of the City on a Hill: The Making and Unmaking of an American Myth*. New York: Continuum Intl. Publishing Group, 2012.

Gill, Gillian. *Mary Baker Eddy*. Cambridge, MA: Perseus Books, 1998.

Glover, Mary Baker. *Science and Health*. First edition. Boston: Christian Scientist Publishing Company, 1875.

Goldsmith, Barbara. *Other Powers: The Age of Suffrage, Spiritualism, and the Scandalous Victoria Woodhull*. New York: Alfred A. Knopf, 1998.

Goodspeed, Robert C. *Metaphors in the Study of Christian Science: And the Light they Shed on its Founder, Mary Baker Eddy*. Xlibris, 2010.

Gordon, Sarah Barringer. *The Mormon Question: Polygamy and Constitutional Conflict in Nineteenth Century America*. Chapel Hill: University of North Carolina Press, 2002.

Gottschaulk, Stephen. *The Emergence of Christian Science in American Religious Life*. Berkeley: University of California Press, 1973.

Grossberg, Michael. *Governing the Hearth: Law and the Family in Nineteenth Century America*. Chapel Hill: University of North Carolina Press, 1985.

Havelin, Kate. *Fearless Feminist: Victoria Woodhull*. Minneapolis: Twenty-First Century Books, 2007.

Hitchens, Christopher. *Thomas Paine's Rights of Man: A Biography*. New York: Atlantic Monthly Press, 2006.

Holifield, E. Brooks. *Theology in America: Christian Thought from the Age of the Puritans to the Civil War*. New Haven: Yale University Press, 2003.

Holton, Woody. *Abigail Adams*. New York: Free Press, 2009.

Hosmer, James Kendall. *Winthrop's Journal: "History of New England" 1630-1649, vol. 1*. New York: Barnes and Noble, 1908.

Human Life Articles on Mary Baker Eddy by Sibyl Wilbur, 1907-1907. Chestnut Hill, MA: Longyear Museum Press, 2000.

In My True Light and Life: Mary Baker Eddy Collections. Boston: The Writings of Mary Baker Eddy and The Mary Baker Eddy Library for the Betterment of Humanity, 2002.

Johnston, Julia Michael. *Mary Baker Eddy: Her Mission and Triumph*. Boston: The Christian Science Publishing Society, 1946.

Jonnes, Jill. *Eiffel's Tower: And the World's Fair Where Buffalo Bill Beguiled Paris, the Artists Quarreled, and Thomas Edison Became a Count*. New York: Viking, 2009.

Kerr, Andrea Moore. *Lucy Stone: Speaking Out for Equality*. New Brunswick, NJ: Rutgers University Press, 1992.

Keyssar, Alexander. *The Right to Vote: The Contested History of Democracy in the United States*. New York: Basic Books, 2000.

Klaw, Spencer. *Without Sin: The Life and Death of the Oneida Community*. New York: Penguin Press, 1993.

La Plante, Eve. *American Jezebel: The Uncommon Life of Anne Hutchinson, the Woman Who Defied the Puritans*. San Francisco: HarperSanFrancisco, 2004.

Longyear, Mary Beecher. *The Genealogy and Life of Asa Gilbert Eddy*. Boston: G. H. Ellis Press, 1922.

MacPherson, Myra. *The Scarlet Sisters: Sex, Suffrage, and Scandal in the Gilded Age*. New York: Twelve, 2014.

Matthews, Jean V. *The Rise of the New Woman: The Women's Movement in America, 1875-1930*. Chicago: Ivan R. Dee, 2003.

McCullough, David. *John Adams*. New York: Simon & Schuster Paperbacks, 2001.

McMillen, Sally G. *Seneca Falls and the Origins of the Women's Rights Movement*. New York: Oxford University Press, 2008.

Morgan, Edmund S. *The Puritan Family: Religion and Domestic Relations in Seventeenth-Century New England*. New York: Harper and Row, 1966.

Mosely, James G. *John Winthrop's World: History as a Story, the Story as History*. Madison: University of Wisconsin Press, 1992.

Nenneman, Richard A. *Persistent Pilgrim: The Life of Mary Baker Eddy*. Etna, NH: Nebbadoon Press, 1997.

—— *The New Birth of Christianity: Why Religion Persists in a Scientific Age*. San Francisco: HarperSanFrancisco, 1992.

Norgren, Jill. *Belva Lockwood: The Woman Who Would be President*. New York: New York University Press, 2007.

Noyes, John Humphrey. *History of American Socialisms*. Philadelphia, 1870.

Packer, J. I., *A Quest For Godliness: The Puritan Vision of the Christian Life*. Wheaton, IL: Crossway Books, 1990.

Parker, Mary Godfrey. "A Friendship Through Two Generations," in *We Knew Mary Baker Eddy*. Boston: Christian Science Publishing Society, 1979. Expanded edition, vol. 1, 2011.

Peel, Robert. *Christian Science: Its Encounter with American Culture*. New York: Holt, Rinehart and Winston, 1958.

—— *Mary Baker Eddy: The Years of Discovery, 1821–1875*. New York: Holt, Rinehart and Winston, 1966.

—— *Mary Baker Eddy: The Years of Trial, 1876–1891*. New York: Holt, Rinehart and Winston, 1971.

Perry, Michael, W. *Lady Eugenist: Feminist Eugenics in the Speeches and Writings of Victoria Woodhull*. Seattle: Inkling Books, 2005.

Phillips, Roderick. *Untying the Knot: A Short History of Divorce*. Ottawa: Cambridge University Press, 1991.

Robinson, Joseph S. *Waymarks in the Life of Mary Baker Eddy*. Springfield, MA: Pond-Ekberg, 1942.

Rosen, Roberts. *A Short History of Charleston*. San Francisco: Lexikos, 1982.

Rutter, Michael. *Upstairs Girls: Prostitution in the American West*. Helena, MT: Farcountry Press, 2005.

Ryken, Leland. *Worldly Saints: The Puritans as They Really Were*. Grand Rapids, MI: Zondervan Publishing House, 1986.

Sears, Hal D. *The Sex Radicals: Free Love in High Victorian America*. Lawrence: The Regents Press of Kansas, 1977.

Shirley, John M. *The Early Jurisprudence of New Hampshire: An Address Delivered at the Annual Meeting of the N.H. Historical Society, June 13, 1883*. Concord, NH, 1885.

Smaus, Jewel Spangler. *Mary Baker Eddy: The Golden Days*. Boston: Christian Science Publishing Society, 1966.

Smith, Clifford P. *Historical Sketches: From the Life of Mary Baker Eddy and the History of Christian Science*. Boston: Christian Science Publishing Society, 1941.

Snay, Mitchell. *Horace Greeley and the Politics of Reform in Nineteenth-Century America*. Lanham, MD: Rowman & Littlefield Publishers, 2011.

Spurlock, John C. *Free Love: Marriage and Middle-Class Radicalism in America, 1825-1860*. New York: New York University Press, 1988.

Stern, Madeline, ed. *The Victoria Woodhull Reader*. Weston, MA: M&S Press, 1974.

Stiles, Henry Reed. *Bundling: Its Origin, Progress and Decline in America*. Albany, NY, 1871. Reprint, New York: Eugenics Publishing, undated.

Stoeher, Taylor, ed. *Free Love in America: A Documentary History*. New York: AMS Press, 1979.

Stowe, Harriet Beecher. *My Wife and I: Or, Harry Henderson's History*. New York, 1871.

Stuart, Nancy Rubin. *The Reluctant Spiritualist: The Life of Maggie Fox*. Orlando, FL: Harcourt, 2005.

Tilton, Theodore. *Victoria C. Woodhull, A Biographical Sketch: Mr. Tilton's Account of Mrs. Woodhull*. New York, 1871.

Tomlinson, Irving. *Twelve Years with Mary Baker Eddy: Recollections and Experiences*. Boston: Christian Science Publishing Society, 1945. Amplified edition, 1996.

Twain, Mark [Samuel L. Clemens]. *Christian Science: With Notes Containing Corrections to Date*. New York, 1907.

Underhill, Lois Beachy. *The Woman Who Ran For President: The Many Lives of Victoria Woodhull*. Bridgehampton, NY: Bridge Works Publishing, 1995.

Van Wagoner, Richard S. *Mormon Polygamy: A History*. Salt Lake City, UT: Signature Books, 1989.

von Fettweis, Yvonne Cache, and Warneck, Robert Townsend. *Mary Baker Eddy: Christian Healer*. Boston: Christian Science Publishing Society, 1998. Amplified edition, 2009.

Ward, Kyle. *History in the Making: An Absorbing Look at How American History Has Changed in the Telling Over the Last 200 Years*. New York: The New Press, 2006.

Wells, H. G. *Mankind in the Making*. London: Chapman & Hall, 1904.

White, Barbara A. *The Beecher Sisters*. New Haven: Yale University, 2003.

Wilbur, Sybil. *The Life of Mary Baker Eddy*. Boston: Christian Science Publishing Society, 1907.

Williams, Mary E., ed. *The Sexual Revolution*. San Diego, CA: Greenhaven Press, 2002.

Woodard, Colin. *American Nations: A History of the Eleven Rival Regional Cultures of North America*. Penguin Group, New York, 2011.

Woodhull, Victoria, C. "The Principles of Social Freedom." New York: Woodhull & Claflin, 1871. Reprint in Stern, *Reader,* 1974.

—— "The Naked Truth; or the Situation Reviewed." *Woodhull & Claflin Weekly*, January 25, 1873. Reprint in Stern, *Reader,* 1974.

—— "Tried As By Fire; Or the True and the False, Socially." New York: Woodhull & Claflin, 1874. Reprint in Stern, *Reader,* 1974.

—— "Victoria C. Woohull's Complete and Detailed Version of the Beecher-Tilton Affair." Washington, DC, 1872. Reprint in Stern, *Reader,* 1974.

—— "The Scientific Propagation of the Human Race; Or Humanitarian Aspects of Finance and Marriage. The Science of Well Being." November 20, 1893. Reprint in Perry, *Lady Eugenist,* 2005.

Woodhull-Martin, Victoria Claflin. "Some Thoughts About America," 1888. Reprint in Stern, *Reader,* 1974.

—— "Stirpiculture; or The Scientific Propagation of the Human Race," London, England, February 1888. Reprint in Perry, *Lady Eugenist,* 2005.

Notes

1. *"Figuratively speaking"*: Twain, 78, 54, 38, 82.

2. *"Mrs. Eddy has accumulated power"*: Brisbane, 44-45. Gottshalk, 24; *"No man ever"*: Christian Science Sentinel, Dec. 14, 1899, 245. See also, *"Science and Health* owned by Susan B. Anthony," Mar. 1, 2011, The Mary Baker Eddy Library website.

3. *"In natural law"*: Eddy, *No & Yes*, 45.

4. *"the most prominent woman"*: Underhill, 185, citing *Pittsburgh Dispatch*, Dec. 2, 1871.

5. *"It was about the year 1875"*: Eddy, "Wedlock," *Miscellaneous Writings*, 285. Slight variation in "Conjugal Rights," *Christian Science Journal*, Jun. 1889.

6. *"I am conducting a campaign"*: Woodhull, "Tried as by Fire," 5.

7. *Body as master*: Glover, *S&H*, 1st ed., 157-158. See also Eddy, *S&H*, final ed., 225-226; *"It is a revolutionary struggle"*: Eddy, *Miscellaneous Writings*, 101.

8. *"flamboyant exponent of free-love"*: Peel, *Trial*, 14.

9. *"My ancestors came"*: "Veritas Odium Parit," *Christian Science Journal*, (Apr. 1885): 2. See also, Eddy, *No & Yes*, 46.

10. *"Puritan parents"*: Eddy, *S&H*, final ed., 359; *"puritanical honesty"*: Glover, *S&H*, 1st ed., 322, 317; *"For one, we honor"*: "Lynn Morals and Woodhull," *Lynn Transcript*, Oct. 14, 1876.

11. *Marriage as cultural achievement*: Ryken, 40. *"dutiful descendants of Puritans"*: Eddy, *No & Yes*, 46.

12. *June 6, 1630*: Banks, 42; *11 ships*: Gamble, 25; "we must consider that we shall be": John Winthrop, "A Model of Christian Charity."

13. *designed for freight*: Banks, 24; *cargo*: Anderson, 26; *20,000*: Anderson, 3.

14. Banks, 13, 19.

15. *"such power of faith"*: Aronson, 27, citing Charles Lloyd Cohen, *God's Caress: The Psychology of Puritan Religious Experience* (New York: Oxford, 1986), 247-50.

16. *"dangerous errors"*: Hosmer, 195.

17. *Controversy over banishment*: Mosely, 123; *Legalists vs. opinionists*: La Plante, 52; *"dangerous errors"*: Hosmer, 195; *"more dangerous evils"*: La Plante, 188.

18. *"tended to the frustration"*: Mosely, 136, citing Winthrop's Journal, June 4, 1646; *"quietly and cheerfully submit"*: John Winthrop, "Little Speech on Liberty," 1645.

19. *"that great enemy of truth"*: John Winthrop, "Little Speech on Liberty," 1645.

20. *"Father of New England"*: Gamble, 73.

21. *"The civilization of New England"*: Gamble, 88-89.

22. *Puritan term*: Packer, 21, 50.

23. *"written in thine heart"* Packer, 67, citing William Tyndale, *Doctrinal Treatises* (Cambridge, 1848), 464f; *Key to the Scriptures*: see *We Knew Mary Baker Eddy*, expanded edition, vol. 2, 437-438.

24. La Plante, 20-22.

25. *"the great licentiousness"*: William Bradford, *Of Plymouth Plantation: 1620-1647*, ch. IV.

26. *Best educated community*: Ryken, 7. Woodard, 59; *Boston as educational center*: Woodard, 61.

27. Packer, 28, 40, 98; *Sports and fashions*: Ryken, 3.

28. *John Cotton and Congregational Church*: La Plante, 91, 98.

29. *Catholic celibacy*: Ryken, 40. Phillips, 11.

30. *God's design*: Packer, 261; *"of the devil"*: Ryken, 232 n. 14, citing Ewald M. Plass, ed. *What Luther Says: An Anthology*, 3 vols. (St. Louis: Concordia, 1959), 2:890; *"For if we judge the tree"*: Phillips, 13, citing Heinrich Bullinger.

31. *Divorce and annulment*: Phillips, 1-6. Morgan, 34.

32. *Annulment of Henry VIII*: Phillips, 20.

33. *Marriage as civil contract*: Phillips, 37; *Marriage as holy*: Ryken, 49.

34. *Divorce to prevent family disintegration*: Phillips, 41; *England divorce*: Phillips, 64.

35. *Required cohabitation*: Morgan, 39.

36. *Rule of thumb*: Phillips, 98; *"The Great God commands thee"*: Morgan, 47, citing Benjamin Wadsworth, *Well-Ordered Family*, 25, 36.

37. *"There is no society"*: Ryken, 42, quoting Thomas Gataker, *A Wife Indeed*, from Robert Victor Schnucker, *Views of Selected Puritans, 1560-1630, on Mar-*

riage and Human Sexuality (PhD Dissertation, University of Iowa, 1969) 139-140.

38. *"two sweet friends"*: Ryken, 50, quoting Daniel Rogers, *A Complete Body of Divinity*, from Philip Greven, *The Protestant Temperament: Patterns of Child-Rearing, Religious Experience, and the Self in Early America* (New York: Knopf, 1977); *"a friend and comfort"*: Ryken, 44, quoting Alexander Niccholes, *A Good Wife*, from Charles H. George and Katherine George, *The Protestant Mind of the English Reformation, 1570-1640* (Princeton: Princeton University Press, 1961), 287; *"It is a mercy"*: Ryken, 43, quoting Richard Baxter, *A Christian Directory*, from John Halkett, *Milton and the Ideal of Matrimony* (New Haven: Yale University Press, 1970), 20.

39. *Selecting partner*: Morgan, 54. Packer, 268; *Parental involvement*: Morgan, 56-58; *"warm and tender and gracious"*: Morgan, 60.

40. Coontz, 7, 23.

41. *"no marrying in Heaven"*: Morgan, 48, quoting Thomas Hooker, *A Comment upon Christ's Last Prayer*, 193; *"Look not for Perfection"*: Morgan, 52, citing Thomas Thatcher, "Boston Sermons," Sept. 30, 1672.

42. *Definition of chastity*: Ryken, 40-47; *"active, hone, and devoted love"*: Ryken, 46, quoting Edmund Spenser, *The Faerie Queene*, from Graham Hough, *A Preface to the Faerie Queene* (New York: Norton, 1962), 170.

43. *Bundling*: Stiles, 50-73.

44. Friedman, 33, 35-36; *"ante-nuptial defilement"*: Shirley, 46.

45. *"Hail wedded love"*: Ryken, 54, citing John Milton, *Paradise Lost*, bk. 4, lines 750-61.

46. *Marriage love subordinate*: Packer, 265; *"lewd and unseemly"*: Woodard, 58; *"Not for their own ends"*: Ryken, 49, quoting John Cotton, *Practical Commentary upon John*, 200.

47. *Stages of regeneration*: Holifield, 42-44.

48. Morgan, 106, 134-143.

49. Morgan, 132.

50. Morgan, 88. Holifield, 61-64.

51. *"nearest to an equality"*: Ryken, 53, quoting Samuel Willard, *Compleat Body of Divinity*, from Laurel Thatcher Ulrich, *Good Wives: Image and Reality in the Lives of Women in Northern New England, 1650-1750* (New York: Knopf, 1982),

8; "*for tho' the husband be the head*": Morgan, 46, quoting Samuel Willard, *Compleat Body of Divinity*, 610.

52. "*All the Members in a Family*": Morgan, 117-118, citing Samuel Willard, *Compleat Body of Divinity*, 616.

53. "*Soules have no sexes*": Packer, 267, citing Robert Bolton, *Works 1631-1641*, IV:245f.

54. *Women's status in Puritan colonies*: Clinton, 3. Epstein, 31; *Not servants*: Morgan, 45.

55. *Women's theological discussions*: La Plante, 44-45; "*Women are capable*": Ryken, 77, quoting Samuel Torshell, *The Woman's Glory*, from R. C. Richardson, *Puritanism in North-West England: A Regional Study of Chester to 1642* (Manchester: Manchester University Press, 1972), 106.

56. "*As dutiful descendents*": Eddy, *No and Yes*, 46.

57. *Divinity degree*: Eddy, *Church Manual*, 67-68.

58. *Puritan growth rate*: Woodard, 59; *Calvinism standard*: Holifield, 25.

59. *90%*: Nenneman, *The New Birth*, 102-103; *First settlers' influence*: Woodard, 16.

60. *Protestant domination*: Gottschalk, *Emergence*, 2; *Illegal sexuality*: Eskridge, 23; *Puritan law model*: Shirley, 52.

61. *Abigail's financial independence*: Holton, ix-xii; "*best, dearest, worthiest*": McCullough, 148, citing *Adams Family Correspondence*, II, 83.

62. Phillips, 42.

63. Grossberg, 15.

64. John Adams quotes: *Revolutionary Services and Civil Life of General William Hull*, (New York, 1848), 266, citing Letters to the Officers of the First Brigade of the Third Division of the Militia of Massachusetts, Oct. 11, 1798.

65. "*Why I loved Christians*": Eddy, *Message of 1901*, 32.

66. "*When America realizes*": Martin-Woodhull, "Some Thoughts About America."

67. "*I know how long*": Woodhull, "Principles of Social Freedom," 42.

68. *Term "free love"*: Gabriel, 96. Spurlock, 48-49. Henry David Thoreau, "Free Love," *The Dial* (Oct. 1842): 199.

69. "*Under the old covenant*": Klaw, 28.

70. *"When the will of God"*: Stoeher, 497, quoting John Humphrey Noyes, letter to *Battle Axe*, Jan. 15, 1837 and published a few months later.

71. *"Step by step"*: Spurlock, 81, quoting *First Annual Report of the Oneida Association: Exhibiting its History, Principles, and Transactions to Jan. 1, 1849*, (Oneida Reserve, 1849), 2.

72. *Dutch slave trade in NYC*: Woodard, 71.

73. *"I can see him now"*: Goldsmith, 43, quoting Elizabeth Cady Stanton, *Eighty Years and More: Reminiscences 1815-1897 (New York, 1898)*, 42.

74. *"Burned-over district"*: Stuart, 11.

75. Spurlock, 26.

76. *Term "feminist"*: Wikipedia topic "Charles Fourier"; *"Perpetual fidelity in love"*: Spurlock, 64, quoting Charles Fourier, *The Utopian Vision of Charles Fourier: Selected Texts on Work, Love, and Passionate Attraction*, trans. Johnathan Beecher and Richard Bienvenu (Boston: Beacan Press, 1971), 172-173.

77. *Noyes' writings*: Spurlock, 26; *Marx and Engels*: Wikipedia article "Utopian Societies." "Manifesto of the Communist Party," Feb. 1848, (marxists.org).

78. *"amative"*: Klaw, 156; *"ascending fellowship"*: Klaw, 209. See also Stoeher, 533; *"the last citadel"*: Klaw, 206.

79. *Noyes' publicity*: Stoeher, 486.

80. *Mind your own business*: Spurlock, 135.

81. *Noyes' Bible Communism*: Stoeher, 35.

82. *"Judged by its fruits"*: Woodhull, "Tried as by Fire," 18.

83. *Mormon synonymous with free love*: "with a large share of the Mormon (to express it mildly) thrown in" from "The Valcour Community," *New York Times*, Feb. 14, 1875. Also "A New Community," *New York Times*, Sept. 12, 1874. Gordon, 31; *Bigamy as felony*: Gordon, 129.

84. Van Wagoner, 27, 43.

85. *"exterminated"*: Gordon, 107, quoting Governor L.W. Boggs to General John B. Clark, Oct. 27, 1838, reprinted in William Mulder and A. Russell Mortensen, eds. *Among the Mormons: Historic Accounts by Contemporary Observers*, (New York, 1958), 102-3.

86. Gordon, 1.

87. *"twin relics of barbarism"*: Gordon, 55.

88. Gordon, 102.

89. *"Consistency is a jewel"*: Woodhull, "Tried as by Fire," 23; *"I need not tell you"*: Woodhull, "Principles of Social Freedom," 34. A recent source estimated the number of prostitutes in New York City as 10,000 out of 1,000,000. McMillen, 44.

90. *Revolution-era women*: Clinton, 12; "remember the ladies": Abigail Adams to John Adams, Mar. 31, 1776.

91. *Economic shift*: Snay, 11; *Separate spheres*: Epstein, 62.

92. *Intentionally little organization*: McMillen, 105, 113.

93. *American shift to English law*: Clinton, 8. Epstein, 31. Friedman, 3; *"unlimited power to the husband"*: Abigail Adams to Mercy Otis Warren, Apr. 27, 1776; *Blackstone's "one flesh"*: Gordon, 66.

94. *Stanton's marriage contract*: McMillen, 118. See also Brody, 77.

95. *NY Tribune on women's rights in 1850s*: Braude, 93. Snay, 99.

96. *"a Paradise of free-lovers"*: "Divorce-Woman's Rights," *NY Tribune*, Mar. 1, 1860, 4.

97. *"God forgive you"*: "Divorce," *NY Tribune*, Mar. 5, 1860, 7.

98. *"what is Marriage?"*: *NY Tribune*, Mar. 6, 1860, 4; *NY Tribune's influence*: Snay, 49; *Greeley's Irish district*: Snay, 95; *Greeley turned enemy*: Kerr, 126. Snay, 174.

99. *"Now, it must strike"*: "Marriage and Divorce," *NY Tribune*, May 30, 1860, 8.

100. *"E.C.S. write us"*: "Marriage": *NY Tribune*, May 30, 1860, 4.

101. *"From a woman's standpoint"*: Spurlock, 210, quoting Stanton, 1871, from William L. O'Neill, *Everyone was Brave*, 1969, 21.

102. *"all this loose, pestiferous talk"*: Kerr, 156, citing *Woman's Journal*, Oct. 22, 1870; *"legitimately carried out"*: Kerr, 156, citing *Woman's Journal*, Nov. 5, 1870.

103. *"Mrs. Stanton and the free love roost"*: White, 209, citing Harriet Beecher Stowe to Mary Claflin, Aug. 22, 1874, Harriet Beecher Stowe Center, Hartford, CT; *"The men and women who are dabbling"*: Brody, 77, citing Elizabeth Cady Stanton, "On Marriage and Divorce," [1871 convention speech].

104. *Rappings as a prank*: Stuart, 298.

105. *Mesmer influence in séance*: Gottschaulk, *Emergence*, 143; $100 to $150: Stuart, 48.

106. *"spiritual telegraph"*: Isaac Post coined the term. Stuart, 37.

107. *NYC $5*: Stuart, 58. *In millions*: Estimate of 4 million by Judge Edmonds, in Ellis, 415. Braude, 25; *100 spiritualist periodicals*: Richardson, 412.

108. Friedman, 33-34. Corrigan, 34.

109. *Mixed audiences*: Goldsmith, 35; *Trans speakers*: Braude, 86.

110. *"inner union of souls"*: Benz, 416, 409, quoting Swedenborg, *Conjugal Love*, §49, §50, §177.

111. *"one true marriage"*: Spurlock, 94, quoting Andrew Jackson Davis, *Memoranda of Persons, Places, and Events: Embracing Authentic Facts, Visions, Impressions, Discoveries, in Magnetism, Clairvoyance, Spiritualism* (Boston, 1868), 248; *Elective affinities*: Armstrong, 356-359; "Doctrine of Affinities": Spurlock, 96, 193, citing "The Doctrine of Affinities," *Spiritual Telegraph*, Jun. 12, 1852.

112. Stoeher, 35. *"Spiritualism undermined"*: "Towler's Confession," Mar. 25, 1867, in Ellis, 422.

113. Braude, 2, 34, 41, 56; *"free love is the doctrine"*: Braude, 129, citing Alfred Cridge, "Spiritualism, Socialism, and Free Love," *Social Revolutionist* (1854):124.

114. *"Undoubtedly, he shocked"*: Victoria C. Woodhull, introduction to *Elective Affinities* by Johann Wolfgang Goethe (Boston, 1872).

115. *"To preach the doctrine"*: Goldsmith, 304.

116. *"Do you not now begin"*: Woodhull, "The Naked Truth," 16.

117. *"promiscuousness, variety, or monogamy"*: Woodhull, "Tried as by Fire," 16, 24.

118. *"Society, like everything else"*: Woodhull, "Tried as by Fire," 43; *"it is the question of a new gospel"*: Woodhull, "The Naked Truth," 6.

119. *"graciously preparing"*: Eddy, *S&H*, final ed., 107; "wretched condition": Eddy, *Miscellaneous Writings*, 52; *"points to the revelation"*: Eddy, *S&H*, final ed., 107; *"outgrowth of my whole life"*: In My True Light and Life, vii-viii, citing V00838, Eddy to Katie Swarts, Sept. 30, 1884 ©The Mary Baker Eddy Collection.

120. *Protestant rebel ancestor*: Peel, *Discovery*, 18; *Boston homestead*: Peel, *Discovery*, 18. *Bow bend*: Robinson, 2.

121. *Revolutionary riders*: Smaus, 27.

122. Wilbur, 16. *"grandmother's treasures"*: Eddy, *Retrospection*, 2.

123. *Most valuable land*: Robinson, 7.

124. *Esquire*: Smaus, 44; *"treated all men"*: Smith, 14, referencing Deacon Gardner S. Abbott; *Cousin in Congress*: Hon. Henry M. Baker. Tomlinson, 219.

125. *"a living illustration"*: Eddy, *Retrospection*, 5, 6.

126. *School until 21*: Gill, 50; *Wealth educational divide*: Epstein, 72; *"After school"*: Tomlinson, 7, citing A11416, Dec. 26, 1901, ©The Mary Baker Eddy Collection.

127. *"The Bible and I"*: Tomlinson, 105, citing A11884, Aug. 29, 1907, ©The Mary Baker Eddy Collection.

128. *"relentless theology"*: Eddy, *Retrospection*, 13.

129. *Congregational revivals*: Smaus, 62; *"old-school expounder"*: Eddy, *Retrospection*, 14, 15.

130. *Desire to write a book*: Wilbur, 27. Gill, 50-51.

131. *"often convenient, sometimes pleasant"*: Eddy, *Miscellaneous Writings*, 52; *"tender devotion"*: Eddy, *Retrospection*, 19.

132. *"The Colonel placed me"*: Gill, 55, citing *Retrospection*, 1st ed., 24.

133. *Haiti*: Gill, 63. Peel, *Discovery*, 69.

134. *Love letters confiscated*: Tomlinson, 13.

135. *"so far away"*: Tomlinson, 13, ©The Mary Baker Eddy Collection; *Unhealthy climate*: Nenneman, *Pilgrim*, 41, in Mark Baker to Mary Glover, Feb. 6, 1844. Original at Longyear Museum; *Average marriage age*: Smaus, 33; *Glover's level of education*: Gill, 98, 601 n. 29. Peel, *Discovery*, 68.

136. *"thoroughly impregnated"*: Tomlinson, 18, ©The Mary Baker Eddy Collection; *Glover's letters to Sullivan*: Gill, 22-23.

137. *Social acceptability in SC*: Rosen, 34. *SC marriage law*: Phillips, 142, 145.

138. *Mark Baker's politics*: Peel, *Discovery*, 60.

139. *"rash, passionate"*: *George Sullivan Baker Journal*, by permission of Longyear Museum; *NYC prostitutes*: Gill, 23; *"a fine man"*: Tomlinson, 13, ©The Mary Baker Eddy Collection.

140. *Sullivan's romantic fiction*: Gill, 55.

141. *Emma Clinton*: Gill, 57.

142. *Ship from Boston*: Peel, *Discovery*, 67. *Pregnancy and sea sickness*: Gill, 61.

143. Rosen, 9, 34, 41, 63, 66.

144. *"under the paternal roof"*: Eddy, *Retrospection*, 19; *"I can say with Job"*: Nenneman, *Pilgrim*, 41, quoting Mark Baker to Mary Glover, Feb. 6, 1844. Original at Longyear Museum.

145. *Nearby slave auctions*: Ferguson and Frederick, 31, citing *Longyear Museum Quarterly News* (Autumn 1987); *Issues between Glovers*: Tomlinson, 18-20; *"I never could believe"*: Eddy, *Message 1902*, 15.

146. Eddy, *Retrospection*, 19, 20. Gill, 55.

147. *"regular mother"*: Jewel Spangler Smaus, "Family: From New England to the Black Hills, Part VI," *Longyear Museum Quarterly News* (Spring 1984):322. *"mortal life-battle"*: Eddy, *Retrospection*, 22.

148. *widows ineligible for employment*: Gill, 75; *40 students*: Frederick, 34.

149. *Marriage prospects*: Powell, 88; *secret engagement to Bartlett*: Peel, *Discovery*, 92.

150. *Inheritance to the youngest son*: Shirley, 81.

151. *Jefferson and inheritance*: Grossberg, 212.

152. *Inheritance issues as motive*: Deduced from a study of American family law, then affirmed by "Interview with Mary Baker Eddy at Pleasant View, Aug. 31, 1890" in Carpenter, *Miscellaneous Documents*, 103. Excerpt: "They knew that he had an inheritance from his father and grandfather, and they seemed to desire to get his guardianship away from me."

153. *Mark Baker's will*: Gill, 155; *Mark Baker's inheritance*: Gill, 6; Smaus, 18.

154. *"The night before my child"*: Eddy, *Retrospection*, 20.

155. *"very unfortunate"*: Eddy, *Retrospection*, 20; *"acquaintance commenced strangely"*: In My True Light and Life, 96; *"one of strong dislike"*: Janet E. Weller, "The Human Side of Mrs. Eddy" in *In My True Light and Life*, 573, citing Janette W. Weller reminiscence, ©The Mary Baker Eddy Collection.

156. *"his attentions"*: In My True Light and Life, 573, 575.

157. *"heresy"*: Peel, *Discovery*, 109; *Church compromise*: Peel, *Discovery*, 115; *Free dentistry*: Gill, 97.

158. *"love standing at the very threshold"*: Gill, 98. *In My True Light and Life*, 95, citing L16252.

159. *"hopes raised only to be dashed"*: In My True Light and Life, 95, citing L16252.

160. *Legal documents*: Gill, 102, citing Smaus research.

161. *Small furnished house*: Gill, 102; *Decline in practice*: Gill, 103.

162. *Head of household authority*: Morgan, 120; *Visits continued*: Gill, 111. Wilbur, 62.

163. *Baker family conspiracy*: Gill, 112; Jewel Smaus, "Family: From New England to the Black Hills," *Longyear Quarterly News* (Spring 1983); *"a plot was consummated"*: Eddy, *Retrospection*, p. 20.

164. *"a helpless cripple"*: Powell, 96. Gill, 105, citing Mrs. Eddy's "Letters and Miscellany," vol. 55:199:7796. L07796, Mary Baker Eddy to Julius Dresser, Feb. 15, 1866, ©The Mary Baker Eddy Collection.

165. *"Oh! How long must I bear"*: *Mary Baker Eddy: Speaking For Herself*, xxxvi, citing Scrapbook 1, 8A, ©The Mary Baker Eddy Collection.

166. *"long and lingering passage"*: *Mary Baker Eddy: Speaking For Herself*, xxxvi; *"The heavenly intent"*: Eddy, *Retrospection*, 21.

167. Peel, *Discovery*, 138. Smith, 46.

168. *Alternative medicine*: Peel, *Discovery*, 135; *Homeopathy*: Eddy, *S&H*, final ed., 152-3, 156.

169. *Arguing*: Peel, *Discovery*, 125; *Seduction of Sarah Crosby*: Gill, 154.

170. *"ruinous expense"*: Shirley, 101.

171. *"in the poorhouse"*: Powell, 118; *house fire*: Longyear, *Human Life*, 34; *hermitage*: Peel, *Discovery*, 202.

172. *Divorce scandalous*: Gill, 171; *Abandonment*: Shirley, 102; *Fear of arrest*: Wilbur, 210.

173. *"if it had not been for that man"*: Janette E. Weller, "The Human Side of Mrs. Eddy," in *In My True Light and Life*, 572. Janette Weller reminiscence, ©The Mary Baker Eddy Collection.

174. *"Ode to Adversity"*: Peel, *Discovery*, 143. Poem ©The Mary Baker Eddy Collection.

175. *"Sorrow has its reward"*: Glover, *S&H*, 1st ed., 324. See Eddy, *S&H*, final ed., 66:30-67:1.

176. *"heart's bridal"*: Eddy, *Retrospection*, 23.

177. *"hot little hell"*: Gabriel, 254; *"unconsciously dragging out"*: Woodhull, "The Naked Truth," 26.

178. *"I supposed that to marry"*: Gabriel, 13, citing *Woodhull & Claflin Weekly*, Oct. 18, 1873.

179. *"realization of the hollowness"*: Woodhull, "Principles of Social Freedom," 29; *"the most terrible curse"*: Goldsmith, 274, citing *Woodhull & Claflin Weekly*, May 27, 1871.

180. *Logger, riverman*: Underhill, 12; *"could see more deviltry"*: Gabriel, 7, citing Homer Historical Society Collection, Grace Goulder article, Nov. 3, 1957.

181. *"Nowhere"*: Goldsmith, 14, citing *Chicago Daily Mail*, May 9, 1892.

182. Goldsmith, 14.

183. *"pour forth passionate hallelujahs"*: Tilton, 5; *Methodist*: Underhill, 15.

184. Goldsmith, 15-16.

185. Goldsmith, 95.

186. *"impartial in his cruelty"*: Tilton, 4-6.

187. Goldsmith, 24. *"a child without a childhood"*: Tilton, 4; 7.

188. Gabriel, 9.

189. *"be a good listener"*: Gabriel, 11, citing Boston Public Library Woodhull Collection, Zula Maud Woodhull notes.

190. *"an escape"*: Tilton, 14; *Sexual abuse*: Goldsmith, 51-52.

191. *"She was stung to the quick"*: Tilton, 14. Goldsmith, 51-52.

192. *"in almost mortal agony"*: Tilton, 15. Goldsmith, 64; *"When I found that I had given birth"*: Gabriel, 14, citing British Museum transcript of *Martin v. British Museum*, Feb. 24, 1894, 27.

193. *"habitually unchaste"*: Tilton, 14.

194. *"Sodom-by-the-Sea"*: Dale L. Walker, *Eldorado: The California Gold Rush* (New York: Tom Doherty Associates, 2003). Goldsmith, 65.

195. Rutter, 4-24.

196. Rutter, 59-77.

197. Rutter, 41-51, 131-132.

198. Gabriel, 15. Goldsmith, 65.

199. Goldsmith, 65.

200. Goldsmith, 65-66. *"Victoria, come home!"*: Tilton, 18.

201. *"Clairvoyant Medium and Magnetic Healer"*: Goldsmith, 70.

202. *"She can see and point out"*: Goldsmith, 66, citing "Victoria Woodhull Prophesy," *Boston Post*, Oct. 20, 1876; *$1 a visit, $2 a bottle*: Goldsmith, 66; *$100/day, $100K/year*: Gabriel, 18; *Life elixir recipe*: Goldsmith, 26.

203. Braude, 143-145.

204. *"It was a hard life"*: Goldsmith, 66, citing court testimony of Tennessee Claflin in *Roxanna Claflin v. Colonel James H. Blood*, May 15, 1871, Essex Market Police Court, New York City.

205. *20 people*: Goldsmith, 276; *"But for years there has been"*: Tilton, 6-7.

206. Gabriel, 21.

207. Goldsmith, 70. *"Why should I any longer"*: Tilton, 21.

208. *Uncertain divorces*: Underhill, 37; *"the old and still prevalent"*: Woodhull, "Principles of Social Freedom," 42.

209. Underhill, 35-37.

210. *"wonderful cures of female complaints"*: Goldsmith, 107, citing handbill in Victoria Claflin Woodhull (Martin) Papers; *"to their mutual amazement"*: Tilton, 24.

211. Underhill, 73.

212. *"wretched wreck"*: Tilton, 26.

213. Underhill, 37.

214. *King of Cancers*: Goldsmith, 80-81.

215. *Entertaining men*: Goldsmith, 108-109, citing Joseph Treat, 1874; *Misunderstanding*: Gabriel, 21.

216. *"My God, have I got to"*: Goldsmith, 109, citing Joseph Treat, M.D., *Beecher, Tilton, Woodhull, The Creation of Society: All Four of Them Exposed, and if Possible Reformed and Forgiven, in Dr. Treat's Celebrated Letter to Victoria C. Woodhull*, New York: Published by the author, 1874. *"I was almost lost"*: Goldsmith, 109, citing court testimony of Tennessee Claflin in Roxanna Claflin v. Colonel James H. Blood trial, May 15, 1871, Essex Market Police Court; *"two united defiers"*: Tilton, 23; *$100,000*: Tilton, 20.

217. *"calling"*: Morgan, 70; *"reinstate primitive Christianity"*: Eddy, *Church Manual*, 17; *"The miracles recorded in the Bible"*: Eddy, *Retrospection*, 26.

218. *Matthew 9*: Nenneman, *Pilgrim*, 86. Eddy, *Retrospection*, 24.

219. *"pregnant years"*: Eddy, "Footprints Fadeless," *Mary Baker Eddy: Speaking for Herself*, 106, ©The Mary Baker Eddy Collection.

220. *Incessant writing*: Nenneman, *Pilgrim*, 93; *"buoyant with hope"*: S&H, final ed., 109; *"When a new spiritual idea"*: Eddy, *S&H*, final ed., 109.

221. *"Oh, how I thank you"*: von Fettweis and Warneck, 81, citing *Boston Traveller*, 1900. See also Eddy, *Miscellaneous Writings*, 69. Tomlinson, 56.

222. *"Healing morally and physically"*: Eddy, *Miscellaneous Writings*, 300.

223. *"Error will hate more"*: Eddy, *Miscellaneous Writings*, 278.

224. *"She straightened the feet"*: Tilton, 19; *"gliding through the air"*: Tilton, 11; *"at her pleasure"*: Tilton, 33.

225. *Rooftop temple*: Tilton, 8, 33; *"At about eleven"*: Tilton, 24-25.

226. Underhill, 43-45.

227. 1.5%: "Riches Americans in History," *Forbes.com*, 1998.

228. *Just a few doors down*: Underhill, 43-44.

229. Underhill, 48-50. Goldsmith, 106.

230. Underhill, 75-76.

231. *"We would have every arbitrary barrier"*: Fuller, 30, 168.

232. Margaret Fuller and Nathanial Hawthorn's ideal woman correlated in Peel, *Encounter*, 25-26.

233. *"The need of his hour"*: Goldsmith, 214, from American Equal Rights Association convention, May 1869.

234. *"Visions of the offices"*: Underhill, 52, citing Victoria Woodhull autobiographical papers in Holland-Martin Family Archives, London, England.

235. *"I am the evangel"*: Goldsmith, 214, citing *Woodhull & Claflin Weekly*, Nov. 2, 1872, 12, and "I am an evangel" variation in Woodhull, "Beecher-Tilton Affair," 13.

236. *"The Spirits have entrusted me"*: Goldsmith, 384, citing Emanie Sachs, *The Terrible Siren: Victoria Woodhull (1838-1927)*. 1928. Reprint (New York, Arno Press, 1978).

237. *Vanderbilt leverage*: Underhill, 61.

238. Underhill, 94-97. *Rumors about Butler*: Goldsmith, 212.

239. White, 139, 164.

240. Kerr, 119. McMillan, 163.

241. McMillan, 98. Kerr, 1, 49, 243; *"the first person by whom"*: Wikipedia topic "Lucy Stone," citing Alice Stone Blackwell, *Lucy Stone: Pioneer of Woman's Rights* (Charlottesville: University Press of Virginia, 2001), 94.

242. McMillan, 168, 173. Kerr, 129, 133.

243. White, 139. McMillen, 207. Kerr, 146-147.

244. *"fascinated," "peculiar"*: Goldsmith, 5, citing interview between John Martin and Isabella Beecher Hook at the Sherman House, May 1, 1892, typed May 13, 1892. Victoria Claflin Woodhull (Martin) Papers, reel 2:37-40.

245. *"All the past efforts"*: Applegate, 412. Underhill, 104, citing *New York Tribune*, Jan. 16, 1871; *"She seems to be"*: Underhill, 115, citing *New York Herald*, Feb. 17, 1871; *Woodhull-Hooker association*: White, 164.

246. *"But why do I war upon marriage?"*: Woodhull, "Tried as by Fire," 7; *"The Woodhull Convention"*: Kerr, 164.

247. *NWSA on Woodhull*: Kerr, 164; *"Victoria Woodhull stands before us"*: Gabriel, 92, citing Elizabeth Cady Stanton to Lucretia Mott, Apr. 1, 1871. Smith College.

248. *"the worst gang"*: Goldsmith, 276, citing *Roxanna Claflin v. Colonel James Blood*, Essex Market Police Court (May 10, 15, 16, 1871); *Legitimacy questioned*: Kerr, 165.

249. *"Free Love!"*: "Free Love!" *New York Daily Tribune*, May 12, 1871; *Sporting illustrations*: Frisken, 2, 16.

250. *$10,000*: Kerr, 161.

251. *"I believe in Spiritualism"*: "Mrs. Woodhull and Her Critics," *New York Times*, May 22, 1871.

252. *IWA*: Frisken, 34. Sterns, 5.

253. *"God's first, last, and best law"*: Frisken, 38; *"seats, aisles, and galleries"*: "Mrs. Woodhull's Lecture": *New York Tribune*, Nov. 21, 1871; *"the first distinct announcement"*: Introduction to "Principles of Social Freedom" in Stern's *Reader*, citing *Woodhull & Claflin Weekly*, Aug. 16, 1873.

254. *"a rather tedious sketch"*: "Mrs. Woodhull's Lecture," *New York Tribune*, Nov. 21, 1871; *"It must be concluded, then"*: Woodhull, "Principles of Social Freedom," 15-16.

255. *"Two persons, a male and a female"*: Woodhull, "Principles of Social Freedom," 15.

256. *"The novelty of the doctrines"*: "The Principle of Social Freedom, Involving Free Love, Marriage, Divorce, &cs – Lecture by Victoria C. Woodhull," *New York Times*, Nov. 21, 1871.

257. *"as she boldly stood"*: "The Principle of Social Freedom, Involving Free Love, Marriage, Divorce, &cs – Lecture by Victoria C. Woodhull," *New York Times*, Nov. 21, 1871.

258. *"How would you like"*: Goldsmith, 301; *"not such a terrible thing"*: "Mrs. Woodhull on Free Love," *Cedar Falls Gazette*, Dec. 8, 1871.

259. *"Yes, I am a free lover!"*: Woodhull, "Principles of Social Freedom," 23-24; *Loud hisses*: "Mrs. Woodhull's Lecture," *New York Tribune*, Nov. 21, 1871.

260. *"run the machine"*: Frisken, 120, citing *Woodhull & Claflin Weekly*, Nov. 28, 1874.

261. *Marx interview*: Frisken, 35; *"Lower Million"*: Frisken, 121.

262. *Early political writings*: Nenneman, *Pilgrim*, 45; *Eddy's lectures*: Peel, *Discovery*, 178, 184, 186, 225; *Lynn political activism*: Gill, 154; *Presiding officer*: Fettweis and Warneck, 55. Peel, *Discovery*, 188; *Journalist*: Longyear, *Human Life*, 34; *"seemed to fill the room"*: Peel, *Discovery*, 209, citing Charles Allen Taber affidavit, Jan. 14, 1913, ©The Mary Baker Eddy Collection.

263. *"I can love only"*: Nenneman, *Pilgrim*, 78, citing Quimby Manuscripts, 154-56, Apr. 24, 1864, ©The Mary Baker Eddy Collection; *"lost element of healing"*: Eddy, *Church Manual*, 17; *"A few sentences"*: *S&H*, 1st ed., 158. See also *S&H*, final ed., 227:24-26.

264. *Science of Man*: Peel, *Trial*, 6. Nenneman, *Pilgrim*, 105.

265. *"Mrs. Eddy did not claim"*: Fettweis and Warneck, 87-88. Bancroft, vi; *Moral requirement*: Tomlinson, 105.

266. *1st year revenues*: Peel, *Discovery*, 257; *Partnership*: Peel, *Discovery*, 239.

267. *"Richard, this is a very spiritual life"*: von Fettweis and Warneck, 85. Eddy to Richard Kennedy, excerpted from Wilbur, 186-187. Courtesy of The Mary Baker Eddy Collection; *"notorious"*: Nenneman, *Pilgrim*, 140.

268. *Tuition*: Nenneman, *Pilgrim*, 108, 361 n. 21; *"beyond any money consideration"*: Nenneman, *Pilgrim*, 109, citing Spofford letter, Jun. 27, Original at Longyear Museum.

269. *Born again*: Peel, *Encounter*, 61. Peel, *Trial*, 10; *"A student of Moral Science"*: Fettweis and Warneck, 89. Bancroft, 119. *The Science of Man*. Courtesy of The Mary Baker Eddy Collection.

270. *Spiritualism opposite*: Eddy, *Retrospection*, 24; *Early students spiritualists*: Gottschalk, *Emergence*, 142; *North Groton Spiritualist*: Gill, 109; *Eddy at séances*: Peel, *Discovery*, 211, 220.

271. *"liberal, kind-hearted"*: Gill, 179, citing Alfred Farlow papers, excerpted from Mary Baker Eddy by Gillian Gill © 1998, quote ©The Mary Baker Eddy Collection; *Banner of Light*: Peel, *Discovery*, 221; *"loose morals"*: Glover, *S&H*, 1st ed., 95.

272. *Love interests*: Gill, 197, 238, 632 n. 28; *Spofford expelled*: Gill, 250; *Lewd cohabitation*: Eskridge, 21.

273. *Moral teachings*: Gill, 198; *"You cannot destroy error"*: Gill, 632 n. 25, citing manuscript *Questions and Answers in Moral Science*. Courtesy of The Mary Baker Eddy Collection.

274. *Earliest rubbing*: Gill, 201; *Abuses*: Gill, 633 n. 30; *Magnetized water*: Peel, *Discovery*, 155.

275. *Phasing out*: Fettweis and Warneck, 86, citing L11061; *"habit more pernicious"*: *S&H*, 1st ed., 382.

276. *"In warfare with error"*: Glover, *S&H*, 1st ed., 368; *Lustful purposes*: Gill, 203; *Secret sins*: Gill, 205. Peel, *Trial*, 49, citing L&M 84-12422. *Homosexuality speculation*: Gill, 207. *"crime against nature"*: Eskridge, 394.

277. *"spurning a Christian life"*: Gill, 205, citing *S&H*, 3rd ed., 1. Courtesy of The Mary Baker Eddy Collection; *Several refused to obey*: Bancroft, vii; *Never really understood*: Wilbur, 205; *"the hands of lust and lies"*: Gill, 203, citing L08302, Eddy letter to Sarah O. Bagley, Apr. 18, 1872, ©The Mary Baker Eddy Collection.

278. *"Masseuse"*: Nenneman, *Pilgrim*, 117; *Kennedy's lucrative practice*: Gill, 643 n. 34.

279. *Kennedy spreading rumors*: Gill, 203; *Efforts years later*: Gill, 625 n. 7; *Age difference*: Gill, 188; *Mother and son*: Gill, 189, citing Wilbur, 186; *"a medium, controlled"*: Bancroft, 36; *"Dr. Kennedy had his apartment"*: Gill, 188 n. 1, citing Farlow papers collected statement of Mrs. Carrie Colby, Eddy's landlord, excerpted from Gill, quote ©The Mary Baker Eddy Collection.

280. *"Dear student"*: F00342, Eddy letter to Samuel Putnam Bancroft, Apr. 28, 1871, ©The Mary Baker Eddy Collection.

281. *"Why is this all?"*: F00353, Eddy letter to Samuel Putnam Bancroft, Jan. 27, 1875, ©The Mary Baker Eddy Collection.

282. *"While I do not question"*: von Fettweis and Warneck, 97. "Moral Science and Mesmerism," *Lynn Transcript*, Jan. 13, 1872.

283. *"I am preparing a work"*: *In My True Light and Life*, 249, citing *Lynn Transcript*, Feb. 3, 1872.

284. *"From the time we dissolved"*: von Fettweis and Warneck, 559 n. 7, citing Eddy, *S&H*, 3rd ed., vol. II, 13. Courtesy of The Mary Baker Eddy Collection.

285. *"What sort of brazen tramp"*: Stowe, 263.

286. *"the most stirring and exciting"*: Stowe, 5, vi.

287. *"Miss Anthony and Mrs. Stanton"*: Stowe, 3.

288. *"Mercy upon us!"*: Stowe, 244.

289. *"I found [it] to be an exposition"*: Stowe, 259.

290. *"quiet, calm, warming"*: Stowe, 38, 263.

291. *Marx and Woodhull*: Frisken, 35, 43-46; See also Karl Marx, "The International Working Men's Association, 1872: Notes of the 'American Split,'" (marxists.org). *Marx on marriage*: Phillips, 168; *Spiritualists divided*: Braude, 173.

292. *"precipitated a storm of criticism"*: Kerr, 162, citing Ida Husted Harper, *Life and Work of Susan B Anthony* (New York: Arno, 1969) vol. 1, 377; *"Died of Free Love"*: Kerr, 169, citing *Lancaster Gazette*, Nov. 25, 1871.

293. *Woodhull's pamphlets*: Kerr, 168; *"social epidemic"*: "Marriage vs. Free Love," *Boston Globe*, Oct. 24, 1872; *"the sanctity and permanence"*: Kerr, 177, citing *Woman's Journal*, Dec. 7, 1872.

294. *"the Free Love incubus"*: Kerr, 172, citing *Woman's Journal*, May 18, 1872; *Moderates convinced*: "Political Notes," *Boston Globe*, Sept. 17, 1872; *"the Free Love panic"*: Goldsmith, 304, citing Martha Coffin Wright to Elizabeth Cady Stanton, Mar. 22, 1872, in Martha Coffin Wright Correspondence; *Free love conflict*: Kerr, 166, 168, 177.

295. *"The American Pope"*: Woodhull, "Tried as by Fire," 28.

296. *Brooklyn culture*: Fox, 29-30.

297. *"the New England doctrine"*: Fox, 74.

298. *"It is not, therefore, Mr. Beecher"*: Woodhull, "Beecher-Tilton Affair," 5, 18.

299. *"My judges preach against"*: Applegate, 412, citing *New York World* article, a variation of phrasing from "Mrs. Woodhull and Her Critics," *New York*

Times, May 22, 1871; *"I intend that this article"*: Woodhull, "Beecher-Tilton Affair," 3; *Price for scandal issue*: Applegate, 422.

300. *Woodhull's 1871 vote activism*: Underhill, 176; *"knowingly voting"*: Norgren, 60.

301. Applegate, 436, 451. *400,000 issues*: Fox, 56.

302. Fox, 74. *Woodhull's court appearance*: "The Tilton-Beecher Trial," *New York Tribune*, May 13, 1875, 3.

303. *Beecher's salary*: Fox, 20.

304. *Blackmail of women leaders*: Kerr, 171; *"to shut the mouths"*: Macpherson, 163, citing *Woodhull & Claflin Weekly*, Apr. 2, 1873.

305. *Newspaper reaction*: Macpherson, 168; *"Ku Klux spirit"*: Victoria Sandwick Schmitt, "Rochester's Frederick Douglass: Part Two," *Rochester History*, vol. LXVII no. 4 (Fall 2005):17, citing "Frederick Douglas vs. the People and Hotel Keepers of Rochester," *Rochester Union and Advertiser*, Jun. 17, 1872.

306. *Spiritualist organization dissolved*: Braude, 173.

307. *60 pages by June*: Gill, 211; *"I have known her"*: Nenneman, *Pilgrim*, 124, citing Bancroft, 127.

308. *"I have a very nice time"*: Nenneman, *Pilgrim*, 122, citing L07802, Eddy to Sarah O. Bagley, Dec. 13, 1872, ©The Mary Baker Eddy Collection; *Daylight writing*: Tomlinson, 131.

309. Peel, *Discovery*, 275; *"Truths remain the same"*: Henry Ward Beecher, *The Life of Jesus, The Christ* (New York, 1871), 6, 7.

310. *"hopelessly original"*: Eddy, *Miscellaneous Writings*, 371; *Copyright claim*: Stephen R. Howard, "Homeward Part 1: Lynn," *A Report to Members*, Longyear Museum (Spring/Summer 2007):4.

311. *Rewriting manuscript*: Peel, *Discovery*, 282.

312. *Spiritualist publisher's revisions*: Gill, 238; *"a hard thrust at spiritualism"*: Peel, *Discovery*, 291; *Thousands of words*: "I Bought the House for That Purpose," *The Mary Baker Eddy Library for the Betterment of Humanity Quarterly Magazine* (Summer 2001):19, citing Eddy to student, Aug. 12, 1895; *Printer's intentions*: Stephen R. Howard, "Homeward Part 1: Lynn," *A Report to Members*, Longyear Museum (Spring/Summer 2007):3, citing Eddy to Hermann S. Hering, Mar. 7, 1904; *"tired to death"*: F00350, Eddy letter to Samuel Putnam Bancroft, 1874, ©The Mary Baker Eddy Collection.

313. *Christian Scientists*: Peel, *Discovery*, 287; *Summer activities*: Nenneman, *Pilgrim*, 126; *Happy period*: Bancroft, 22; *"solemn, earnest and eloquent"*: "The Best Sermon Ever Preached," *Magazine of The Mary Baker Eddy Library for the Betterment of Humanity* (Winter/Spring 2002):7, citing *Lynn Transcript*, Jul. 10, 1875.

314. *July 4 sermon*: Peel, *Discovery*, 288; *Spiritualists disrupt sermons*: Gill, 238.

315. *Final 16 pages*: von Fettweis and Warneck, 104. Eddy, *Retrospection*, 38. *Oct. 30 printing*: Peel, *Discovery*, 291.

316. *"my babe!"*: Eddy, "Footprints Fadeless," *Mary Baker Eddy: Speaking for Herself*, 144, ©The Mary Baker Eddy Collection.

317. *"crossed swords"*: Eddy, *Miscellaneous Writings*, 285; *"school of virtue"*: Glover, *S&H*, 1st ed., 322; *"those who would learn"*: Glover, *S&H*, 1st ed., 5.

318. *Spiritualism opposite*: Eddy, *Retrospection*, 29.

319. *"The Rochester rappings"*: Glover, *S&H*, 1st ed., 92, 95.

320. *"To-day sin offers a premium"*: Glover, *S&H*, 1st ed., 84.

321. *"the majority of what is termed mediumship"*: Glover, *S&H*, 1st ed., 96.

322. *"But for these false views"*: Glover, *S&H*, 1st ed., 313.

323. *"The time cometh"*: Glover, *S&H*, 1st ed., 322. See Eddy, *S&H*, final ed., 64:17-25. Also, Matt. 22:30.

324. *New Hampshire connection*: Peel, *Discovery*, 115; *"Marriage is a contract"*: Noah Webster, *American Dictionary of the English Language* (1824).

325. *"Marriage is the only"*: Glover, S&H, 1st ed., 314, 318. See Eddy, *S&H*, final ed., 56:7-14, 60:16-18.

326. *"Infidelity to the marriage covenant"*: Glover, *S&H*, 1st ed., 314. See Eddy, *S&H*, final ed., 56:15-57:3.

327. *"Owing to the shocking depravity"*: Glover, *S&H*, 1st ed., 314-315.

328. *"discussed on grounds"*: Glover, *S&H*, 1st ed., 321; *Livermore lecture*: Peel, *Discovery*, 277.

329. *"difficulties of a greater magnitude"*: Glover, *S&H*, 1st ed., 321. See Eddy, *S&H*, final ed., 63:22.

330. *"Wisdom will ultimately separate"*: Glover, *S&H*, 1st ed., 318. See Eddy, *S&H*, final ed., 60:13-15; *"if there is no moral demand"*: Glover, *S&H*, 1st ed., 323. See Eddy, *S&H*, final ed., 66:21-22.

331. *American divorce rates*: Phillips, 137; "*slight temporary fermentation*": Fuller, 30. "*The broad-cast power*": Glover, *S&H,* 1st ed., 322, 323. See Eddy, *S&H,* final ed., 65:13-16, 29-32.

332. "*indissolubly*": Eddy, *S&H,* final ed., 60.

333. "*be not in haste*": Glover, *S&H,* 1st ed., 326. See Eddy, *S&H,* final ed., 68:11-15.

334. *Eddy's reading of "Night Thoughts"*: Peel, *Discovery*, 47.

335. "*What do you say*": F00352, Eddy letter to Samuel Putnam Bancroft, Jan. 1875, ©The Mary Baker Eddy Collection.

336. "*The greatest hindrance*": Glover, *S&H,* 1st ed., 429.

337. "*age of Christian Science*": Samuel Miller, *A Brief Retrospect of the Eighteenth Century: Containing a Sketch of the Revolutions and Improvements in Science, Art, and Literature During that Period*, vol. 2, 433; Holifield, 173; "*beginning to diffuse the cheering beams*": Peel, *Discovery*, 139.

338. "*In the nineteenth century*": Peel, *Trial*, 6, citing *The Science of Man*. Courtesy of The Mary Baker Eddy Collection.

339. *Wycliffe phrase*: Eddy, *Message 1901*, 16; "*We have faith this book*": Glover, *S&H,* 1st ed., 414.

340. "*remarkable volume*": Johnston, 66; *Alcott's reputation*: Peel, *Encounter*, 35; "*In times like ours*": Johnston, 66, citing *The Journals of Bronson Alcott*; ed. Odell Shepard, 464; *S&H sent to influencers*: Nenneman, *Pilgrim*, 129.

341. "*a Christian*": Peel, *Encounter*, 52; "*wholesome views*": Peel, *Encounter*, 81; "*The Doctrines of this book*": Bancroft, 33.

342. Margaret Beecher White, "Beecher and Christian Science," *Cosmopolitan Magazine*, vol. XLV no. 3 (Aug. 1908). Brisbane, 54. "An Interview with Mrs. Eddy," *Cosmopolitan Magazine*, (Aug. 1907).

343. "*the great anniversary festival*": McCullough, 130, citing Adams Family Correspondence, II, 30; "*Champion of Independence*": Robert C. Winthrop, Jul. 4, 1876 speech at Boston Music Hall. Fourth of July Orations Collection, University of Missouri Digital Library; "*a delirium of patriotic fervor*": Peel, *Trial*, 11.

344. "*the shot heard round the world*": Ralph Waldo Emerson's Concord Hymn, 1836, Centennial Exhibition Digital Collection, Free Library of Philadelphia, (freelibrary.org).

345. *Robert C. Winthrop on John Winthrop*: Gamble, 89, 111-112; *"Yet what can I say?"*: Robert C Winthrop, Jul. 4, 1876 speech at Boston Music Hall. Fourth of July Orations Collection, University of Missouri Digital Library.

346. *NWSA at Independence Hall*: Norgren, 53; *CSA formed*: Peel, *Trial*, 11.

347. *2500 on July 4, 1897*: Tomlinson, 226; *"commemorate not only"*: "Saw 'Mother' Eddy," *Boston Globe*, Jul. 6, 1897. Also, Eddy, *Miscellaneous Writings*, 251; *Speeches*: James R. Suber, "'For Our Dear Cause': The 1897 Visit to Pleasant View," Longyear Museum, *A Report to Members* (Spring/Summer 2013):4-11.

348. *"self-evident Truth"*: Glover, *S&H*, 1st ed., 12. See Eddy, *S&H*, final ed., 113:10; *"better than going to Philadelphia"*: Carpenter, *Items by and About*, 55, quoting "Freedom of Speech and Liberty of the Press," *Boston Investigator*; *"that man has dominion"*: Glover, *S&H*, 1st ed., 399; *"that man was made in the image"*: Glover, *S&H*, 1st ed., 257; *"Like our nation"*: Glover, *S&H*, final ed., 106:6-11.

349. *Eddy's visit to Centennial show*: Peel, *Trial*, 11; *"Having returned so gushing"*: "The Great Exhibition," *Lynn Transcript*, Nov. 25, 1876, reprinted in Carpenter, *Items by and About*, 61; *Communion Hymn poem*: Peel, *Trial*, 12. Hymn 298-301 in *Christian Science Hymnal*.

350. *Woman's Rights poem*: Peel, *Trial*, 317 n. 24.

351. *"of course I believe"*: Peel, *Trial*, 14, citing Elvira Newhall reminiscence. Courtesy of The Mary Baker Eddy Collection.

352. *"some naughty words"*: Woodhull, "Beecher-Tilton Affair," 8; *"obnoxious"*: Gabriel, 179, citing Emanie Sachs, *The Terrible Siren, Victoria Woodhull* (New York: Harper & Brothers, 1928), 171; *Impossible to speak in Boston*: Perry, 50.

353. Frisken, 91, 104, 106, 121; *Stowe's influence*: White, 203. Gabriel, 198; *MA governor's influence*: Clark, 208; "The Labor League," *Boston Post*, Feb. 24, 1873; *1873 Boston hall rental*: Macpherson, 133.

354. Frisken, 140, 145; *Woodhull synonymous with licentiousness*: McMillen, 189, referencing Alice Stone Blackwell.

355. *First and second lectures*: Perry, 47.

356. *"when she paces the platform"*: Frisken, 124, citing *Leavenworth Daily Times*, Jan. 11, 1874, 4; *"For the benefit of those"*: "Victoria Woodhull's Lecture," *Lynn Record*, Nov. 8, 1873, 2.

357. *"Men and ladies"*: Frisken, 143, citing *St. Louis Republican*, Feb. 2, 1876.

358. *"The South has always been free"*: "Victoria Woodhull in the South," *Herald and Mail*, Feb. 11, 1876, 2.

359. "Mrs. Woodhull Aroused: She Turns on her Foes and Spiritedly Defends Herself," *The Sun*, Aug. 3, 1876.

360. "Victoria Woodhull," *Boston Daily Globe*, Sept. 26, 1876, 1.

361. *"'free-love' trio"*: "The Beecher Scandal Revived," *Daily Free Press* (Ontario), Sept. 26, 1876.

362. *"Many will ask"*: "Mrs. Woodhull's Case," *Boston Daily Globe*, Sept. 27, 1876, 5.

363. *Deist theology*: Holifield, 162-167.

364. *"Temple to Free Thought"*: "Thomas Paine: Dedication the New Memorial Building," *Boston Daily Globe*, Jan. 30, 1875, 5; *"strike a blow"*: "Off-Color Reformers," *Boston Daily Globe*, Mar. 1, 1875, 8.

365. *"In beginning the exposition"*: "The Temple of God," *Boston Daily Globe*, Oct. 2, 1876, 5.

366. *"God's most holy"*: "Mrs. Woodhull and Her Critics," *New York Times*, May 22, 1871; *"The passions, instead"*: Woodhull, "The Naked Truth," 26.

367. *"no more sickness"*: Woodhull, "Tried as by Fire," 43.

368. *"When she learned"*: "The Temple of God," *Boston Daily Globe*, Oct. 2, 1876, 5.

369. *"hurled in her face"*: "Temple of God," *Boston Daily Globe*, Oct. 2, 1876, 5; *"You hear people say"*: "Victoria Woodhull," *Public Ledger* (Memphis), Feb. 7, 1876, 3.

370. *"Not so awfully shocking"*: "The Temple of God," *Boston Daily Globe*, Oct. 2, 1876, 5.

371. Display Ad, *Lynn Semi-Weekly Reporter*, Oct. 4, 1876; *"Mrs. Victoria C. Woodhull lectured"*: *Lynn Transcript*, Oct. 7, 1876.

372. *"Mrs. Woodhull's language"*: "Lecture by Mrs. Woodhull," *Lynn Semi-Weekly Reporter*, Oct. 7, 1876.

373. *Eddy's support of Cook*: Peel, *Discovery*, 245; *"truly Christian stand"*: "A Card," *Lynn Semi-Weekly Reporter*, Feb. 1, 1871, reprinted in Carpenter, *Items By and About*, 41.

374. *Lorette*: Courtney Ann Sullivan, "Classification, Containment, Contamination, and the Courtesan: The Grisette, Lorette, and the Demi-Mondaine in

19th Century French Fiction." (PhD dissertation, University of Texas. May 2003) 10, 14, 297.

375. *"the acme"*: S&H, final ed., 577; *"culminates"*: Eddy, *Miscellaneous Writings*, 21; *"true sense of Love"*: Eddy, S&H, final ed., 574.

376. *A type*: Gottschalk, 275; Denninger, ix, xi, 110, 177; *Hypocrisy and lust*: Denninger, 181; *"The hour is come"*: Eddy, *Miscellany*, 125-126.

377. *"It is hard to bear"*: Woodhull, "Beecher-Tilton Affair," 17-18.

378. *Breeding the human animal*: Woodhull, "Beecher-Tilton Affair," 3; *Noyes on selective breeding*: Stoeher, 524, 527; "The religion of the future": Perry, 142. Woodhull-Martin, "Stirpiculture," 23.

379. *"hereditary taints"*: Tomlinson, 172, citing lecture notice, first advertisement for *Science and Health*. Courtesy of The Mary Baker Eddy Collection; *"The good we possess"*: Glover, S&H, 1st ed., 318, 319, 322. See Eddy, S&H, final ed., 61:4-13, 64:26-29.

380. "A Reply to Mrs. Woodhull," *Boston Daily Globe*, Oct. 20, 1876, 8.

381. "Victoria Woodhull's Farewell," *Boston Daily Globe*, Oct. 23, 1876, 8.

382. "Henry Ward Beecher," *Boston Daily Globe*, Oct. 10, 1876, 1; *"look for Divine aid"*: "The Platform," *Boston Daily Globe*, Oct. 12, 1876, 5.

383. *"The mercury of my mind"*: Peel, *Trial*, 17. L07810, Eddy letter to Daniel H. Spofford, Oct. 22, 1876, ©The Mary Baker Eddy Collection.

384. *"my loved precious one"*: Nenneman, *Pilgrim*, 161. L02059, Eddy letter to Eldridge J. Smith, Jun. 27, 1882, ©The Mary Baker Eddy Collection; *"a union of the affections"*: Eddy, *Miscellaneous Writings*, 52.

385. *"sought in marriage by several"*: Bancroft, 24; *"striking appearance"*: Peel, *Trial*, 54, citing *Philadelphia Evening Bulletin*, Mar. 5, 1907; *"never a hair out of place"*: Parker, 34. Mary Godfrey Parker reminiscence. Courtesy of The Mary Baker Eddy Collection; "Her features were regular": Bancroft, 35.

386. *Youthful appearance*: Smith, 89. Peel, *Trial*, 12, citing AJ Henry Jones reminiscences. Eddy, *Pulpit & Press*, 32; *Younger men*: Gill, 241.

387. *Hitchings as suitor*: Bancroft, 17; *Hitchings as book financer*: Peel, *Trial*, 318 n. 40.

388. *Spofford's introduction*: Wilbur, 223; *Marriage proposal at gunpoint*: Peel, *Trial*, 17, 319 n. 51. Gill, 243; *Spofford as tenant*: Gill, 238. Peel, *Trial*, 319 n. 47.

389. *"quit thinking of me"*: Peel, *Trial*, 18. Nenneman, *Pilgrim*, 132. L07811, Eddy letter to Daniel H. Spofford, Dec. 30, 1876, ©The Mary Baker Eddy Collection; *"Sin is thought"*: Glover, *S&H*, 1st ed., 193.

390. Peel, *Trial*, 5-6; *Baptist*: Eddy, *Footprints Fadeless*, 112; *Gilbert's mother*: Longyear, 10; *Gilbert and spiritualism*: Longyear, 10-11; *Godfrey and Gilbert*: Parker, 10.

391. *"No Medicine, Mediumship"*: Ferguson, 89.

392. *"The day after my return"*: Nenneman, 131. L09897, Eddy letter to Hattie Baker, Jul. 14, 1876, ©The Mary Baker Eddy Collection; Peel, *Trial*, 16, citing Archive L&M 70-9897; *11 years younger*: Gill, 244.

393. *"A union of the masculine and feminine"*: Glover, *S&H*, 1st ed., 315. See Eddy, *S&H*, final ed., 57:4-14.

394. *"on the ground alone"*: Powel, 119. Von Fettweis and Warneck, 110. L08737, Eddy letter to Anna I. Kingsbury, Jan. 12, 1877. ©The Mary Baker Eddy Collection; *"latent noble qualities"*: Nenneman, *Pilgrim*, 135. L07812, Eddy letter to Daniel H. Spofford, Jan. 3, 1877, ©The Mary Baker Eddy Collection; *"There was always"*: Parker, 8. Mary Godfrey Parker reminiscence. Courtesy of The Mary Baker Eddy Collection; *Gilbert's character*: Longyear, 17-19, 28, citing Dr. Arthur Buswell. See also Clara Choate reminiscences, 7.

395, *"No, I must rely wholly on God"*: Longyear, 16; *"She seemed to be standing"*: Peel, *Trial*, 18. Clara Shannon reminiscence, ©The Mary Baker Eddy Collection.

396. *one-day engagement*: Peel, *Trial*, 17-19; *"A bridal altar"*: Glover, *S&H*, 1st ed., 326. See Eddy, *S&H*, final ed., 68:11-12; *"a quiet affair"*: Longyear, 21.

397. *Disapproval of the marriage*: Clara Choate's reminiscences; *"union of affection"*: Nenneman, *Pilgrim*, 137. L02048, Eddy letter to Eldridge J. Smith, Oct. 19, 1877, ©The Mary Baker Eddy Collection; *"with a view to promote"*: von Fettweis and Warneck, 110. L08737, Eddy letter to Anna I. Kingsbury, Jan. 12, 1877, ©The Mary Baker Eddy Collection; *"To happify existence"*: Glover, *S&H*, 1st ed., 315-316. See Eddy, *S&H*, final ed., 57:32-58:4, 58:7-12.

398. *5 years old*: Peel, *Trial*, 10. Peel, *Discovery*, 278; *"O, mother mine"*: Wilbur, 228. Peel, *Trial*, 23.

399. *March 1877 Barry suit*: Gill, 245. Peel, *Trial*, 22.

400. *Personal idol*: Peel, *Trial*, 18, 21; *"momentary hatred"*: Peel, *Trial*, 26; *"incapable as a leader"*: Wilbur, 238; *"unworthy to be the standard bearer"*: Peel, *Trial*, 26. Letter to Eddy from Daniel H. Spofford, May 30, 1877; *"immorality"*: von

Fettweis and Warneck, 112; *Spofford cohabitation*: Gill, 250; *Spofford expelled*: Peel, *Trial*, 28; "*strictly moral*": von Fettweis and Warneck, 115. L02655, Aug. 9, 1879, ©The Mary Baker Eddy Collection.

401. "*like a snake*": Wilbur, 245; *Years of trial*: Nenneman, *Pilgrim*, 134, citing Bancroft, 54; "*sleepless nights*": Clara Choate reminiscences, 9.

402. "*The highest friendship*": Clara Choate reminiscences, 8, 10-11. Courtesy of The Mary Baker Eddy Collection.

403. "*invariably deferred*": Clara Choate reminiscences, 7. Courtesy of The Mary Baker Eddy Collection, "*Never record ages*": Eddy, *S&H*, final ed., 246:17; *Marriage license*: Peel, *Trial*, 20.

404. "*lively talker*": Longyear, 10.

405. *Eddy family heritage*: Longyear, 6, 9. *Longyear Historical Society Quarterly News*, vol. 1 no. 2 (Summer 1964): 6-7, vol. 6 no. 3 (Autumn 1969):89-91, vol. 6 no. 4 (Winter 1969-1970):93-96; "*fulfilling the different demands*": Glover, *S&H*, 1st ed., 317. See Eddy, *S&H*, final ed., 59:11-16.

406. "*the very soul of conservatism*": Gabriel, 287, citing Woodhull's notes in Holland-Martin Family Archives, London, England.

407. "*appear as the dupe*": Underhill, 284, citing Holland-Martin Family Archives. *Relationship with in-laws*: Underhill, 286, 290.

408. *Interdependence Day*: Underhill, 290.

409. "*We no longer look*": Woodhull, "The Scientific Propagation of the Human Race," 6, 34.

410. *Republishing illustrations*: Frisken, 148; "*Oh could we but live*": Gabriel, 282-283, citing letter from Woodhull to John Martin dated Feb 26, 1897, Boston Public Library Woodhull Collection.

411. *Circle of acquaintances*: Gabriel, 287; "*her monthly organ*": Wells, 38-39; *Credit for promoting Eugenics*: Solveig C. Robinson, "Victoria Woodhull-Martin and *The Humanitarian* (1892-1901): Feminism and Eugenics at the Fin de Siècle," *Nineteenth-Century Gender Studies* (ncgsjournal.com), Summer 2010; *Eugenics endowment*: Underhill, 310.

412. *Avoiding germs*: Goldsmith, 446.

413. *Sisters' estrangement*: Macpherson, 267.

414. *Eugenics research*: Frisken, 146; "*I now openly avow*": Goldsmith, 441, citing Victoria Claflin Woodhull (Martin) Papers, reel 3 no. 136. Also, Gabriel, 253, citing *Woodhall & Claflin's Journal*, London, England, Jan. 29, 1881.

415. *Reply to clergy*: "Let the People Judge," *Christian Science Journal*, (Apr. 1885); *Eddy's instructions*: "Separation of Truth and Error," *Christian Science Journal*, (Jul. 1889): 188.

416. Eddy, *Church Manual*, 46, 49.

417. *"equal rights and privileges"*: Eddy, *Miscellany*, 247; *First Readers and Practitioners*: *Christian Science Journal*, (Mar. 1911); *"placed woman by the side of man"*: Carol Norton, "Woman's Cause: What the Work of the Founder of Christian Science Has Done For It," *Christian Science Journal*, (Jul. 1895):151-152; *Women ministers*: Matthews, 42. Clinton, 141.

418. *Suffrage appeal*: Alice Stone Blackwell, "Woman Suffrage," *Christian Science Journal*, (Apr. 1887):15.

419. *Anthony and CS*: "*Science and Health* owned by Susan B. Anthony," The Mary Baker Eddy Library newsletter, Mar. 2011.

420. *Beechers and CS*: Margaret Beecher White, "How and Why I Became a Christian Scientist," *Christian Science Sentinel*, (May 16, 1908). Reprinted from *New York American*. "Letters of Special Interest," *Christian Science Sentinel*, (Jun. 8, 1907).

421. *Beecher mention*: "Smooth Words," *Christian Science Sentinel*, (Jan. 26, 1899): 14; *"We stand on a far-reaching"*: "Mrs. Eddy's Preaching," *Christian Science Journal*, (Apr. 1887):32.

422. Brisbane, 54; Beecher hymn #276.

423. *Strongest statements*: "Let the People Judge," *Christian Science Journal* (Apr. 1885). "Separation of Truth and Error," *Christian Science Journal*, (Jul. 1889):188. "A Word From Our Leader," *Christian Science Journal*, (Oct. 1895):267.

424. *"The truth is that I am"*: Underhill, 294, from interview with a reporter on Election Day 1892.

425. *"new-style conjugality"*: Eddy, *Miscellaneous Writings*, 285. "Conjugal Rights," *Christian Science Journal*, (Jun. 1889); *"I have tried to remove"*: Eddy, *Miscellaneous Writings*, xi-xii.

Index

abandonment, 24, 86, 87, 88, 96

abolition of marriage, 38, 133, 190

abolition of slavery, 41, 49, 153, 154

abortion, 97

abstinence, 27

Adam and Eve, 19, 23, 202

Adams, Abigail, 34, 48, 50

Adams, John, 34, 35, 177

adultery, 23, 28, 86, 87, 88, 157, 158

affinities, 37, 56, 60, 61, 131

African slavery, 6, 39, 47, 55, 152

Age of Reason, 190

Alcott, Bronson, 172

alimony, 87, 137

alternative medicine, 86, 99

American Association of Spiritualists, 160, 205

American Woman Suffrage Assoc, 150, 159

American Woman Suffrage Association, 125

Andover Theological Seminary, 38

Andrews, Stephen Pearl, 43, 128, 200, 222

Anglicans, 33

annulment, 24

ante-nuptial defilement, 28

Anthony, Susan B., 4, 50, 55, 122, 123, 129, 155, 178, 232

antiwoman suffrage organizations, 151

Applegate, Debby, 158

Arbella, 14, 15, 34

Armageddon, 198

Around the World in 80 Days, 125

ascending fellowship, 43

atonement, 60, 166

Babylonish woman, 199

Bagley, Sarah, 109

Baker, Abigail, 69, 73, 79

Baker, George Sullivan, 72, 74, 78, 81, 109

Baker, Hattie, 212

Baker, Mark, 69, 73, 74, 81, 109

Baker, Samuel, 72

Bancroft, Samuel Putney, 136, 142, 171, 209

Banner of Light, 138

Baptist church, 83, 211

Barnum, P.T., 57

Barry, George, 215, 216

Bartlett, John, 79

Battle Axe, 39

Baxter, Richard, 26

Beaumont, Colonel, 75

Beecher, Catherine, 169

Beecher, Eunice, 159

Beecher, Henry Ward, 152, 155, 158, 162, 173, 183, 188, 191, 204, 205, 233

Beecher, Lyman, 71, 124

Beecher-Tilton affair, 155, 158, 177, 184, 222, 224

Bible Communism, 44

Bible quotations and references
    Genesis, 23, 50, 202
    I Corinthians, 190
    Luke, 7, 172, 197
    Matthew, 7, 15, 38, 107, 108, 167
    Revelation, 198

bigamy, 44, 113

Black Friday, 121

blackmail, 113, 155, 159, 187, 223

Blackstone, William, 50, 168

Blackwell, Alice Stone, 232

Blackwell, Antoinette Brown, 181

Blood, James Harvey, 102, 103, 111, 121, 129, 133, 187, 205, 222

Bolton, Robert, 31

Book of Mormon, 41

Boston Daily Globe, 187, 188, 189, 193, 205

Boston Investigator, 179
Bradford, William, 21
Brooker, Utica Claflin, 132
Bullinger, Heinrich, 23
bundling, 28
burnt-over district, 40, 45
Butler, Benjamin, 122

Calvin, John, 20
Calvinism, 20, 30, 33
catechism, 30
Catholics, 33, 71
celestial marriage, 45
celibacy, 23
Centennial Exhibition, 177, 179
chastity, 27, 168
Cheney, Mahala, 78, 84
Cheney, Russell, 79, 84
Chinese slave trade, 97
Choate, Clara, 217
Christian Science, 3, 110, 179, 216, 219
    churches, 3, 232
    Eddy's definition, 172
    origins of term, 171
    treatment, 209, 211
Christian Science Association, 178, 212, 214, 216, 217
Christian Science class instruction, 136, 233
Christian Science Journal, 13, 232
Christian Science Monitor, 4
Christian Science practitioner, 136, 173, 212, 232
Christian Union, 154
Church of England, 15, 18, 24
Cincinnati Enquirer, 187
city on a hill, 14, 15, 18, 178
Clafin, Utica. *See* Brooker, Utica Claflin
Claflin, Reuben Buckman, 90, 91, 92, 94, 99, 103
Claflin, Roxanna Hummel, 90, 91, 92, 100

Claflin, Tennessee Celeste, 92, 94, 99, 103, 104, 111, 113, 186, 187, 221, 226
Cleveland, Grover, 223
Clinton, Catherine, 32
Clinton, Emma, 75
Cochran, Jacob, 45
Cogswell, Anna, 99
Common Sense, 189
Communion Hymn, 180
Communist Manifesto, 42, 133
complex marriage, 192
Comstock, Anthony, 156, 183
concubinage, 53
Congregational church, 36, 69, 71, 83, 152
    democratic governance, 22
    theology, 20
Conjugal Love, 59
Constitution for the United States of the World, 122
Cook, Frances, 226
Cook, Joseph, 197
Corsican Brothers, 99
Cosmopolitan Magazine, 173, 225
Cotton, John, 16, 22
coverture, 50, 150, 168
Crafts, Hiram, 109
cribs, 97
Cridge, Alfred, 61
crime against nature, 140
criminal intimacy, 158
Cruden's Bible Concordance, 161
custody rights, 90

Daily Free Press, 189
Dangyereyes, Audacia, 147, 148
Darwin, Charles, 226
Davis, Andrew Jackson, 59, 60, 112
Declaration of Independence, 34, 35, 48, 51, 177
Declaration of Rights and Sentiments, 51
Deism, 190

Democracy in America, 17
Demosthenes, 111
Denninger, George, 199
dictates of conscience, 13, 19
divorce law, 25, 51, 52, 53, 86, 169
divorce rate, 169
doctrine of affinities. *See* affinities
Douglas, Frederick, 41, 160
Duncan, Elizabeth Patterson, 80, 82

Eddy, Asa, 219
Eddy, Asa Gilbert, 211, 213, 214, 217
Eddy, Betsy Smith, 219
Eddy, John, 219
Eddy, Mary Baker
    Boston Pope, 3
    Congregational membership, 22,
      70
    divorce, 87, 162
    education, 70
    healing of injuries, 108
    household, 33
    letter on Woodhull, 195
    marriage to Eddy, 209, 214, 216
    marriage to Glover, 72, 75
    marriage to Patterson, 82, 83
    on free love, 167
    on homeopathy, 86
    on woman's hour, 4
    on women's rights, 168, 180
    partnership with Kennedy, 136,
      144, 161
    Puritan heritage, 13, 32, 68
    son taken away, 81
    widowhood, 77
educated suffrage, 125
Elective Affinities, 59, 61
Emancipated Woman, 148
Emerson, Ralph Waldo, 177
Engels, Friedrich, 42, 133
English Common Law, 50
Epstein, Barbara, 32
eugenics, 226
extramarital sex, 28, 60

feminist, 42
Finney, Charles Grandison, 40, 51
fornication, 28
Fourier, Charles, 42
Fox sisters, 56, 57, 94, 165
Franklin, Benjamin, 190
Free Thought movement, 190
Frisk, Jim, 121
Fuller, Margaret, 52, 115, 116, 169

Galton, Francis, 226
Garrison, William Lloyd, 41, 124
Gataker, Thomas, 26
Gill, Gillian, 74, 138, 140, 141
Glover, George Washington, 72, 73,
    74, 75
Glover, George Washington Jr., 78,
    79, 80, 109
Godliness, 30
Goethe, Johann Wolfgang, 59, 61
Goldsmith, Barbara, 94, 102
Gottschalk, Steven, 199
Grant, Ulysses, 122
Great Migration, 14, 21, 33, 68, 219
Greeley, Horace, 51, 52, 122
Grundy, Mrs., 200
Gulliver's Travels, 200

Handmaid, 219
Hard Times, 205
Harper, Ida Husted, 150
Harvard College, 21, 34, 79, 210
Hawthorne, Nathaniel, 115
Hayes, Rutherford, 205
Henderson, Harry, 148
hereditary taints, 202
History of American Socialism, 42
History of Woman Suffrage, 233
Hitchings, Edward, 210
homeopathy, 83, 86
homosexuality, 140
Hooker Convention, 123, 126, 127

Hooker, Isabella Beecher, 123, 126, 129, 154, 155, 159, 233
Hooker, Thomas, 27, 29, 67
Human Body, the Temple of God, 190, 191, 221
Humanitarian, 223, 225
Hutchinson, Anne, 16, 32

illegitimate child, 24, 90, 95, 132
incest, 43, 94
indentured servant, 91, 97
Independence Day, 94, 177, 179, 180
indissoluble bond, 23, 52, 170
infanticide, 46
inheritance rights, 27, 42, 81, 90
Interdependence Day, 223
International Workingman's Association, 130, 149
involuntary servitude, 91, 153

Jackson, Andrew, 74
James, Henry Sr., 52
Jefferson, Thomas, 35, 80, 190
Jesus, 15, 211, 234
Jews, 39
John the Apostle, 198
John the Baptist, 166
Judicial Committee, 123
Junius, 200

Kennedy, Richard, 136, 137, 138, 140, 144, 161, 164, 217
King Charles I, 21
King Edward VII, 225
King George III, 35
King Henry VIII, 24

Lathrop, Laura, 233
Liberty Bell, 177
Life of Jesus, The Christ, 152, 162
Lincoln, Abraham, 8, 46, 153, 234
Livermore, Mary, 151, 168
lorette, 196, 198
Luther, Martin, 19, 23, 234

Lynn Record, 185
Lynn Semi-Weekly Reporter, 195
Lynn Transcript, 143, 180, 194, 195, 200, 202, 203

Mankind in the Making, 225
marriage defined, 23, 53, 131, 167
marriage eligibility, 24
marriage vows, 23
Marriage vs. Free Love, 151
Martin, John Biddulph, 221, 224
Martin, Richard, 225
Marx, Karl, 42, 130, 133, 149
Massachusetts Metaphysical College, 79
masseuse, 141
Mayflower, 18
mediumship, 57, 58, 166
Mesmer, Anton, 57, 92
Methodist church, 91
Miller, Samuel, 171
Milton, John, 28
Ministry of Wealth, 205
Model of Christian Charity, 15
Modern Times, 43
Monroe, James, 42
Moral Science, 110, 138, 140, 141
Moral Science and Mesmerism Contrasted, 163
Morgan, Edmund, 26
Mormon religion, 44
Morse Code, 57
Morse, Samuel, 57
Mosaic law, 23, 192, 198, 202
Moses, 15
Mott, Lucretia, 128, 135
Muslims, 39
My Wife and I, 147, 154

Naked Truth, 183
Napoleon's Imperial Guard, 213
National Woman Suffrage Association, 123, 126, 127, 129, 159, 178

new departure, 123
New England doctrine, 154
New England Free Love League, 190
New England Way, 22
New Harmony, 41, 51, 52
new school theology, 71
New York by Gaslight, 99
New York Herald, 127, 158
New York Sun, 187
New York Times, 129, 132
New York Tribune, 51, 53, 126, 131, 158
Newton, Isaac, 107
Night Thoughts, 170
no-fault divorce, 47
Noyes, John Humphrey, 38, 41, 192

Ode to Adversity, 88
old school theology, 71
Oneida community, 41, 42, 43, 60, 192, 231
open marriage, 103
original sin, 19
Owen, Robert Dale, 52
Owen, Robert Sr., 41, 42, 51, 52

Paine, Thomas, 189, 190
Paradise Lost, 28
Patterson, Daniel, 82, 83, 84, 87, 88, 109, 162
Paul, 13, 234
Peel, Robert, 7, 115, 162, 177, 209
Philips, Wendell, 124
Pierce, Franklyn, 68
plural marriage, 37, 44, 45, 231, *See* polygamy
Plymouth Church, 152, 153, 155, 156, 159, 189, 233
Plymouth Colony, 219
Plymouth Rock, 18
polygamy, 37, 44, 47, 53, *See* plural marriage
Powell, Lyman, 87
predestination, 20, 70

premarital sex, 28, 96
Presbyterian, 20, 22, 40, 71, 93, 171
Principia, 107
Principle (Mormon), 44
Principles of Social Freedom, 130, 150, 155, 183
Prodigal Son, 74, 197
prostitution, 46, 51, 53, 96, 99, 101, 104, 196
Protestant Christians, 18
Prynne, Hester, 116
public display of affection, 29
public women. *See* prostitution
Puritan
    companionship marriage, 26
    equality, 31
    household, 30
    leaving England, 21
    marriage law, 24
    Sabbath observance, 20
    term coined, 18
    theology, 20, 29, 30

Quakers, 33, 39, 41
Queen Victoria, 115, 117, 225
Quimby, Phineas P., 107, 135, 139, 181

Radical Republicans, 122
Rapid Multiplication of Unfit, 223
rappings of Rochester, 56, 165
Reformed Protestants, 20
removal of obstructions. *See* abortion
Republican Party, 46, 47, 124
Revelation, 198
Revere, Paul, 68
Revolution, 122, 125
Rights of Man, 189
Roman Catholic Church, 18
Royal Institution of Great Britain, 226
rubbing treatment, 139
rule of thumb, 25

Salem witch trials, 58

salvation, 19

Sanborn, Mahala. *See* Cheney,
     Mahala

Scarlet Letter, 116

Science and Health
     claims of cures, 179
     first printing, 164
     inspiration, 107
     Key to the Scriptures, 20, 164
     on free love, 5, 164, 235
     sales, 4, 210
     writing, 143, 161, 162

Science of Man, 135

Scientific Propagation of Human
     Race, 223

séance. *See* Spiritualism

selective breeding, 192, 201

Seneca Falls convention, 51

separate spheres, 49

Sermon on the Mount, 15

Seventh Day Adventists, 41

sex industry. *See* prostitution

sexual abuse, 94, 153

sexual misconduct, 139

Shakers, 41

sin, 19, 20, 29, 38, 130, 140, 165,
     166, 168, 211

Smaus, Jewel Spangler, 68

Smith, Joseph, 41, 45

social freedom, 61

sodomy laws, 140

soul mate, 59

spiritual affinities. *See* affinities

spiritual marriage, 37, 45, 131

spiritual telegraph, 57

Spiritualism
     affinities. *See* affinities
     origins, 56
     séances, 57, 94, 99, 138
     theology, 58

Spofford, Addie, 139, 210

Spofford, Daniel Harry, 139, 209, 210,
     213, 216

Springfield Republican, 173

St. Louis Republican, 186

St. Louis Society of Spiritualists, 102

Stanton, Elizabeth Cady, 40, 48, 50,
     53, 55, 116, 122, 123, 129, 131,
     155, 186

Statue of Liberty, 178

stirpiculture, 192, 201

Stone, Lucy, 55, 124, 125, 150, 160,
     169, 232

Stowe, Harriet Beecher, 55, 58, 147,
     149, 152, 154, 183

Swedenborg, Emmanuel, 58

Synder, John, 91

temperance movement, 49

Thanksgiving Day Proclamation, 18

Thatcher, Thomas, 27

therapeutic magnets, 92

Thirteenth Ammendment, 91

Thoreau, Henry David, 38

Tilton, Elizabeth, 154, 158

Tilton, Theodore, 92, 100, 111, 154,
     156, 158, 188

Tocqueville, Alexis de, 17

Tomlinson, Irving, 73, 161

Torshell, Samuel, 32

Towner, James, 60

Train, George Francis, 125

true marriage, 59

Twain, Mark, 3

twin relics of barbarism, 46

Tyndale, William, 19

Uncle Tom's Cabin, 55, 58, 153

Underground Railroad, 153

Underhill, Lois, 112

Unitarians, 71, 214

universal suffrage, 124

unmarried cohabitation, 24, 25

utopian communities, 41

Vanderbilt, Cornelius, 112, 121, 134, 221
Vanderbilt, William, 113, 221
venereal disease, 97, 98
Verne, Jules, 125
virgin Mary, 115

Wadsworth, Benjamin, 25
Washington, George, 68, 199
Webster's Dictionary, 53, 167
Well Ordered Family, 25
Weller, Janette, 88
Wells, H. G., 225
Wentworth, Sally, 109
White, Margaret Beecher, 173
wife beating, 25
Wilbur, Sibyl, 87
Willard, Samuel, 31
Williams, Roger, 16
Winthrop Fleet, 14
Winthrop, Elizabeth, 204
Winthrop, John, 14, 32, 178
Winthrop, Robert, 180, 204
Winthrop, Robert C., 178
Woman in the Nineteenth Century, 115, 169
Woman's Glory, 32
Woman's Journal, 125, 151
Woman's Rights, 180
women's rights defined, 49, 115
Woodhall & Claflin's Journal, 222
Woodhull & Claflin Weekly, 122, 133, 155, 156, 159, 187
Woodhull Convention, 127, 128
Woodhull, Byron, 95, 103, 191, 226
Woodhull, Canning, 94, 98, 101, 103, 128
Woodhull, Claflin & Company, 121
Woodhull, Victoria Claflin
    achievements, 4
    Audacia Dangyereyes, 147
    childhood, 90
    clairvoyant, 94, 99
    Communist, 133, 149
    Congressional speach, 123
    divorce, 186
    education, 93
    letter on Eddy, 203
    marriage to Blood, 101, 102
    marriage to Martin, 221, 222
    marriage to Woodhull, 95
    most prominent woman quote, 4
    on Goethe, 61
    on Mormon polygamy, 47
    on Oneida community, 44
    presidential candidacy, 122
    stage actress, 99
    Stanton support, 55
    Steinway Hall speach, 130
    stock brokerage, 121
    widowhood, 225
Woodhull, Zula Maude, 101, 103, 226
World's Fair, 177
Wright, Wallace, 139, 143
Wycliffe, John, 172

Yale Divinity School, 38
Young, Brigham, 44, 46, 233
Young, Brigham Bicknell, 233
Young, Edward, 170